New SAT
Blue Writing

Version 2.0

Printed in the United States of America
International Standard Book Number:
978-0990670407

Published by Reetiforp, LLC Publishing, a division of Reetiforp, LLC Reetiforp

Publishing books are available at special quantity discounts to use for sales promotions, employee premiums, or educational purposes. Please email our Marketing Department to order or for more information at workbooks@c2educate.com. Please report any errors or corrections to corrections@c2educate.com.

Letter to Students and Parents

To Students and Parents

C2 Education's Redesigned SAT workbooks focus on curriculum that will help students build key foundation skills and learn problem-solving methods to tackle the new SAT to be released in 2016. We strongly recommend that students use these workbooks aligned with instructions and guidance from our tutors at a C2 Education center.

This book contains a number of exercises designed to guide the student through a careful, progressive process that will build layers of understanding and present problems with an increasing degree of difficulty. Each colored (belt) level will confront a variety of topics within the realms of Writing, Essay, Reading, and Math; some topics may re-appear in other workbooks of different difficulties while some topics may only appear once. The ultimate goal of C2 Education's workbooks is to cover the academic content in a comprehensive manner with sufficient practice sets and homework review.

Students will obtain the greatest benefit and improvement from these workbooks by following the workbooks from Lesson 1 to the end. Each lesson will contain the following:

- A diagnostic assessment designed to help our C2 tutors gauge the student's understanding prior to the lesson
- Instructional text and information focused on methodology and problem-solving thought processes
- Practice problems about the concepts presented and any connecting concepts from other lessons
- Test-like practice problems geared to emulate the real exam
- Homework problems to review academic information covered in class and the workbook

We wish you the best of luck in your academic endeavors and we hope that our workbooks will provide you with strong improvements, facilitated understanding, and expanded problem-solving skills. Thank you for being a part of the C2 family; we hope that you enjoy your time learning with us!

- C2 Education's Curriculum Team

SAT Blue Writing
Table of Contents

BLUE WRITING LESSON 1: COMMAS AND SEMICOLONS
Getting Your Feet Wet

Directions: The following questions are intended as a short diagnostic exam.

1. The last three host countries to win the World Cup were France, in 1998, Argentina, in 1978, and Germany, in 1974.

   A) NO CHANGE
   B) in 1998, Argentina in 1978, and
   C) in 1998; Argentina, in 1978; and
   D) in 1998 Argentina in 1978 and

2. My guidance counselor was a Marine sergeant and he told me that becoming a professional soccer player was not a realistic goal.

   A) NO CHANGE
   B) counselor was a former Marine sergeant, therefore
   C) counselor, who was formerly a sergeant in the Marines, he
   D) counselor, a former Marine sergeant,

3. If not for the popularity of their star Mia Hamm, the U.S. Women's Soccer Team may not have become as popular as it is today.

   A) NO CHANGE
   B) Mia Hamm; the U.S. Women's Soccer Team
   C) Mia Hamm, it is clear that the U.S. Women's Soccer Team
   D) Mia Hamm, the U.S. Women's Soccer Team,

4. Until the corruption of its officials can be curtailed, international soccer's governing body, FIFA, will be plagued by public doubt and financial insecurities.

   A) NO CHANGE
   B) public doubt, and financial insecurities.
   C) public doubt, or financial insecurities.
   D) public doubt; and financial insecurities.

BLUE WRITING LESSON 1: COMMAS AND SEMICOLONS
Wading In

TOPIC OVERVIEW: SEMICOLONS AND COMMAS

Commas and **semicolons** fulfill similar but subtly different tasks in English. On the SAT, there are four major types of comma and semicolon questions. We'll review each of these in this lesson.

LISTS

If we have a list of at least three things, we use commas or semicolons to separate the different items.

Example 1: The first four World Cup tournaments were won by Uruguay and Italy.

Because this list only contains two items, we don't need a comma.

Example 2: The last three winners were Spain, Italy, and Brazil.

This example has three items in the list; therefore, we need to separate them with commas.

Example 3: The last three World Cup tournaments took place in Johannesburg, South Africa; Berlin, Germany; and Yokohama, Japan.

Because the items in this list contain commas, we need to use semicolons to separate them. Note that if even <u>one item</u> in the list contains a comma, semicolons must be used to separate the items. ✳

SEPARATING NON-RESTRICTIVE CLAUSES

A **non-restrictive clause**, or parenthetical phrase, is a phrase that contains information that relates to the topic of a sentence but is not essential for the sentence to be grammatically correct. A non-restrictive element must be set off from the sentence using commas.

Example 4: My favorite team, the U.S. National Team, has never won the World Cup.

In Example 4, the phrase "the U.S. National Team" is useful information, but not necessary for the sentence to make sense.

Example 5: Only the player in the yellow jersey is the goalie.

In Example 5, the words "in the yellow jersey" specifically identify the word "player" and are necessary for the sentence to make sense. In general, we use

commas to separate clauses that are not necessary or not restrictive to the sentence.

SENTENCE BOUNDARIES

If a sentence contains two independent clauses, we must connect them either with a comma and a conjunction or with a semicolon. We never connect two independent clauses with just a comma or with a semicolon and a conjunction.

A comma can also be used to connect a dependent clause and an independent clause, but this is done *without* a conjunction.

Example 6: Despite the protests of the Brazilian citizens, the Arena Amazonia was built in Manaus, Brazil.

In this example, the phrase "Despite the protests of the Brazilian citizens," is a dependent clause, therefore we use just a comma (with no conjunction).

Example 7: The best result for the U.S. Men's National Team came in 1980, when they finished third; the U.S. Women's Team won in 1991 and in 1999.

In Example 7 we see the use of a semicolon to join two independent clauses — both sentences could stand on their own.

UNNECESSARY COMMAS

The SAT will sometimes test your ability to *remove* commas from a sentence. One way this is tested is in compound nouns and compound verbs:

Example 8: Great skill and timing are necessary to be an international soccer star.

Example 9: The two skills most great players have are heading and trapping.

When there are only two items, as in these two examples, we never put commas in between the elements of a compound verb or noun.

BLUE WRITING LESSON 1: COMMAS AND SEMICOLONS
Learning to Swim

CONCEPT EXERCISE:

Directions: Find and correct errors in the following sentences. Some sentences will not have any errors.

1. A dinosaur refers to a specific type of land creature that roamed the Earth during the Triassic, Jurassic, and Cretaceous Periods, most children use the term more loosely, including pterodactyls and some marine animals as well.

2. Scientists estimate the intelligence of dinosaurs using a ratio called the "encephalization quotient;" which is the ratio of the actual size of an animal's brain to its expected brain size.

3. The dinosaur, with the highest encephalization quotient, is the Troodon, which was likely about as smart as a modern possum.

4. On the other side of the spectrum is the Stegosaurus, a large dinosaur with lines of plates on its back, which had a brain the size of a walnut but weighed over 4,000 pounds.

5. One place you will not find any dinosaur fossils is in Greenland, which is northeast of the United States.

6. Three of the best cities to see dinosaur exhibits at museums are Thermopolis, Wyoming, Woodland Park, Colorado, and Washington, D.C.

7. The largest dinosaurs were sauropods, enormous plant-eating grazers, the smallest were likely micro-raptors, which may have only grown to 16 inches long.

8. The longest dinosaur ever discovered is named Seismosaurus, which is a type of a sauropod measuring over 130 feet long.

9. Many scientists, including Jack Horner, the inspiration for Dr. Grant in *Jurassic Park*, believe that birds are the direct descendants of dinosaurs.

10. Some people believe that a sudden event, like a meteor strike, killed the dinosaurs, but others believe it was a more gradual change.

11. Luis Alvarez, who was a physicist, was the man who discovered the impact crater of the meteor that many believe killed the dinosaurs.

12. The other likely candidates are changes in volcanic activity, accelerated tectonic plate movement, and gradual climate changes that destroyed the dinosaurs' food supply.

13. Paleontologists subscribe to the "gradualist" theories, and physicists subscribe to the "catastrophic" theories.

14. Another competing theory is that the shells of dinosaur eggs became either too thin or too thick; either of these problems would result in the premature death of the embryo.

15. Most pictures of dinosaurs that appear today depict them as having a pebbled leathery brown skin, but many dinosaurs likely had a thin covering of fluffy hair called proto-feathers.

BLUE WRITING LESSON 1: COMMAS AND SEMICOLONS
Diving into the Deep End

PRACTICE EXERCISE:

Directions: Answer the questions that accompany the following passage.

Taking Too Many Fish

Tropical fish make for beautiful aquarium pets, but they've become a little bit too popular. **(1)** In Hawaii a major source of aquarium life, people are taking too many tropical fish out of the water, and the coral reefs that the fish help maintain are suffering.

The water around Hawaii and the people who fish in it are at odds with each other. The area's coral reefs depend on tropical fish to eat algae that would otherwise overtake the **(2)** coral but fish collectors take the beautiful marine creatures so they can sell them to pet stores. If the collectors take too many fish, the coral reefs can lose their beauty, and eventually die from too much algae.

That's exactly what is happening in Hawaii, **(3)** where, according to state data, collectors took over half a million marine creatures in 2004. Many people say that's just too many, and they have evidence to substantiate their claim — the coral reefs are losing their luster.

"It just doesn't look as pretty any more as it used to," said Brian **(4)** Tissot a professor of environmental science at Washington State University. That may seem like a superficial problem, but for a state that depends on its own **(5)** natural beauty, to attract the tourists that drive its economy, it could be an economic nightmare.

"There's no place else in America that has what we **(6)** have", said Robert Wintner, whose dive shop takes tourists to see the reefs. "And you know the cookie jar is wide open and the bad kids are robbing it."

The problem goes beyond the aesthetic, however — the fish depend on the coral as much as the coral needs the fish. If the coral **(7)** dies, the fish will begin to die out too, and pet store owners —

1. A) NO CHANGE
   B) Hawaii a major source of aquarium life
   C) Hawaii, a major source of aquarium life,
   D) Hawaii; a major source of aquarium life,

2. A) NO CHANGE
   B) coral, but fish collectors take
   C) coral, so fish collectors take
   D) coral; therefore fish collectors take

3. A) NO CHANGE
   B) where, according to state data; collectors
   C) where according to state data collectors
   D) where; according to state data; collectors

4. A) NO CHANGE
   B) Tissot, a professor,
   C) Tissot, whose a professor
   D) Tissot, a professor

5. A) NO CHANGE
   B) natural beauty; to attract
   C) natural beauty to attract
   D) natural, beauty to attract

6. A) NO CHANGE
   B) have" said
   C) have." said
   D) have," said

7. A) NO CHANGE
   B) dies the fish will begin to die out too and
   C) dies, the fish will begin to die out too; and
   D) dies; the fish will begin to die out too, and

the very people who are causing the problem, will lose their livelihood.

Pet store owner Randy Fernley understands **(8)** <u>this and</u> he says he's trying to prevent it by collecting his fish from many **(9)** <u>different areas, in order</u> to allow fish populations a chance to replenish themselves.

"I'm into protecting the reef because I know that's my life," said Fernley. "And I need to have that reef around the rest of my life."

Although Fernley is conscientious, scientists say that many other collectors take advantage of the fact that Hawaii has few laws to regulate their activities. Some scientists have persuaded officials to tighten **(10)** <u>restrictions however, and</u> things are starting to turn around. Collecting is now prohibited in certain areas, and the number of fish is on the rise. Scientists say that if collecting is **(11)** <u>limited shop</u> owners will have to be more responsible about how they acquire fish.

That way, this beautiful state will stay beautiful for a long time to come.

8. A) NO CHANGE
   B) this, and
   C) this, but
   D) this although

9. A) NO CHANGE
   B) different areas in order,
   C) different areas in order
   D) different areas so he could

10. A) NO CHANGE
    B) restrictions however and
    C) restrictions; however, and
    D) restrictions, however, and

11. A) NO CHANGE
    B) limited, shop
    C) limited then it will be the shop
    D) limited, unless the shop

TEST EXERCISE:

Directions: Answer the questions that accompany the following passage.

A Plague of Great Dimensions

In the 1300s a terrible disease called the bubonic plague swept across Europe, killing **(1)** <u>about a third of the population on the continent</u>. **(2)** <u>Today, a plague</u> still exists in some parts of the world, but it's not nearly as deadly, and scientists aren't sure why. Is it because of advancements in medical practices, or is there some other reason — some difference between the plague of today and the plague of medieval times? Recently, **(3)** <u>they tried to</u> find out.

The bubonic plague is initially transmitted among rodents by infected fleas. When the rodents, often rats, come into contact with **(4)** <u>people, the fleas can move from the rats and infect the people through bites.</u> Symptoms of the plague include a swollen lymph node called a "bubo," as well as fever, exhaustion, and infections of the blood and lungs.

[1] When the bubonic plague infected Europe from 1347 to 1353, it was so virulent that it became known as the "Black Death." [2] Doctors had no idea what caused the disease or how to treat it effectively; some administered a poultice of garlic over the bubo or used "medicines" made from dried toads or various roots. [3] These treatments were futile, and the healthy fled their villages or isolated themselves — even from family members — for fear of getting sick. [4] It was a terrifying time. {5}

1. If added to the end of the sentence, which of the following phrases would best emphasize the significance of the original sentence?

   A) or around 100 million people.
   B) less than the number of people who died in the recent Crusades.
   C) millions of men, women, and children from every nation.
   D) and affecting people at every social and economic level.

2. A) NO CHANGE
   B) Today, the plague
   C) Today, plagues
   D) Today, some plagues

3. A) NO CHANGE
   B) journalists are trying to
   C) someone tried to
   D) researchers tried to

4. A) NO CHANGE
   B) people, the fleas can transmit the infection through bites.
   C) people, fleas bite people after fleeing the rats, and cause infection to spread.
   D) a person, the fleas can bite them and give them plague.

5. For the sake of the focus of the paragraph, Sentence 4 should

   A) remain where it is.
   B) be deleted.
   C) be combined with Sentence 1.
   D) be moved to the next paragraph.

(6) <u>Although</u> the modern plague is still serious, it is not as frightening as the disease that **(7)** <u>afflicted</u> Europe centuries ago. There are now pesticides to control fleas and the rats that carry them, and today's doctors have a greater understanding of **(8)** <u>how germs work.</u> Doctors know that the disease is caused by bacteria, and they have developed antibiotics and even vaccines to prevent outbreaks.

However, even without modern medicine, today's plague is less serious than the Black Death. Scientists are researching the plague because they want to prevent a more serious epidemic from developing again.

Researchers in the recent study believed the modern plague and the plague of the 14th century were both caused by the same bacterium: *Yersinia pestis* (*Y. pestis*). They suspected, though, that there **(9)** <u>are</u> different versions of *Y. pestis* — one that caused the very serious plague years ago, and one that causes the less serious plague today.

"The Black Death in medieval Europe was caused by a variant of *Y. pestis* that may no longer exist," wrote the researchers, led by Hendrik Poinar and Johannes Krause. **{10}**

In the study, they looked at the DNA of *Y. pestis* from the 1300s (extracted from victims' remains) and today in hopes of identifying the differences.

"With any ancient pathogen, understanding why it **(11)** <u>might be</u> so virulent in the past is important to be able to predict possible reemergence today," Poinar said. "If it did ... perhaps we might be prepared."

6. Which of the following transitions would provide the best link between these two paragraphs?

   (A) NO CHANGE
   B) Consequently
   C) Furthermore
   D) In spite of

7. (A) NO CHANGE
   B) affected
   C) effected
   D) distressed

8. A) NO CHANGE
   B) the ways in which germs can function.
   (C) the nature of diseases.
   D) the inner workings and functioning of germs.

9. A) NO CHANGE
   B) is
   C) had been
   (D) might exist

10. To provide the most logical sequence of ideas, this paragraph ("The Black Death…Krause") should be placed

    A) where it is now.
    (B) before the sixth paragraph ("Researchers…today").
    C) after the eighth paragraph ("In the study…differences").
    D) at the end of the passage.

11. A) NO CHANGE
    B) was
    (C) had been
    D) might be behaving

BLUE WRITING LESSON 1: COMMAS AND SEMICOLONS
Race to the Finish

HOMEWORK EXERCISE 1:

Directions: Find and correct errors in the following sentences. Some sentences will not have any errors.

1. Many of the world's great cities have transportation issues; there are too many people for them to all use cars to get around.

2. Charles Pearson, who was a solicitor in London, first proposed the Metropolitan Railway in 1845; this would become the world's first subway.

3. Some of the best subway systems in the world are in the Eastern Hemisphere.

4. Hong Kong; Seoul, Korea; and Singapore have the three top-rated mass transit systems in the world.

5. The MTR in Hong Kong carries more than 3 million passengers per day, has over 150 stations, and comprises more than 200 kilometers of track.

6. The Seoul Metropolitan System is considered by many to be the longest system by length; it is, however, operated by multiple carriers.

7. One of Seoul's most popular innovations, which is being copied by other transit systems, is the use of RFID chips to process payment for travel automatically.

8. These Radio Frequency Identification chips can be in smartphones, ID cards, or credit cards.
   NE

9. These cards note passengers' arrival and departure stations and charge the passengers' accounts accordingly.

10. Another technological marvel available on this subway is the Seolleung Station Virtual Market, where passengers can do their virtual shopping while waiting for a train.

11. A shopper simply finds an item he wants, takes a photograph of the bar code with his smartphone, and then takes delivery of the item at home the same day.

12. One of the categories transportation engineers use to measure efficiency of a subway system is density, which measures how many stations there are in a given area of the city.
    NE

13. The best density depends on the density of the surrounding city; for example, in Los Angeles less density is required than in New York City.

14. Bus transfers, which are a vital component of any transit system, depend on the distance between streets in the city's grid.

15. Most engineers agree that the worst public transit systems are in Mumbai, India; Manila, the capital of the Philippines; and Sao Paulo, Brazil.

HOMEWORK EXERCISE 2:.

Directions: Answer the questions that accompany the passage

Modern Segregation

In 1963, only 1 percent of black children in the South attended school with white children. Over the next decade, that number **(1)** raised to 90 percent. This remarkable change was brought about largely by federal judges, who faced death threats and violence while issuing hundreds of court orders to ensure the elimination of racial segregation in schools. Federal agencies then used the authority of the courts to monitor school systems, denying federal dollars to districts that refused to desegregate.

{2} We would like to believe that this period in our history is a relic of a bygone era, but studies show our schools are just as, if not more, racially segregated than they were in the 1960s. Across the country, 80% of Latino students and 74% of black students attend schools where the student population is more than half minority.

The re-segregation of American schools stems, at least in part, from the dissolution of the once-great force of courts and federal agencies **(3)** that issued desegregation orders, enforced desegregation orders, and monitored desegregation orders. At the height of the country's integration **(4)** efforts some 750 school districts were placed under desegregation orders. Today, these orders remain active in more than 300 districts, **(5)** but they are no longer aggressively monitored or enforced.

1. A) NO CHANGE
   B) rose
   C) rises
   D) had risen

2. Which of the following facts would best support the claims put forth in this paragraph?

   A) Today, the most segregated schools are not in the South, but in states like New York.
   B) 43% of Latino students and 38% of black students attend schools where fewer than 10% of their classmates are white.
   C) In 1968, when desegregation efforts began, 55% of Latino students and 77% of black students attended schools where the student population was more than half minority.
   D) Black and Latino students account for just 15% of the student population at the nation's top 468 four-year colleges.

3. A) NO CHANGE
   B) that had to deal with desegregation.
   C) that desegregated the schools.
   D) involved with school integration.

4. A) NO CHANGE
   B) efforts: some
   C) efforts, some
   D) efforts, for example, some

5. Which of the following revisions to the underlined portion of the sentence would best develop the main idea of the paragraph?

   A) NO CHANGE
   B) far fewer than there used to be.
   C) which shows that the courts still make some efforts to battle segregation.
   D) but many of these districts no longer need court orders.

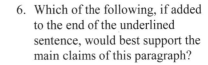
Many question whether modern racial segregation in schools is truly a product of racist public policy, as segregation most assuredly was in the Jim Crow South. Data from the Department of Education shows that schools with very high minority populations also tend to be schools with high levels of poverty **(6)**. In most parts of the country, students are assigned to schools based on the neighborhoods in which they live, thus students from low-income neighborhoods tend to go to one school **(7)** while schools in high-income neighborhoods are attended by students from higher income families. Statistically, **(8)** they are more likely to live in high poverty areas than white or Asian children. **(9)** For all intensive purposes, this situation results in segregation by socioeconomic class.

[1] While this theory of classist segregation has some merit, it ignores the importance of the steady decline of integration efforts at the federal level. [2] After decades of fighting segregation, federal courts and agencies buckled under what some civil-rights experts call integration fatigue. [3] Upon taking office in 1981, President Ronald Reagan immediately cut federal financial support for desegregation efforts. [4] Reagan's Justice Department, far from working to enforce existing court orders, focused on curtailing and ending court orders, a trend that accelerated under President George W. Bush. [5] Both the presidencies of both Reagan and Bush were plagued by problems abroad, which perhaps explains the decline in attention to school integration. [6] Today, no one — not the Justice Department, not the Department of Education, and certainly not the local school districts — knows exactly how many desegregation orders are still active. {10}

As long as **(11)** public school's continue to practice de facto racial segregation, our bitter racial history remains in the present, an albatross around the neck of future generations.

6. Which of the following, if added to the end of the underlined sentence, would best support the main claims of this paragraph?

   A) , an interesting correlation but likely not a causal relationship
   B) , suggesting that modern segregation may be more a result of classism than of racism
   C) , so clearly segregation has little to do with race
   D) , and these schools have lower test scores than rich schools

7. A) NO CHANGE
   B) while schools in high-income neighborhoods are attended by other students.
   C) while students from higher-income neighborhoods go to another.
   D) and then students from high-income neighborhoods attend schools in high-income neighborhoods.

8. A) NO CHANGE
   B) minorities
   C) students
   D) black or Latino children

9. A) NO CHANGE
   B) For all intents and purposes
   C) As a result
   D) Realistically

10. Which of the following changes would improve the focus of the paragraph?

    A) NO CHANGE
    B) Move Sentence 5 so that it comes before Sentence 3
    C) Delete Sentence 5
    D) Move Sentence 1 to the end of the paragraph

11. A) NO CHANGE
    B) public schools continue
    C) public school's continued
    D) public school continues

BLUE WRITING LESSON 2: SUBJECT-VERB AGREEMENT
Getting Your Feet Wet

Directions: The following questions are intended as a short diagnostic exam.

1. Most of the basic <u>tenets</u> of these religions seem to have no common <u>ground</u> <u>but ends up</u> arriving at the same concepts for human rights.

    A) NO CHANGE
    B) ground and ends
    C) ground but end
    D) ground, and ending

2. The beauty of the houses of worship of all different <u>religions are a testament</u> <u>to</u> the dedication of their adherents.

    A) NO CHANGE
    B) religions are testaments to
    C) religions, are a testament to
    D) religions is a testament to

BLUE WRITING LESSON 2: SUBJECT-VERB AGREEMENT
Wading In

TOPIC OVERVIEW: SUBJECT-VERB AGREEMENT

Subject-verb agreement is generally a straightforward topic, and one which is made easier because sentences with this type of mistake sound wrong when we read them. In this lesson, we'll look at three situations which make detecting mistakes in subject-verb agreement more difficult: separation between subject and verb, indefinite pronouns, and inverted sentence order.

SEPARATION BETWEEN SUBJECT AND VERB

One way that the SAT makes finding subject-verb agreement more difficult is to put words between the subject and the verb.

Example 1: The five largest **religions** in the world, listed in order of size, **are** Christianity, Islam, Hinduism, Buddhism, and Shinto.

In this example, the verb is *to be*, and is conjugated in the plural form because its subject is *religions*.

Example 2: **Shinto**, a classification which includes many different traditional Japanese religions, **is** not as well known in the United States as it is in many Eastern Hemisphere countries.

Again the verb is *to be*, but now it is conjugated in the singular form because its subject is *Shinto*. Notice that the word directly preceding it, *religions*, is a plural noun, but because *religions* is not the subject of the sentence, it doesn't affect the form of the verb.

INDEFINITE PRONOUNS

When the subject of a sentence is an **indefinite pronoun**, we often have more difficulty deciding whether to use a singular or plural form of a verb. We'll list the more common indefinite pronouns and whether they are singular or plural here:

Singular Pronouns:
everyone/everything/everybody
anyone/anything/anybody
someone/something/somebody
no one/nothing/nobody
each, much, one
either, neither
the number

Plural Pronouns:
both
many
few
several
a number

The following list contains pronouns that can be either plural or singular, depending on what type of noun they are replacing:

Singular/Plural Pronouns:

any	some	more
all	most	none

Note the last two items in the singular and plural pronouns lists: we consider *a number* to be plural, while *the number* is singular. The next two examples demonstrate each of these situations:

Example 3: **The number** of religions in the world **is** not known, mostly because it depends on how you divide them; estimates range from 19 to 17,000!

Example 4: **A number** of religions **have** only one major deity, while others have many — some have hundreds or even thousands of gods!

The most confusing situations arise with the indefinite pronouns in the third list above, which can be either singular or plural, depending on their use. The best rule for this is to ask ourselves if the pronoun is referring to individual items or to a group of items — the context of the sentence will give us the answer. In the next two examples, the pronoun takes the number of the noun in the prepositional phrase.

Example 5: **Some** of the largest **religions** in the world **are** concentrated in very specific parts of the world — for example, almost one billion Hindus live in India.

Example 6: The world has seen many wars fought over religions, and **some** of this **contentiousness has** made people doubt the practicality of religion.

Note that in Example 5, the subject is *Some*, but it's replacing *religions*. Because it's referring to many things, we use the plural form of the verb *to be*. In Example 6, the pronoun refers to *contentiousness*, which is one individual thing, so we use the singular form of *to have*.

INVERTED SUBJECT-VERB ORDER

English is a subject-verb-object language, which means that there is an order in which we are used to seeing sentences written. When this order is switched, it can be difficult to determine subject-verb agreement.

Example 7: In the Middle East **lies** the **intersection** of three major religions: Judaism, Christianity, and Islam.

Example 8: Within most the world's religions **resides** one important **premise**: Act towards others as you would like them to act towards you.

In Example 7, the subject *intersection* follows the verb *lies*. This is a perfect example of why you should pick out the subject and verb of the sentence and read them in a subject-verb order. Saying "the intersection lie" and "the intersection lies" makes it clear which one is correct. Example 8 follows a similar pattern. One clue that a sentence may be in an inverted order is if it begins with a preposition.

BLUE WRITING LESSON 2: SUBJECT-VERB AGREEMENT
Learning to Swim

CONCEPT EXERCISE:

Directions: Find and correct errors in the following sentences. Some sentences will not have any errors.

1. If we lived in an era centuries past, we might have taken a tour among the Seven Wonders of the Ancient World, which remains some of the most daring constructions undertaken by humans.

2. While today many of these great monuments have been destroyed, hundreds (or thousands) of years ago most was still standing. *were*

3. The Colossus, a great statue built from iron tie bars and brass plates, were built as evidence of a battle won by the islanders against the Greeks. *was*

4. Most of the mortar used to build the three Great Pyramids was produced using the plentiful sand from the desert, held together by water carried across the desert by thousands of workers. *NE*

5. Off the coast of Alexandria, towering over the waves, stand the great Lighthouse, for many years standing as the tallest structure in the world. *stands*

6. The Statue of Zeus, although disassembled and then reassembled in Constantinople by the Turks, tower over the eponymously named temple. *towers*

7. We could even go see the Hanging Gardens of Babylon of which no trace remain today – no one even knows its exact location. *NE* *s*

8. Perhaps the least-known of the Seven Wonders are the Mausoleum at Halicarnassus, a great tomb built and named for Mausolus, a governor in the Persian Empire. *is*

9. The word *mausoleum*, among others, persist to this day in the English language, although many people do not know its origins. *persists*

10. The other lesser-known Ancient Wonder is the Temple of Artemis, built from beautiful white stones, which stand near the ancient city of Ephesus. *stands*

11. Moving forward in time, we find that the list of Wonders change as people envision and build new and fantastic creations. *changed*

12. Recently a group made up of the public, historians, and archaeologists has put together a list of Wonders made up of monuments that are still standing. *had*

13. The great statue Christ the Redeemer in Brazil, built by an army of engineers and technicians, stand as one of the modern symbols of Christianity, and is considered one of the New Wonders. *stands*

14. Another structure which made the cut is Petra, a temple whose walls, cut out of the living rock of a canyon in modern-day Jordan, rises over 2000 feet. *NE*

15. The Great Wall of China, while in reality a series of walls and fortifications, are a Wonder often thought to be Ancient, but which instead resides on the New Wonders list. *is*

BLUE WRITING LESSON 2: SUBJECT-VERB AGREEMENT
Diving into the Deep End

PRACTICE EXERCISE:

Directions: Answer the questions that accompany the following passage.

Your Brain is Smaller Than a Caveman's

Over the past 20,000 years, the human brain has gotten smaller. The average male brain 20,000 years ago, during the middle and late **(1)** Stone Ages, were 1,500 cubic centimeters. Now it's 1,350. Paleontologists and anthropologists aren't sure why this has happened, though they offer a variety of explanations.

Some point out that our bodies are smaller than those of our caveman ancestors, so it stands to reason that our brains would have grown smaller as well. **(2)** Others suggest that our brains grew smaller because they became more efficient over time. Still others, including a neuroscientist at one of America's top **(3)** universities, offers a third explanation: Our brains are smaller because we've become more social. The rationale, first advanced by Brian Hare of Duke University and other **(4)** top scientists, are that the process by which we became better able to live and work together also shrunk our brains.

The theory grew out of Hare's realization that bonobos, a famously sociable chimpanzee **(5)** species, was smaller in size than common chimps. Hare examined work by the Russian geneticist Dmitri Belyaev in the 1950s examining the process by which species, like the cow or the **(6)** common cat, has become domesticated. Belyaev did this by picking a wild animal, the Siberian silver fox, and trying to domesticate it. It took only a dozen generations of choosing the least aggressive foxes from a population and crossbreeding them before he got foxes that shared many common traits with domestic dogs. Not only were they tamer than wild foxes, they also had floppy ears — and smaller brains.

1. A) NO CHANGE
   B) Stone Ages were 1,500
   C) Stone Ages was 1,500
   D) Stone Ages, was 1,500

2. A) NO CHANGE
   B) Others are suggesting
   C) Others suggests
   D) Others, suggest

3. A) NO CHANGE
   B) universities, offering a third
   C) universities, offer a third
   D) universities offers a third

4. A) NO CHANGE
   B) top scientists, is that
   C) top scientists are that
   D) top scientists, being that

5. A) NO CHANGE
   B) species, were smaller
   C) species, is smaller
   D) species has been smaller

6. A) NO CHANGE
   B) common cat has become
   C) common cat, have become
   D) common cat, becomes

Testosterone, one of the hormones produced by **(7)** the brain's many glands, control both size and aggression. More docile animals have less testosterone, and testosterone determines brain size. Human beings, of course, aren't domesticated in the way dogs are, but the process of **(8)** civilizing humans are similar to self-domestication. As we transitioned from hunter-gatherer societies to subsistence farmers to bureaucrats, aggression became less useful. Those members considered **(9)** overly aggressive were eliminated from the tribe, sent to the gallows, or considered unmarriageable and so prevented from reproducing. Today's modern human, **(10)** in other words, are the bonobo of the human family.

The shrinking of the human brain does not necessarily translate to a decrease in intelligence because the connections between brain **(11)** size and intelligence is far from straightforward. Moreover, it seems that the decreasing size of human brains has begun to reverse itself in the past few hundred years, perhaps because improved nutrition has allowed our bodies to allocate greater resources to our energy-hungry brains. Even if our smaller brains do translate to lower intelligence, our social communities more than compensate for any decline. After all, we no longer need to solve all problems on our own — we can turn to one another for help.

7. A) NO CHANGE
    B) the brain's many glands, control only
    C) the brain's many glands, controlling both
    D) the brain's many glands, controls both

8. A) NO CHANGE
    B) civilizing humanity are similar to
    C) civilizing humans is similar to
    D) civilizing, humans, are similar to

9. A) NO CHANGE
    B) overly aggressive was eliminated
    C) overly aggressive eliminated
    D) overly aggressive has been

10. A) NO CHANGE
    B) in other words, have been determined to be the
    C) in other words, is the
    D) in other words, are

11. A) NO CHANGE
    B) size and intelligence are far from straightforward.
    C) size and intelligence isn't far from straightforward.
    D) size and intelligence aren't too terribly straightforward.

TEST EXERCISE:

Directions: Answer the questions that accompany the following passage.

Conflict in South Sudan

South Sudan's conflict has devastated communities and polarized society and, unless the root causes of

(1) the conflict is addressed now, the world's youngest country may find itself once more in crisis.

(2) South Sudan became an independent country in 2011. The new nation has seen near-constant conflict. South Sudan is at war with at least seven armed groups in 9 of its 10 states. The fighters accuse the South Sudanese government of plotting to stay in power indefinitely, not fairly representing and supporting all tribal groups, and neglecting development in rural areas. At the end of 2013, a political power struggle broke out between President Kiir and his ex-deputy Riek Machar. Kiir accused Machar of plotting to overthrow the **(3)** government, however, Machar accused Kiir of attempting to establish a dictatorship. Although both men have supporters from across South Sudan's ethnic divides, fighting has become communal, with rebels targeting the Kinka ethnic group and government soldiers attacking Nuers.

As a result of the conflict, more than half a million people have been displaced and thousands have been killed. More than half of those **(4)** displaced have not received any aid. **(5)** Although many have sought shelter in U.N. compounds, many others have been moving quickly from one place to another in an attempt to escape violence, making it difficult for aid agencies to reach people. Looting has **(6)** exasperated the problem as fighters have stolen food, aid agency vehicles, and medical supplies.

1. A) NO CHANGE
   B) the conflict are addressed
   C) the conflicts is addressed
   D) the conflict was addressed

2. Which choice most effectively combines the two sentences?

   A) NO CHANGE
   B) South Sudan became an independent country in 2011; since then, the new nation has seen near-constant conflict.
   C) Before South Sudan became an independent country in 2011, it had seen near-constant conflict.
   D) South Sudan became an independent country in 2011; therefore, the new nation has seen near-constant conflict.

3. A) NO CHANGE
   B) government; and
   C) government, while
   D) government, so

4. A) NO CHANGE
   B) displaced has not received
   C) displaced is not receiving
   D) displaced have not been found to receive

5. A) NO CHANGE
   B) Since
   C) If
   D) When

6. A) NO CHANGE
   B) exonerated
   C) exhibited
   D) exacerbated

{7} Aid workers are also concerned about the host communities coping with huge numbers of displaced people. For example, one town in central South Sudan that was home to 10,000 people before the conflict is now host to more than 85,000 displaced people. To make matters worse, harvests have been destroyed in large parts of the country, which will make it all the more difficult for people to feed themselves in the months to come. **(8)** Aid workers are struggling for answers to these problems.

This conflict has likely set the nation back by decades. South Sudan will continue to face a critical humanitarian crisis for years to come. In addition to the **(9)** social needs of people, such as food, water, and healthcare, entire communities have been devastated. Friends and former colleagues **(10)** has become enemies, creating a very polarized citizenry. The on-going conflict has also halted development as foreign investment is unlikely to resume in such an unstable country. **(11)** Just as the damage that has been done cannot be undone by a cessation of hostilities and the people of South Sudan cannot hope for a simple solution from international forces. Once the fighting stops, only time will heal South Sudan.

7. Which choice most effectively establishes the main topic of this paragraph?

A) Aid workers cannot cope with the massive population of South Sudan and its need for food.
B) Based on the small population of South Sudan, aid workers believe they have adequate food supplies.
C) Hunger is the main challenge facing aid workers.
D) There are two major challenges that have consistently concerned aid workers: population size and food supplies.

8. Which of the following changes to the underlined sentence most effectively concludes this paragraph?

A) NO CHANGE
B) Delete it. It is unnecessary.
C) Aid workers have nearly given up hope.
D) Aid workers are looking to the U.N. for help with these complex problems.

9. A) NO CHANGE
B) long-term
C) physical
D) less important

10. A) NO CHANGE
B) had become
C) will become
D) have become

11. A) NO CHANGE
B) Just as the damage that has been done cannot be undone by a cessation of hostilities,
C) Just as the damage that has been done cannot be undone by a cessation of hostilities;
D) Just as the damage that has been done cannot be undone by a cessation of hostilities

11/11

BLUE WRITING LESSON 2: SUBJECT-VERB AGREEMENT
Race to the Finish

HOMEWORK EXERCISE 1:

Directions: Find and correct errors in the following sentences. Some sentences will not have any errors.

1. Some of the greatest American books, even when compared with the works of Mark Twain and Tom Wolfe, ~~was~~ written by Edgar Allen Poe.
were

2. Among his most famous works is both lyric poetry and short stories. *are*

3. His contributions, in addition to the vast amount of literature he produced in his lifetime, includes the invention of the detective story.

4. The story, "The Murders in the Rue Morgue," written in 1841, is thought to be the first modern detective story.

5. Some scholars maintain that two other men, including the famous French author Voltaire, ~~was~~ actually responsible for the first story in this genre. *were*

6. Most of the characteristics of the classic detective story ~~is~~ present in Poe's story, though, including a partner who narrates and mysterious, seemingly unconnected pieces of evidence. *are*

7. Subsequent fictional detectives, including the famous Sherlock Holmes or Hercule Poirot, seems to be based on the mold set forth in this novel, though.

8. Another of Poe's most notable characteristics ~~were~~ being the first eminent American author to attempt to be a writer and nothing else; at the time, most writers had additional jobs besides their writing. *was*

9. A famous story about Poe, which was thought to be the stuff of rumors, concern his marriage to his first cousin, Virginia Clemm. *s*

10. "The Raven," arguably among Poe's most popular works, ~~bring~~ together Poe's spooky prose and the tribulations of his life — many thought it was written about his wife. *brings*

11. Most of his famous works, including "The Fall of the House of Usher," ~~is~~ gathered in a book entitled *Tales of Mystery and Imagination*. *are*

12. Among the stories contained in this book ~~is~~ "The Pit and the Pendulum" and "The Tell-Tale Heart," which are famous for building suspense. *are*

13. Poe's legacy as a poet, author, and a champion of the rights of writers are the reasons he is still such a popular figure today.

14. Poe's death, likely caused by both grief for his wife and a variety of self-destructive habits, elicited a vicious attack on his character by one of his colleagues. *NE*

15. Ironically, this had the opposite effect as intended, and Poe's books, particularly his poetry, ~~was~~ more popular than ever before. *were*

14/15

HOMEWORK EXERCISE 2:

Directions: Answer the questions that accompany the following passage.

The Race to Develop Graphene

The newest material in the world of technology has the **(1)** knowledge to change the way we look at mobile technology, medical diagnoses, and energy sources. Graphene is a super-thin touchscreen material that is transparent, **(2)** pliable, and efficient at conducting electricity. Stretched across the surface of a phone or a tablet, graphene can turn any device into a touchscreen. Thinner, stronger, and more pliable than materials currently on the market, **(3)** they are ideal for wearable devices like smartwatches and for tablets that can fold into the size of a small smartphone. Graphene is so thin that when Andre Geim and Konstantin Novoselov from the University of Manchester won the Nobel Prize in Physics in 2010 for their work with it, the material was classified as two-dimensional. With graphene, we **(4)** definitely may find a future context of development where mobile devices can be folded and unfolded.

[1] The conductive film now most commonly used for mobile-device touchscreens, indium tin oxide, is too brittle for bendable displays. [2] Moreover, it isn't particularly durable, and its effectiveness diminishes with larger screen sizes. [3] Researchers have yet to find a way to make indium tin oxide work on larger screen sizes. [4] Conversely, graphene can be made into sheets as large as 50 inches, about five times the size of an Apple iPad. {5}

1. A) NO CHANGE
   B) cost
   C) potential
   D) effectiveness

2. A) NO CHANGE
   B) besides being pliable and conducting electricity.
   C) pliable, as well as efficient at conducting electricity.
   D) and pliable, and conducts electricity.

3. A) NO CHANGE
   B) it is
   C) they will be
   D) it will be

4. A) NO CHANGE
   B) might possibly see technological improvement such that
   C) may see rapid changes so that
   D) may see an era in which

5. Which sentence should be eliminated in order to improve the focus of the paragraph?

   A) NO CHANGE
   B) Sentence 2
   C) Sentence 3
   D) Sentence 4

(6) <u>Beyond its applications for touchscreens,</u> graphene also has potential for use in memory chips, televisions, and other electronic devices. Graphene can conduct electricity about 100 times faster than silicon **(7)** , it will likely wind up in many different types of electronics. **(8)** <u>However,</u> Korean researchers have used graphene to make an experimental cell phone battery that can be recharged in just 15 minutes and retains the charge for a week.

Although technology companies are racing to commercialize graphene, its unique attributes may have far greater implications. Among several potential medical applications is its use for rapid, inexpensive electronic DNA sequencing, which could make graphene an excellent diagnostic tool. Graphene also has a unique combination of high electrical conductivity and optical transparency, **(9)** <u>which makes them an excellent candidate</u> for use in solar cells. Such technology has the potential to make solar energy more commercially viable.

{10} It is likely that companies like Apple, Google, and Samsung will be the first to discover ways to bring graphene into widespread use, but it will only be a matter of time before graphene extends beyond mobile devices and into the realms of medicine and green energy. Whether that will happen because of the tech giants or in spite of them **(11)** <u>remains</u> to be seen.

6. Which choice most effectively transitions between paragraphs?

A) NO CHANGE
B) Other than its importance to touchscreens;
C) Because touchscreens are such an important technology,
D) Though many would dispute this,

7. A) NO CHANGE
B) , therefore,
C) , so
D) ;

8. A) NO CHANGE
B) Heretofore,
C) In consequence,
D) In fact,

9. A) NO CHANGE
B) which makes it the most excellent candidates
C) which makes them excellent
D) which makes it an excellent candidate

10. Which choice most effectively establishes the main topic of the paragraph?

A) Big companies like Apple, Google, and Samsung usually make technological breakthroughs first because they have more resources.
B) While there is no dispute about the usefulness of graphene, there is dispute over who will succeed in its development first.
C) Researchers will likely develop graphene before the tech giants because tech giants are too focused on other issues.
D) No one is making much progress in developing graphene.

11. A) NO CHANGE
B) remain
C) is remaining
D) are remaining

BLUE WRITING LESSON 3: RUN-ONS AND FRAGMENTS
Getting Your Feet Wet

Directions: The following is intended as a short diagnostic exam.

1. Although Katie wanted a country music band and her fiancée <u>preferred a DJ. They managed</u> to compromise on a local blues band.

    A) NO CHANGE
    B) preferred a DJ: they managed
    C) preferred a DJ, they managed
    D) preferred a DJ, and they managed

2. The size of the bridal party for her wedding was a source of distress <u>for Katie she didn't</u> want to leave anyone out.

    A) NO CHANGE
    B) for Katie so she didn't
    C) for Katie, and she didn't
    D) for Katie because she didn't

3. After the ceremony was over, Katie was happy that she hadn't pressed any of the issues <u>too hard; marriage is</u> more than just the wedding day.

    A) NO CHANGE
    B) too hard; although marriage is
    C) too hard and it is true that marriage is
    D) too hard; because marriage is

BLUE WRITING LESSON 3: RUN-ONS AND FRAGMENTS
Wading In

TOPIC OVERVIEW: RUN-ONS AND FRAGMENTS

English sentence structure can look confusing, but if we focus on a few key concepts, questions like this are fairly easy. First we need a few definitions, and then we'll learn a couple simple rules. And that's all!

A *clause* is a series of words that consists of a subject and a predicate — a noun and a verb. A *dependent* clause cannot stand on its own, but an *independent* clause can.

There are four basic sentence types — these are taught in most English classes, but here is an example of each as a reminder:

Example 1: Katie picked a beautiful farmhouse in Asheville as the site of her wedding.

Example 2: The rental price of the farmhouse was steep, but it was the place she had always dreamed of getting married.

Example 3: Although her father was helping to pay for the wedding, Katie still wanted to keep the cost to a minimum.

Example 4: When her fiancée proposed, Katie was surprised; she didn't think he was ready for that kind of commitment.

Example 1 is a simple sentence — one independent clause. Example 2 is a compound sentence — two independent clauses connected with a semi-colon (we can also connect these with a comma and a conjunction). Example 3 is a complex sentence — one independent and one dependent clause. If the dependent clause comes first, we usually use a comma to connect them (no conjunction!). If the dependent clause comes second, we rarely need a comma — just continue the sentence with the dependent clause. Finally, Example 4 is a compound-complex sentence — two independent clauses and a dependent clause.

TOPIC OVERVIEW: FRAGMENTS

Sentence fragments occur when a sentence is either missing a subject or a verb (this is less common on the SAT) or when a sentence is missing an independent clause.

Example 5: Although Katie didn't have a person in mind to be her bridesmaid.

Example 6: Katie didn't have a person in mind to be her bridesmaid.

In these two examples, we see a dependent clause (Example 5) and an independent clause (Example 6). The two sentences differ by only one word, but that word, *although*, is enough to make the first sentence a fragment. Words like this are called *subordinating conjunctions*, and they signal to you that there may be a sentence boundary error.

Subordinating Conjunctions

After	Although	As
Because	Before	Even
How	If	In order that
Now that	Once	Provided
Rather than	Since	So
So that	Than	That
Though	Unless	Until
When	Whenever	Where
Whereas	Wherever	While

Example 5 is an example of a fragment. There are a number of ways to fix a fragment. One way is already shown in Example 6: remove the subordinating conjunction. Another way is to connect the dependent clause to an independent clause, using either a semicolon or a comma and a conjunction. When we encounter a fragment, follow one of the aforementioned ways.

TOPIC OVERVIEW: RUN-ON SENTENCES

A **run-on sentence** can be created in a number of ways. Two common errors found on the SAT are comma splices and missing connectives.

A **comma splice** occurs when two independent clauses are connected by just a comma, without a conjunction. The best way to identify this is to read each clause individually and determine if it is independent or not. If both are independent, then there are three possible fixes:

1) replace the comma with a semicolon.
2) replace the comma with a period and begin a new sentence.
3) add a coordinating conjunction.

When a question involving a comma splice is presented on the test, one of these fixes will be among the answer choices.

Example 7: The guest list for a wedding is often a point of contention among the participants, limited space means that some people will have to be left out of the occasion.

Example 8: The guest list for a wedding is often a point of contention among the participants; limited space means that some people will have to be left out of the occasion.

Example 7 is an example of a comma splice; Example 8 is an example of a way fix it.

A missing connective occurs when two independent clauses run right into another — no comma, no semicolon, no nothing. In this case, add one of the connectives listed above.

Example 9: Katie wanted to invite all of her parents' cousins her fiancée thought that it would make the wedding party much too large.

Example 10: Katie wanted to invite all of her parents' cousins, but her fiancée thought that it would make the wedding party much too large.

Example 9 is an example a sentence with a missing connective, and Example 10 fixes the problem by adding a comma and the coordinating conjunction *but*.

WRAP-UP: RUN-ONS AND FRAGMENTS

To answer questions about run-ons and fragments, it's important to identify the different types of clauses in the sentence and to understand the rules that tell us how to connect them. Here is a short summary of the information in this lesson:

1. Two independent clauses can be connected by either a semi-colon or a comma and a conjunction. An alternate way to connect two independent clauses is to make them into two separate sentences.
2. A dependent clause can be attached to the front end of an independent clause with a comma, or to the back end without a comma.
3. A fragment is a dependent clause standing by itself; a run-on sentence is two independent clauses that are incorrectly connected.

BLUE WRITING LESSON 3: RUN-ONS AND FRAGMENTS
Learning to Swim

CONCEPT EXERCISE:

Directions: Find and correct errors in the following sentences. Some sentences will not have any errors.

1. Cosmology is the study of the origin and development of the universe, one of its most famous theories is the Big Bang Theory

2. Although there is no direct evidence for it, many scientists do not question the fact that the universe began as a very dense, hot ball of energy.

3. Some of the best observational evidence for the theory comes from Edwin Hubble, who observed that the universe appears to be expanding.

4. Although the red-shifting of galaxies is a persuasive argument in favor of this theory.

5. We observe a red shift in the light coming from an object when it is receding from us, This is true of every galaxy astronomers have ever observed.

6. A good way to understand this is to think of the universe as existing on the surface of a balloon, the expansion of the universe is like someone blowing up the balloon.

7. Now imagine making two marks on the balloon; no matter where you put them, they will always be moving away from each other. NE

8. One theory, although many people find it hard to believe, involving a repeated expansion and contraction of the universe. involves

9. Even though this theory seems unbelievable, it helps to explain some of the apparent paradoxes discovered by physicists.

10. One of the most divisive ideas in cosmology is the "multiverse" concept, this is the idea that there are a vast number of other universes running parallel with ours.

11. Probably the most famous supporter of the multiverse theory is Stephen Hawking, a physicist most notable for his brilliant work despite his devastating illness, ALS. NE

12. Whether or not the multiverse exists, many cosmologists believe that inquiry in this field is unscientific because it explores concepts that have no hope of proof.

13. Although many people associate cosmology with a scientific interpretation of the universe unfolding, almost every religion has a version of their own. NE

14. For example, the major monotheistic religions of the world using the Genesis story found in the Bible as a version of the origin and development of the universe. use

15. Inherent in Hindu cosmology is the concept of a multiverse; additionally, there is a cycle of existence that lasts over 300 trillion years!

BLUE WRITING LESSON 3: RUN-ONS AND FRAGMENTS
Diving into the Deep End

PRACTICE EXERCISE:

Directions: Answer the questions that accompany the following passage.

A New Tool for Early Detection of Heart Failure

Until recently, a reliable, low-cost, non-invasive method to measure changes in the water content of the lungs did not exist. Having such a device could be an important tool for the early detection of heart **(1)** <u>failure, this</u> condition currently afflicts an estimated 5.1 million Americans and is a leading cause of hospitalization and death.

Heart failure costs the nation an estimated $32 billion **(2)** <u>annually; which includes</u> the cost of health care services, medications to treat heart failure, and missed days of work, according to the federal Centers for Disease Control and Prevention. The only condition that has proven more costly is **(3)** <u>cancer. Furthermore,</u> this condition frequently leads to patients being readmitted to hospitals within 30 days of the initial discharge.

A scientist named Magdy Iskander has invented a new type of **(4)** <u>stethoscope. That he believes</u> will prompt significant and positive changes for patients suffering from heart failure and other related conditions. It attaches to the skin of the chest (there is no need to implant it on the lungs or **(5)** <u>within the body), and uses</u> a novel radio frequency (RF) sensor to detect small changes in lung water and monitor vital signs such as heart rate, respiration rate, and stroke volume. Increased <u>levels</u> of water in **(6)** <u>the lungs, a</u> symptom of heightened heart failure risk.

Since the lungs normally do contain **(7)** <u>some water the idea is</u> to first use the device to obtain a baseline so as to more easily identify future changes. After initial treatment, the stethoscope, **(8)** <u>an important component</u> that monitors patients after discharge to prevent readmission, is critical for identifying changes.

1. A) NO CHANGE
   B) failure; this
   C) failure, or this
   D) failure. And this

2. A) NO CHANGE
   B) annually which includes
   C) annually, which includes
   D) annually. Which includes

3. A) NO CHANGE
   B) cancer furthermore,
   C) cancer, furthermore,
   D) cancer; and furthermore,

4. A) NO CHANGE
   B) stethoscope; that he believes
   C) stethoscope that he believes
   D) stethoscope, that he believes

5. A) NO CHANGE
   B) within the body) and uses
   C) within the body); and uses
   D) within the body), uses

6. A) NO CHANGE
   B) the lungs are a
   C) the lungs is a
   D) the lungs; a

7. A) NO CHANGE
   B) some water; the idea is
   C) some water; ideas are
   D) some water, the idea is

8. A) NO CHANGE
   B) the more important component
   C) a more important component
   D) the most important component

The cardio-pulmonary stethoscope evolved from research Iskander conducted years ago for the **(9)** <u>Air Force, when he was</u> developing safety standards for microwave exposure. He was trying to evaluate the biological effects of working with microwaves by exploring the use of microwaves in medical applications. In doing so, he discovered that microwave signals reflect changes in lung water. If the lungs have too much water, the magnitude of the microwave signal is reduced because water absorbs microwaves. More water enters **(10)** <u>the lungs, the signal</u> becomes weaker.

Years ago, when Iskander designed his first cardio-pulmonary stethoscope, no one else had yet considered making a similar device. Today, since many of its components are now used in cell phones, the costs are now impossibly reduced, making it easier for doctors and hospitals to afford this potentially life-saving device. If the stethoscope proves **(11)** <u>affordable enough, it could</u> even be placed in patients' homes, allowing them to transmit their vital health data to doctors without having to visit a hospital.

9. A) NO CHANGE
B) Air Force, he was
C) Air Force; when he was
D) Air Force; and he was

10. A) NO CHANGE
B) the lungs, or the signal
C) the lungs, so the signal
D) the lungs, but the signal

11. A) NO CHANGE
B) affordable enough; it could
C) affordable enough. It could
D) affordable enough, although it could

TEST EXERCISE:

Directions: Answer the questions that accompany the following passage.

Searching the Valley of Death

Amor Masovic has the gaze and mournful air of a man who never gets enough sleep. For nearly two decades, his job has been to find the mass graves containing thousands **(1)** <u>of people who have never been seen again since the Bosnian war.</u> He is very good at what he does. In the summer of 2012, Masovic **(2)** <u>decided</u> that he and his colleagues at the Bosnian government's Missing Persons Institute had found more than 700 mass graves, containing the remains of nearly 25,000 people.

Of all the atrocities committed in Bosnia between 1992 and 1995, the one that compels Masovic the most is **(3)** <u>Srebenica, which has come to symbolize</u> the Bosnian war's unspeakable brutality and the international community's colossal failure in confronting it. Located in a tiny valley in eastern Bosnia, it was the site of one of the war's most desperate contests, where a few thousand soldiers and as many as 40,000 Muslim refugees held out for three years against a siege by Serb separatist fighters.

{4} For much of that time, Srebrenica was considered a United Nations-designated "safe area," a status that proved meaningless when the Serbs launched their assault in July 1995. Instead of resisting, the U.N. Protection Force stood down **(5)** <u>and</u> over the next few days, the Serbs hunted and killed more than 8,000 men and boys. It was the worst slaughter to occur on European soil since World War II.

1. A) NO CHANGE
   B) who disappeared during the Bosnian war.
   C) of lost victims of the terrible genocide during the Bosnian war.
   D) of Bosnians who many thought would be lost forever to history.

2. A) NO CHANGE
   B) hoped
   C) calculated
   D) guessed

3. A) NO CHANGE
   B) Srebrenica, it has come to symbolize
   C) Srebrenica, moreover, it has come to symbolize
   D) Srebrenica and it has come to symbolize

4. Which choice most effectively establishes the main topic of this paragraph?

   A) Historians don't know much about what happened at Srebrenica because there were so few survivors.
   B) Srebrenica was one of many similar mass killings during the Bosnian war.
   C) The U.N. Protection Force is to blame for what happened at Srebrenica.
   D) Srebrenica was the worst tragedy of the Bosnian war.

5. A) NO CHANGE
   B) ; and
   C) , and
   D) Delete it. It is unnecessary.

WH

The massacre in Srebrenica presents a professional challenge to Masovic. Only about a thousand of those fleeing were killed **(6)** <u>by soldiers.</u> The other 7,000 were taken to killing fields and dumped into mass graves. Shortly afterward, Serb commanders ordered the original graves dug up and the remains moved to a series of smaller mass graves along the Drina River basin — the so-called Valley of Death. **(7)** <u>Initially,</u> Masovic's goal is to find those who have been killed so that their families can find closure concerning the situation.

Since 1999, Masovic **(8)** <u>have transferred</u> any remains discovered from Srebrenica to a mortuary built by the International Commission on Missing Persons (ICMP). **(9)** <u>Working off a DNA database of more than 22,000 living relatives of the missing.</u> The ICMP has identified nearly 7,000 of those killed. Such efforts make Srebrenica one of the **(10)** <u>most</u> thoroughly documented war crimes in history.

Masovic's job is not yet finished. There are roughly 1,100 men still unaccounted for. Masovic believes that there are some remains still in the forests surrounding Srebrenica **(11)** <u>but he</u> is worried that many more may have been thrown in the Drina River. If so, many may never be found.

6. Which of the following makes the most sense in the context of the paragraph?

   A) NO CHANGE
   B) delete the word
   C) outright.
   D) at that time.

7. A) NO CHANGE
   B) Lastly
   C) Least importantly
   D) Ultimately

8. A) NO CHANGE
   B) has transferred
   C) had transferred
   D) will have transferred

9. A) NO CHANGE
   B) The ICMP has successfully used a DNA database of more than 22,000 living relatives to identify the missing.
   C) The ICMP working off a DNA database of more than 22,000 living relatives of the missing.
   D) The ICMP, working off, a DNA database of more than 22,000 living relatives to identify the missing.

10. A) NO CHANGE
    B) more
    C) less
    D) least

11. A) NO CHANGE
    B) ; but he
    C) , but he
    D) , but, he

C2 education
be smarter

BLUE WRITING LESSON 3: RUN-ONS AND FRAGMENTS
Race to the Finish

HOMEWORK EXERCISE 1:

Directions: Find and correct errors in the following sentences. Some sentences will not have any errors.

1. Although the most popular of the four major sports in America is football, our official national pastime is baseball.

2. The earliest forms of this bat-and-ball game originated in England though today's modern game hardly resembles these games at all.

3. John Newberry's *A Little Pretty Pocketbook* contains the first description of baseball; it used a triangular field and didn't have bases but used posts instead.

4. Abner Doubleday, the supposed inventor of baseball, who was born in New York in the 1800s.

5. Modern baseball began in the mid-1800s in New York, and journalists began referring to it as the "national game."

6. Oddly, in the first versions of the game, if a player caught a ball after one bounce, the player who hit it was out, this rule was disallowed in 1863.

7. Baseball experienced a massive overhaul in the 1920s when many new rule changes ended the "dead ball" era, when the sport became more hitter-friendly. NE

8. Jackie Robinson, the first black player to play in the major leagues, took the field for the Brooklyn Dodgers in 1947, but it was still 12 years until every major league team had at least one black player.

9. A tradition in existence for many years, the "retiring" of a jersey number for a team; no player for that team will ever wear that number again.

10. In a move that garnered much public approval, Major League Baseball retired Robinson's number, 42, for every team in 1997.

11. Another great tradition that has come about in the past 15 years is Jackie Robinson Day, April 15th, and on this day every player wears the number 42.

12. Baseball is a popular sport in other countries as well, most notably in Venezuela, the Dominican Republic, and Japan.

13. Although it was once an Olympic sport, the International Olympic Committee voted in 2005 to eliminate it from the Games. NE

14. Because the sport is played in summer, and the Olympic Games are also in the summer.

15. Although they are second nature to people who have grown up with the sport, therefore many people find that the complicated rules of baseball make the game less fun to watch.

HOMEWORK EXERCISE 2:

Directions: Answer the questions that accompany the following passage.

Tiananmen, Forgotten

I remember the first time the term *liu si* — meaning June 4, which is how the Tiananmen protests, the widespread 1989 demonstrations that ended in bloodshed, are referred to in China — came up in conversation with my peers. On the 20th anniversary of the crackdown, a friend turned to me and asked what *liu si* was all about. Twenty-five years after the massacre, **(1)** Chinese people still forbidden by the government to speak about June 4.

{2} To my generation, the widespread patriotic liberalism that bonded students in the early 1980s feels as distant as the political fanaticism that defined the preceding decades. Chinese leaders, having learned their lesson during the Tiananmen protests, have kept politics out of **(3)** our lives, channeling our energies to state-sanctioned pursuits like economic advancement. Growing up in the post-Tiananmen years, **(4)** we have found simple life. We study hard, hoping to earn that college degree, that prestigious job, focusing on our personal well-being, rather than the larger issues that bedevil society.

Many of my Chinese peers **(5)** unfamiliar with the stories of Chen Guangcheng and Ai Weiwei, whose courageous struggles against the state are better known among my Western friends. Topics such as the religious repression in Tibet barely enter the collective consciousness of my generation. Perhaps nowhere is this indifference toward politics and civil rights more pronounced than in the insouciance of young people about the Communist Party's attempts to expunge historical truths from public memory.

1. A) NO CHANGE
   B) Chinese people too afraid of the possible government response to speak about June 4.
   C) the Chinese government remaining active in stomping out discussion of June 4.
   D) the topic remains taboo here.

2. Which choice best states the main idea of this paragraph?

   A) Chinese people are no longer bothered by Chinese politics, so they don't protest the government.
   B) The Chinese government has succeeded in getting its people to focus on working hard rather than on political dissent.
   C) The Chinese government has made liberal reforms, which have satisfied the Chinese.
   D) The Chinese people and government have decided that ignoring what happened on June 4th is the best policy.

3. A) NO CHANGE
   B) their lives,
   C) Chinese people's lives,
   D) my life,

4. A) NO CHANGE
   B) a simpler life will be easier to find.
   C) our lives were simpler.
   D) life is simpler.

5. A) NO CHANGE
   B) are unfamiliar with
   C) aware of
   D) cognizant of

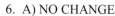

The majority of my generation still believes **(6)** : by way of illustration, that the war against Japanese invasion in the 1930s and '40s was fought primarily by Communist soldiers, while the Nationalist army passively resisted the Japanese and actively combated the Communists **(7)** — a direct contradiction to verifiable fact.

The party is responsible for distorting my **(8)** generations' understanding of history through state education and blocking our access to sensitive information. Yet even those who are well-aware of the state's meddling **(9)** makes little effort to seek truth and push for change. Well-educated and worldly, members of my generation nonetheless see censorship as a mere nuisance to be begrudgingly endured, rather than an infringement on their freedom of speech. If the previous generation learned the cost of political transgression through persecution, today's youth instinctively understand the futility of challenging the system. **(10)** People of my generation are even beginning to believe that the government is right to do censorship.

Outsiders may lament the contrast between the conservative outlook of today's Chinese youth and the unbounded liberalism of the Tiananmen generation **(11)** but between those of my peers who are familiar with *liu si*, the rosy romanticism on the square in 1989 takes on a different hue today, when viewed in the fluorescent light of a plush government office.

10/11

6. A) NO CHANGE
B) ; for example,
C) , for instance,
D) , as a case in point;

7. A) NO CHANGE
B) ; a direct
C) ; and this is a direct
D) –which is a direct

8. A) NO CHANGE
B) generation
C) generation's
D) generations

9. A) NO CHANGE
B) make
C) made
D) will make

10. Which choice most effectively concludes this paragraph?

A) NO CHANGE
B) Every time people of my generation rebel, they are immediately thrown in prison with no legal recourse.
C) Delete it. It is unnecessary.
D) Better, they believe, to simply accept the system and try to excel within its narrow confines, seeking prestigious positions within the government and state-owned enterprises.

11. A) NO CHANGE
B) , but
C) ; but
D) ; although

BLUE WRITING LESSON 4: VERB TENSE, MOOD, AND VOICE
Getting Your Feet Wet

Directions: The questions below are intended as a short diagnostic exam.

1. Although she never gets up on time, my sister <u>wishes she was able to</u> get to school before the late bell.

   A) NO CHANGE
   B) wishes she might
   C) wishes she could be able to
   D) wishes she were able to

2. <u>The penalties were collected by my sister</u> after a month of being late to school every day.

   A) NO CHANGE
   B) The penalty that was collected by my sister
   C) The penalties were collected for my sister
   D) My sister collected penalties

BLUE WRITING LESSON 4: VERB TENSE, MOOD, AND VOICE
Wading In

TOPIC OVERVIEW: VERBS

English is a **verb-intensive** language — there are verbs for almost every action. No matter how small a difference between two things, there is a verb that will distinguish between them. For example, a verb commonly used in writing is *walk*. But people don't just walk, they also *amble, bounce, hike, limp, lumber, march, mosey, pace, parade, plod, prance, sashay, saunter, stagger, sidle, step, stomp, swagger, tread, trip, trot, waddle,* and *wander*. This rich variety is what makes English a very expressive language. In this lesson we will discuss three characteristics of verbs: tense, mood, and voice.

TOPIC OVERVIEW: VERB TENSE

Tenses tell us the time at which the action of a verb occurs. The diagram below outlines when each of the tenses is used — note that there is a diagram for simple tenses, progressive tenses, and perfect tenses.

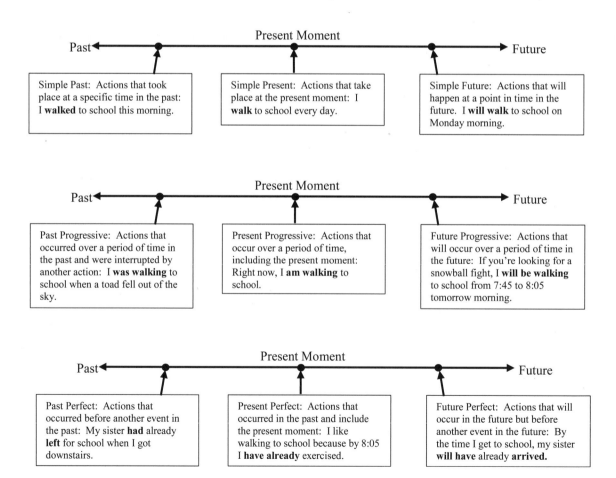

Present Moment

Past ◄————————————————————————► Future

Simple Past: Actions that took place at a specific time in the past: I **walked** to school this morning.

Simple Present: Actions that take place at the present moment: I **walk** to school every day.

Simple Future: Actions that will happen at a point in time in the future. I **will walk** to school on Monday morning.

Present Moment

Past ◄————————————————————————► Future

Past Progressive: Actions that occurred over a period of time in the past and were interrupted by another action: I **was walking** to school when a toad fell out of the sky.

Present Progressive: Actions that occur over a period of time, including the present moment: Right now, I **am walking** to school.

Future Progressive: Actions that will occur over a period of time in the future: If you're looking for a snowball fight, I **will be walking** to school from 7:45 to 8:05 tomorrow morning.

Present Moment

Past ◄————————————————————————► Future

Past Perfect: Actions that occurred before another event in the past: My sister **had** already **left** for school when I got downstairs.

Present Perfect: Actions that occurred in the past and include the present moment: I like walking to school because by 8:05 I **have already** exercised.

Future Perfect: Actions that will occur in the future but before another event in the future: By the time I get to school, my sister **will have** already **arrived.**

For the most part, we can tell the appropriate tense based on the sentence. These are among the easier questions asked about verbs on the New SAT. Below we will discuss the more difficult topics, mood and voice.

TOPIC OVERVIEW: VERB MOOD

There are three **moods** in English: indicative, imperative, and subjunctive.

The *indicative* mood is the one that most writing and speech occurs in, including statements of fact, opinion, and questions:

Example 1: Waking my sister up in the morning **is** not easy.

Example 2: She **doesn't wake up** with her alarm, so my dad **has** to go into her room and **yell** at her.

Example 3: How **is** it possible for someone to **sleep** through that racket?

The *imperative* mood is the one used when giving commands. The subject of sentences written in imperative mood is often assumed to be "you," or the person being addressed in the sentence.

Example 4: **Go** into her room and **wake** her up!

Example 5: **Consider** going to bed a little earlier.

The most difficult mood in English is the *subjunctive* mood, which is used to express states of unreality, such as hopes, wishes, hypothetical situations, and requests:

Example 6: I wish she **were** easier to get out of bed — it would save us a lot of time in the morning.

Example 7: I suggest that she **try** not watching TV while trying to fall asleep.

Often, questions involving the subjunctive mood will include the verb *to be* — either *was* or *were*. When a sentence is expressing something that isn't true, the sentence should use *were*. Such sentences will often — but not always — begin with "if" (as in, "If I were a rich man…").

TOPIC OVERVIEW: VERB VOICE

The **voice** of a verb is either passive or active. Active voice is almost always preferred based on style. A verb is in active voice if the action that it indicates is being performed by the subject. Look at the following examples to see this principle in action:

Example 8: My sister **drives** me to school when she gets up on time.

Example 9: I **am driven** to school by my sister when she gets up on time.

In both sentences, the verb is *to drive*. In Example 8, *My sister* is the subject, and she is the one doing the driving. That means the verb is in active voice. In Example 9, *I* is the subject, but *I* am not doing the driving, my sister is. This is called passive voice and is usually incorrect. As a general rule, choose active voice over passive voice if you have the option.

The only exceptions to this rule occur when the thing being acted upon is more important in the sentence than the actor. This is very rare, and is unlikely to show up on the SAT.

IDENTIFYING VERB QUESTIONS

On the SAT, any verb tense, mood, or voice questions will include a verb in the underlined portion of the sentence. If there is a verb in the underlined portion, examine the rest of the sentence to determine whether the verb features an error in tense, mood, or voice.

WRAP-UP: VERB QUESTIONS

For any verb-related question, follow these steps to find the correct answer:

1. Check to be sure that the verb agrees with the subject. If the verb and the subject disagree, the question is a subject-verb agreement error rather than a verb tense, mood, or voice error.
2. Look for clues within the sentence that might indicate the appropriate verb tense. Eliminate any answer choices that are not in the correct tense.
3. Examine the rest of the sentence to determine the appropriate verb mood. Eliminate any answer choices that are not in the correct mood.
4. Look at the remaining answer choices. Choose the answer that best suits the rest of the sentence.

BLUE WRITING LESSON 4: VERB TENSE, MOOD, AND VOICE
Learning to Swim

CONCEPT EXERCISE:

Directions: Find and correct errors in the following sentences. Some sentences will not have any errors.

1. Many historians ~~have believed~~ that the American dialect of English has to do with the way that English immigrants spoke during the colonial period.

2. We have no way of knowing, however, because there ~~were~~ no recordings from that era.

3. If it ~~was~~ [WERE] not for the fact that historians ~~know~~ [knew] more about European languages before Roman domination, we would not know as much about how modern European Romance languages emerged.

4. Historians believe that before people in modern France began to speak Latin, they ~~spoke~~ Celtic and Germanic languages that contributed to the way the people there ~~ended~~ up speaking Latin.

5. The dialect of Vulgar Latin that then ~~had~~ emerged [had spoken] in Gaul (modern France) led to the way that French sounds today.

6. For example, people in the south of France still ~~are speaking~~ Basque, Catalan, or Provencal.

7. In the early 1800s, Napoleon Bonaparte was responsible for accelerating a movement which ~~was~~ already ~~taking~~ place since medieval times. [had taken]

8. In the early 1800s, Napoleon ~~had~~ decided to try to make Parisian (from Paris) French into the preferred French dialect and language for all French people.

9. This ~~has~~ [had] been a difficult process because people [LIKE] ~~liked~~ to keep their language the same.

10. However, Napoleon wanted to make France into a modern, unified nation-state, and this ~~cannot~~ [COULD NOT] happen without a unifying language. [NE]

11. Napoleon's efforts, aided by all of the other elements of modernity, such as increased travel and communication, had been largely successful.

12. While there are still pockets of places in France where people speak older, regional languages, it is largely the elderly who still use these languages.

13. Linguists speculate what will take place by the year 2100.

14. Some think that modernity will have continued to abolish smaller dialects and languages.

15. But others think that a renewed appreciation for the local is spreading throughout Europe, and that this mood will preserve these linguistic heritages of the past.

BLUE WRITING LESSON 4: VERB TENSE, MOOD, AND VOICE
Diving into the Deep End

PRACTICE EXERCISE:

Directions: Answer the questions that accompany the following passage.

Central African Republic Conflict

The Central African Republic (CAR) **(1)** <u>had been mired</u> in conflict for well over a decade. From 2004 to 2007, the country **(2)** <u>is engaged</u> in civil war. The end of the war **(3)** <u>did not bring</u> an end to violence, and it was only a matter of time before a new conflict **(4)** <u>arosed</u>. On December 10, 2012, rebel groups accused president Francois Bozize of failing to abide by peace agreements signed following the CAR's civil war. By the end of 2012, rebel forces known as Seleka **(5)** <u>captured</u> much of the central and eastern regions of the country, and in March of 2013, Seleka overthrew Bozize's government.

The Seleka are not an overtly religious movement, but they are mostly Muslim, as was Michel Djotodia, the president they installed after taking power. **(6)** <u>During Djotodia's reign, Seleka fighters were able to plunder villages and to kill Christians and supporters of the former president.</u> Although Djotodia claimed that Seleka had been disbanded, the group has continued to commit atrocities including executions, rape, and looting, fomenting religious tension in a country that is 80% Christian.

1. A) NO CHANGE
   B) has been mired
   C) is mired
   D) is being mired

2. A) NO CHANGE
   B) had been engaged
   C) was engaged
   D) has been engaged

3. A) NO CHANGE
   B) does not bring
   C) should not bring
   D) could not bring

4. A) NO CHANGE
   B) arose
   C) has arose
   D) arisen

5. A) NO CHANGE
   B) had been capturing
   C) were capturing
   D) had captured

6. Based on the context of the paragraph it is in, what is the best way to revise this sentence?

   A) NO CHANGE
   B) During Djotodia's reign, Seleka fighters did plunder villages and did kill Christians and supporters of the former president.
   C) During Djotodia's reign, Seleka fighters plundered villages and killed Christians and supporters of the former president.
   D) During Djotodia's reign, Seleka fighters were plundering villages and were killing Christians and supporters of the former president.

Though the current conflict **(7)** <u>is often described as being Christian versus Muslim,</u> this is a dangerous oversimplification. This is not a religious conflict, but a political failure in the CAR. The root of the conflict is the disagreements between Seleka and former President Bozize. The primary fighting parties are the Seleka, commonly considered to be a Muslim group, and the anti-balaka, commonly considered to be a Christian group. But these descriptions are not entirely accurate.

The Seleka **(8)** <u>allow</u> their transgressions to the majority Christian population. They attack anyone they believe **(9)** <u>do support</u> the former president and have been known to attack and loot Muslim property as well as Christian property. Likewise, the anti-balaka groups include Muslims and animists as well as Christians.

Nearly 700,000 people **(10)** <u>have been displaced</u> by the fighting in CAR. Tens of thousands have fled to neighboring countries. Although there are about 8,000 international peacekeepers in the country, this isn't enough to restore peace.

In the absence of international intervention, women and religious leaders have been appealing together for peace. The country's most senior Muslim cleric sought shelter with the Catholic archbishop of Bangui. That month, no one was attacked in Lakounga, one of the oldest parts of the capital, where Christian and Muslim leaders worked together to protect the community. Posters were plastered on every street corner with the message: "Christians and Muslims, the same blood, the same life, the same country."

As long as local and international media continues to define the CAR conflict as a religious conflict, such efforts **(11)** <u>continue</u> to be undermined. And as long as propaganda promoting disunion among African Christians and Muslims continues, so will the CAR conflict.

7. A) NO CHANGE
   B) is often described as Christian versus Muslim
   C) is often being described as being Christian versus Muslim
   D) can often be described as Christian versus Muslim

8. Based on the context of the sentence it is in, what is the best way to revise the underlined portion?

   A) NO CHANGE
   B) do limit
   C) limit
   D) do not limit

9. A) NO CHANGE
   B) should support
   C) might support
   D) support

10. A) NO CHANGE
    B) are being displaced
    C) were displaced
    D) will be displaced

11. A) NO CHANGE
    B) are continuing
    C) have continued
    D) will continue

TEST EXERCISE:

Directions: Answer the questions that accompany the following passage.

Post-War Bosnia

Following World War II, Yugoslavia was set up as a federation of six republics with borders drawn along ethnic and historical lines. To unite these republics, each containing ethnic and religious factions that had long battled one another, **(1)** <u>means being willing to face future, unknown challenges.</u> Only through the firm rule of president-for-life Josip Broz Tito was Yugoslavia able to remain united. Following his death in1980, the weakened federal government **(2)** <u>faced economic and political challenges that were so overwhelming that it could not handle them.</u> One by one, the republics **(3)** <u>created</u> independence, resulting in a string of inter-ethnic incidents, first in Croatia and then, most severely, in multi-ethnic Bosnia and Herzegovina.

Bosnia and Herzegovina was home to a diverse population **(4)** <u>:</u> 44% were Muslim Bosniaks, 31% were Orthodox Serbs, and 17% were Catholic Croats. When Bosnia and Herzegovina declared independence, the Bosnian Serbs mobilized their forces in order to secure a Serbian territory within Bosnia. Bosnian Croats soon followed suit, resulting in three ethnic groups squabbling over a single territory. In 1994, the Washington agreement **(5)** <u>creates</u> the Federation of Bosnia and Herzegovina, uniting the Bosnians and the Croats against the Serbs.

{6} The Bosnian War resulted in well over 100,000 deaths, many the result of ethnic cleansing on the part of the Bosnian Serbs. Finally, after three long years of fighting, President Clinton's special envoy to the Balkans, Richard Holbrooke, compelled the warring factions to the negotiating table. Because neither side had been militarily defeated, the Dayton accords laid out a novel solution: The Bosnia and Herzegovina government would be joined in a confederation with that of the Serbian Republic of Srpska, each maintaining separate

1. A) NO CHANGE
   B) might be to reopen old wounds without knowing how to heal them.
   C) could be an easy solution.
   D) was to court political upheaval.

2. A) NO CHANGE
   B) was unable to find a way to overcome rising political and economic challenges.
   C) struggled to cope with rising economic and political challenges.
   D) had few answers for the questions asked by rising economic and political challenges.

3. A) NO CHANGE
   B) asked for
   C) found
   D) proclaimed

4. A) NO CHANGE
   B) ,
   C) .
   D) Delete it.

5. A) NO CHANGE
   B) had created
   C) has created
   D) created

6. Which choice most effectively establishes the main topic of the paragraph?

   A) The United States did not act quickly enough to prevent the deaths of over 100,000 people in the Bosnian War.
   B) Although the fighting was stopped by effective diplomacy, the solution it created was unique and untested.
   C) Richard Holbrooke should be commended for his leadership.
   D) While the Serbs, Bosniaks, and Croats agreed to the confederation plan, none of them liked it.

status within a single nation.

The blueprint for this nonintegrated integration **(7)** <u>is including</u> a joint parliament, a co-presidency and a mixed judiciary. The linchpin in the plan was the creation of the Office of the High Representative (OHR), an office with the power to appoint, promote, or fire any Bosnian official. **(8)** <u>This solution gave officials from outside the country the chance to intervene before problems became pronounced.</u> **(9)** <u>Because there was</u> no internal mechanism to compel reconciliation between the two entities, the international community <u>had to remain</u> resolute in imposing it. By 2006, with the U.S. mired in far more pressing foreign issues, the European Union had effectively taken over the running of the OHR and displayed little interest in using its power to force reform.

This **(10)** <u>; unfortunately,</u> coincided with the return to power in Srpska of Milorad Dodik. Dodik served as Prime Minister of Srpska in the late 1990s. Then, he was a moderate and conciliatory figure. But with the OHR greatly weakened, Dodik found it to be far more politically expedient to stage his comeback as part of an ultranationalist party. The government of Srpska is now run by this party, which advocates historical revisionism that asserts that Serbians were the victims, **(11)** <u>nor the war criminals,</u> during the Bosnian War. Since taking power, Dodik has frequently advocated the dissolution of Bosnia, suggesting that perhaps the Bosnian War is not over after all.

7. A) NO CHANGE
    B) includes
    C) might include
    D) did include

8. Which choice most effectively connects the previous and the successive sentences?

    A) NO CHANGE
    B) Delete it. It is unnecessary.
    C) This unique solution seemed likely to succeed.
    D) But this situation rests on a risky presumption.

9. A) NO CHANGE
    B) Because there has been
    C) Because there had been
    D) Because there will be

10. A) NO CHANGE
    B) , unfortunately,
    C) unfortunately
    D) unfortunately,

11. A) NO CHANGE
    B) or the war criminals
    C) not the war criminals
    D) rather war criminals

BLUE WRITING LESSON 4: VERB TENSE, MOOD, AND VOICE
Race to the Finish

HOMEWORK EXERCISE 1:

Directions: Find and correct errors in the following sentences. Some sentences will not have any errors.

1. Languages in the British Isles are in some ways even more complex of an issue than they were on the Continent.

2. First off, the language of English itself is a hybrid language, composed mostly from Germanic languages but also with elements from Old French and Old Norse.

3. In many ways, the complexity of the English language is based on the complex history of an island that had been conquered by various language groups over the last few thousand years.

4. Around 1,800 years ago, historians know that many people in England would begin to speak Latin because the Romans conquered England.

5. Before that, English people spoke various dialects of Celtic/Gaelic.

6. There is considerable debate, however, about what language the Picts, the people living in the north of what today is Scotland, had spoken.

7. If linguists and historians were to get a hold of a significant artifact from the Pictish areas, then they could know whether Pictish was a distinct language or just another form of Celtic/Gaelic.

8. While English is the predominant language in England, Scotland, Wales, Northern Ireland, and Ireland today, that was changing over the last 500 years in particular.

9. The Tudors, most notably Henry VIII and Elizabeth I, significantly expanded English rule in the Isles, especially into Ireland, which was completely separate politically from England before that.

10. Starting in Dublin and growing from there, English gradually has begun to take over in Ireland.

11. Even before that, Irish Gaelic speakers conquered western Scotland, which is why people in that region still speak Gaelic today.

12. The fact that western Scotland, often called the Hebrides, and its bordering region of the Highlands, is so isolated from even the rest of Scotland explains why people there still speak Gaelic.

13. Also in the 1500s, the English Reformation means that a more standardized version of English began to conquer regional locations in England.

14. That more standardized or "proper" version of English comes to be called "the King's English", "the Queen's English", or "BBC English".

15. As in France, local dialects and languages are gaining more purchase today than they had as recently as 50 years go.

HOMEWORK EXERCISE 2:

Directions: Answer the questions that accompany the following passage.

Segregation by Ability

New York City's schools chancellor created quite a stir by downplaying the importance of the city's "gifted and talented" programs, sparking a debate about whether public schools **(1)** <u>drain</u> their brightest students into special classrooms. Some label these tracking programs as segregation by ability, pointing out underlying racial trends within such **(2)** <u>systems. Others worry</u> that eliminating gifted programs would leave our brightest students floundering in boring, unchallenging classes.

{**3**} New York City's gifted programs have a long history of exacerbating racial segregation within public schools. As of 2011, roughly 70% of all New York City public school students were black and Latino, but more than 70% of kindergarteners in gifted programs **(4)** <u>are</u> white or Asian. These racial disparities are largely due to socioeconomics. Affluent students generally enter kindergarten with stronger **(5)** <u>reading skills, communication skills, and spatial reasoning skills</u> than their lower-income peers, and white and Asian students — especially in New York City — are more likely to be affluent. Opponents of gifted programs suggest that schools would do well to eliminate such programs in favor of a schoolwide approach to gifted education, incorporating identified students into missed-ability classrooms **(6)** <u>that provide</u> academic enrichment tailored to each student's strengths.

1. A) NO CHANGE
   B) should drain
   C) will drain
   D) could drain

2. Which choice most effectively combines the sentences at the underlined portion?

   A) systems; others worry
   B) systems with others worrying
   C) systems, others worry
   D) systems because others worry

3. Which choice most effectively establishes the main topic of the paragraph?

   A) New York City teachers support plans to integrate gifted students into regular classrooms.
   B) Kindergarten students are the best students to observe to understand segregation by ability.
   C) Because New York City schools have such a large population, it is impossible to create distinct gifted classes.
   D) Because of the long history of segregation in New York City schools, separate gifted programs should be avoided in favor of integrated programs.

4. A) NO CHANGE
   B) were
   C) have been
   D) had been

5. A) NO CHANGE
   B) reading skills, communication, and spatial skills
   C) reading and communication and spatial skills
   D) reading, communication, and spatial reasoning skills

6. A) NO CHANGE
   B) that might provide
   C) that is providing
   D) that will provide

Others claim that such an approach is both unfeasible for teachers and unfair to gifted students. Everything we know about brain plasticity, **(7)** <u>human development and how excellence is the result of copious disciplined practice</u> tells us that we're putting much at risk when we simply hope that overburdened classroom teachers can provide the instruction that gifted students need. In an era in which teachers are largely measured by their ability to close achievement gaps, it should come as no surprise that a Fordham Institute report found that 81% of teachers say that struggling students are most likely to get one-on-one attention. **(8)** <u>As a result, the best performing students in any given classroom are the ones least likely to receive individualized instruction.</u>

Gifted programs not only help to ensure the quality of instruction for gifted students, but may also be our best means of remaining internationally competitive in the years to come. Much has been made of **(9)** <u>its</u> mediocre scores on international assessments, but the test scores of America's top students surpass the test scores of the top students in most other nations. In other words, while our average scores are disappointing, the scores of our brightest students are amazing.

Rather than ignoring the unique instructional needs of gifted students, we should be nurturing **(10)** <u>our gifts</u>. Insisting that gifted children will be fine if we cut gifted programs **(11)** <u>can be</u> a disservice to these children and a horrific waste of an invaluable natural resource.

7. A) NO CHANGE
    B) human development, and being excellent from copious, disciplined practice
    C) human development, and practice-based excellence
    D) human development, and how excellence is the result of copious disciplined practice

8. Which choice most effectively concludes the paragraph?

    A) NO CHANGE
    B) Delete it. It is unnecessary.
    C) This statistic alone is enough to prove to everyone that gifted students deserve distinct instruction.
    D) Experts argue that the remaining 19% is enough to support gifted students.

9. A) NO CHANGE
    B) America's
    C) their
    D) our

10. A) NO CHANGE
    B) our gift
    C) their gifts
    D) his gift

11. A) NO CHANGE
    B) could be
    C) might be
    D) is

BLUE WRITING LESSON 5: MAIN IDEA, TOPIC SENTENCES, AND SUPPORT
Getting Your Feet Wet

Directions: The following questions are intended as a short diagnostic exam.

[1] The practice of the "spoils system," the award of government appointments in return for political support, reinforced the idea that the Department of State and the Diplomatic and Consular Services of the first half of the 1800s were filled with unqualified loafers. [2] President Andrew Jackson believed that "the duties of public officers are so plain and simple that men of intelligence may readily qualify themselves for their performance." [3] Attitudes like this perpetuated both amateurism in government and a disdain for public service. [4] The egalitarian celebration of the common man worked against efforts to improve the quality and status of those who conducted foreign relations. [5] One of the few talented diplomats of the era who made a career in the Diplomatic Service, Henry Wheaton, argued in vain for a professional service that recognized merit and granted tenure to the deserving. [6] Those with necessary qualifications, linguistic skill, awareness of diplomatic forms, and with appropriate experience, should, he thought, "be employed where they can do most service, while incapable men should be turned out without fear or partiality. [7] Those who have served the country faithfully and well ought to be encouraged and transferred from one court to another, which is the only advancement that our system permits."

1. Which choice most effectively establishes the main topic of the passage?

   A) Henry Wheaton was the best diplomat of the 19th century.
   B) Despite efforts by career diplomats, the State Department of 19th century America was thought of as amateurish.
   C) The "spoils system" created many problems for United States foreign policy.
   D) A merit system for the State Department would have solved America's foreign relations problems of the 1800s.

2. Which choice most effectively functions as the topic sentence of the paragraph?

   A) Sentence 2
   B) Sentence 3
   C) Sentence 5
   D) Sentence 6

3. In the first paragraph, which choice would provide the best support for Sentence 2?

   A) Andrew Jackson believed that many of his predecessor political appointees were corrupt.
   B) As the 1800s progressed, many Americans joined the foreign service due to its admirable reputation.
   C) Andrew Jackson served 10 years in the Diplomatic Service before becoming president.
   D) Many of Andrew Jackson's political appointments were people who had little experience in the offices they were in control of.

BLUE WRITING LESSON 5: MAIN IDEA, TOPIC SENTENCES, AND SUPPORT
Wading In

TOPIC OVERVIEW: MAIN IDEA, TOPIC SENTENCES, AND SUPPORT

In addition to the rules of grammar, the SAT Writing section now tests your ability to evaluate and improve the development of ideas in a passage. The test does this by focusing on four major areas, three of which will be addressed in this lesson: determining the main idea of a passage, choosing a topic sentence for a paragraph, and identifying meaningful support for a portion of the text.

TOPIC OVERVIEW: MAIN IDEA

A major obstacle to overcome when determining the **main idea** of a passage or a paragraph is not getting bogged down in the details. Often the answer choices will include items which are valid based on the passage, but which express only a detail about the text, and not the over-arching ideas that are presented in it.

Many passages have a thesis statement, which defines the purpose (and main idea) of the passage; this statement is often the first sentence. Additionally, each paragraph has a topic sentence; often this is the first sentence of the paragraph. Using this information, we can devise a strategy for determining the main idea of a passage:

1) Read the first and last sentence of the passage.
2) Summarize that information.
3) Compare your summary to the answer choices.
4) If none of the choices seem reasonable, read the first sentence of each paragraph.
5) Go back to the answer choices and try again.

TOPIC OVERVIEW: TOPIC SENTENCES

Finding a **topic sentence** for a paragraph follows the same basic principles as finding a main idea for a passage, but it is generally a little easier. To determine a topic sentence, we can look at just a small portion of the whole passage, usually just three or four sentences. Here is a series of steps to follow that will help to determine the best choice:

1) Re-read the paragraph in question.
2) Without looking at the answer choices, write down what *you* think the main idea of the paragraph was.
3) Read each answer choice. If the choice does not match your summary, eliminate it.
4) Choose from the remaining answer choices.

The difficult part of this strategy is the second step. One method for this is to read the paragraph, and then imagine what you would tell someone if they asked

you "What was that paragraph about?" A good answer to that question is the main idea of the paragraph, and a topic sentence will express that idea as well.

TOPIC OVERVIEW: SUPPORT

Providing **supporting evidence** is a crucial skill in crafting a good argument. The support questions on the SAT test this by asking which sentences are best added, removed, or revised in order to improve the claims made in the text. The best way to determine the answer is to identify the argument being made or the main idea of the paragraph. The following steps can help you do this:

1) Read the paragraph or sentence referenced by the question.
2) Determine the argument or main idea — you can use the same strategy described above for finding main ideas.
3) Look at each answer choice, asking if the information provided is specifically about the argument/main idea being referenced.
4) If the information in an answer choice is relevant, check if it supports the information in the passage or contradicts it. If it supports it, it is most likely the correct answer choice.

Use the example on the next page to solidify your understanding of these strategies:

[1] A rare set of international circumstances gave the United States the luxury to concentrate on domestic expansion during the middle of the 19th century, because the country faced no serious external threats until the Civil War (1861-1865). [2] After the defeat of Napoleon in 1812, a stable and complex balance of power evolved in Europe. [3] Maintaining that delicate balance deterred possible aggressors from intervention in the New World, because any nation tempted to interfere in the affairs of the Western Hemisphere would have found itself in considerable difficulty from its neighbors at home. [4] The result was that the United States enjoyed an extended period of tranquility — a very different atmosphere from the days of the early republic.

1. Which choice most effectively establishes the main topic of the paragraph?

   A) The defeat of Napoleon in Russia was a critical event in the development of the United States.
   B) The Civil War kept the United State from taking advantage of the lack of outside influences after Napoleon's defeat.
   C) The United States used the influence of European nations to expand their territory in the New World.
   D) A period of political stability overseas allowed the newly formed United States the opportunity to focus on issues at home.

2. Which choice most effectively functions as the topic sentence of the paragraph?

   A) Sentence 1
   B) Sentence 2
   C) Sentence 3
   D) Sentence 4

3. Which choice best supports the main idea of the paragraph?

   A) The Civil War was the end of a quiet period for the United States of America.
   B) An attempt by Spain to launch a mission to the New World in 1830 was met with aggression from other countries in Europe.
   C) Napoleon's defeat in 1812 created a power vacuum in Europe that was eventually filled by neighboring nations.
   D) The peaceful days of the early United States came to an end after Napoleon's defeat in 1812.

For the first question, use the main idea strategies:

1. Read the first and last sentences of the passage.

2. Summarize the information. The first sentence indicates that a balance of power in another part of the world ("international circumstances") enabled the U.S. to focus on events at home ("concentrate on domestic expansion").

3. Look at the answer choices and match them to the summary you just made. Of the four choices, D matches the best. Choice A is wrong because the word "critical" is too strong, and not indicated by the information in the passage. Choice B indicates that the U.S. didn't take advantage of the period of peace, but the paragraph states that U.S. did experience a period of expansion. Choice C is tempting, but the passage does not say that the U.S. used the influence of other nations, just that it took advantage of a lack of interference. The phrase "used the influence of" implies an active participation, while the passage implies an advantage gained simply by the absence of interference.

We didn't have to use the fourth and fifth steps to answer this question.

For Question 2, we can use the topic sentence strategies.

1. We don't have to re-read, because the sample passage is only one paragraph long.
2. After reading the passage, it seems like a good choice for its main idea would be something like "a balance of power in Europe benefited America."
3. Now look at the answer choices. Sentence 1 sounds good — but let's look at the other choices. Choice B only talks about the situation in Europe, so it's too specific. Choice C describes the mechanism by which the period of peace occurred; this is not a bad choice, so don't eliminate it yet. Choice D is also too specific, speaking only about the climate in America.
4. Of Choices A and C, Choice A is more general, and therefore a better topic sentence. We couldn't use Choice C as a topic sentence, because it references *that balance*, which is defined somewhere else. This makes it an ineffective topic sentence, because it doesn't express the main idea on its own.

The last question asks about a supporting detail. We have a strategy for this as well:

1. We've already read this paragraph. No need to do it again.
2. The argument being made is that the fear of reprisal from their neighbors kept European countries from interfering with America, thus giving America an extended period of peace.
3. Choices A and D don't mention Europe at all, so they can be eliminated quickly. Choice C deals only with events in Europe, so it can also be eliminated. Choice B gives an example of why the period of peace in the United States occurred: countries near Spain were opposed to any interference in the New World, so they attempted to stop the Spanish from doing so ("met with aggression").

Notice that although Choice D contradicts statements in the passage, Choices A and C could easily be accurate statements about history. This does not make them effective supporting details. You need to make sure that the answers you pick specifically support the main ideas of the paragraph or passage in question.

BLUE WRITING LESSON 5: MAIN IDEA, TOPIC SENTENCES, AND SUPPORT
Learning to Swim

CONCEPT EXERCISE:

Directions: Use the following paragraphs to answer each question.

{1, 2, 3} [1]On September 11, 2001, window washer Jan Demczure was ascending One World Trade Center in the elevator with five other men. [2] The elevator came to a sudden halt, pausing for a moment before plunging downward. [3] Thinking quickly, someone in the elevator managed to press the emergency stop button. [4] By some miracle, the elevator stopped, but the men smelled smoke and knew they had to find a way out.

1. Which choice most effectively establishes the main topic of the paragraph?

   A) Elevators are made with an emergency stop in case of emergency.
   B) One of the unwritten yet dynamic stories of September 11, 2001 is that of 6 men who were trapped in an elevator together.
   C) Jan Demczure is one of the unknown heroes of September 11, 2001.
   D) 6 men were trapped in an elevator on September 11, 2001 but were rescued.

2. Which choice most effectively functions as the topic sentence of the paragraph?

   A) Sentence 1
   B) This story has a happy ending.
   C) Many lesser known stories of survival make up the overall narrative of September 11, 2001.
   D) Sentence 4

3. Which choice best supports the main idea of the paragraph?

   A) Jan Demczure had his window washing gear with him in the elevator.
   B) The men were headed to the top floor of the building.
   C) The One World Trade Center had 110 floors.
   D) One World Trade Center was one of two towers.

{4, 5, 6} [1] The men pried open the doors, only to be faced by a wall of Sheetrock. [2] With nothing more than a pocketknife, the men began cutting their way out. [3] Demczure took his turn with the knife, hacking at the unforgiving wall. [4] The knife slipped from his hands, falling down the elevator shaft. [5] With it went his hope.

4. Which choice most effectively establishes the main topic of the paragraph?

   A) Even though there were 6 men in the elevator, that was not enough to find a way out.
   B) The Sheetrock prevented the men from escaping.
   C) Demczure's mistake prevented the men from escaping.
   D) Because of the pocketknife, the men had hope, but once it was lost, they seemed doomed.

5. Which choice most effectively functions as the topic sentence of the paragraph?

   A) Their desperation was not paired with hope.
   B) Sentence 1
   C) Although they were happy to have stopped safely, new obstacles faced the men.
   D) Sentence 4

6. Which choice best supports the main idea of the paragraph?

   A) One of the men realized that he had a pocketknife in his jacket.
   B) Demczure functioned as the leader of the group.
   C) One man was too scared to help.
   D) Several of the men wanted to give up.

{7, 8, 9} [1] One of the men reached into the window washer's bucket and grabbed the Squeegee handle. [2] It was just sharp enough that it might work. [3] The men returned to their work, systematically cutting vertical and horizontal furrows into the Sheetrock, finally creating a sizable depression in the first layers of Sheetrock. [4] They kicked and kicked, breaking through the triple layer of Sheetrock only to find still more Sheetrock. [5] More kicking; more punching; more desperation.

7. Which choice most effectively establishes the main topic of the paragraph?

   A) The Squeegee was not that effective; kicking was more helpful.
   B) Without the idea to use the Squeegee, the men might never have gotten out.
   C) Despite the difficulties of their situation, the men continued fighting to get out.
   D) Despite their efforts, they still were not able to escape.

8. Which choice most effectively functions as the topic sentence of the paragraph?

   A) The loss of the pocketknife did not doom the men because of Demczure's equipment.
   B) Sentence 1
   C) The story doesn't end there.
   D) But new hope came from an unexpected source.

9. Which choice best supports the main idea of the paragraph?

   A) The men thought that they would find their way out into an office.
   B) Demczure continued to feel badly about dropping the pocketknife.
   C) Sheetrock, also called drywall, is a relatively thin layer of paper and plaster which makes up most walls.
   D) The men found that kicking after initially cutting into the Sheetrock was the best formula for breaking through the hole.

{10, 11, 12} [1] Finally, they broke through. [2] They pushed against a thin wall of tile to find themselves beneath a sink in a men's room. [3] All six men escaped the building. [4] It took them 90 minutes from the moment the elevator cab had halted in the shaft, and they reached safety just minutes before the tower collapsed — the second tower to do so.

10. Which choice most effectively establishes the main topic of the paragraph?

    A) The men were surprised to escape out into a men's room.
    B) All of their efforts were worth it because they managed to escape minutes before the tower collapsed.
    C) The men never learned why there were so many layers of Sheetrock.
    D) The men grew extremely tired from their 90 minutes of hard work.

11. Which choice most effectively functions as the topic sentence of the paragraph?

    A) Sentence 1
    B) Sentence 2
    C) Sentence 3
    D) Sentence 4

12. Which choice best supports the main idea of the paragraph?

A) While the story is not known by many, the cooperation of the men makes for one of the best escape stories of September 11.
B) The men's room that they broke out into was flooded.
C) The men wondered why there were so many layers of wall.
D) Demczure left his bucket in the tower when he escaped.

{13, 14, 15} [1]The tool that saved their lives, a humble Squeegee handle, found a home in the collections of the National Museum of American History in 2002 when Congress designated the museum as the official repository for materials honoring the victims of the September 11 attacks, when 2,996 people were killed at the World Trade Center in New York City, the Pentagon in Virginia, and aboard Flight 93 when it crashed into a Pennsylvania field. [2] Today, that Squeegee handle joins other 9/11 artifacts at the newly opened National September 11 Memorial and Museum. [3] In addition to items on loan from the National Museum of American History, the new museum features the personal belongings of several 9/11 victims — recovered purses and wallets, FDNY Chief Peter Ganci's radio, the gloves and helmets of several firemen, and a packet of personal letters — as well as mementos from survivors and rescue workers. [4] These items tell the story of 9/11 in a way that words never could.

13. Which choice most effectively establishes the main topic of the paragraph?

A) The National September 11 Memorial and Museum are trying to collect every artifact they can to remember the day.
B) While small, the Squeegee handle represents the idea that all kinds of artifacts are important to remember and honor September 11, 2001.
C) Americans can go look at the Squeegee handle, which is now on display at the National September 11 Memorial and Museum.
D) It is lucky that Demczure brought the Squeegee out with him because it otherwise would never have ended up in the museum.

14. Which choice most effectively functions as the topic sentence of the paragraph?

A) Sentence 1
B) Sentence 2
C) The National September 11 Memorial and Museum still needs many more artifacts to accomplish its mission.
D) Sentence 4

15. Which choice best supports the main idea of the paragraph?

A) The directors of the National September 11 Memorial and Museum have intentionally sought out artifacts that tell the story of what happened to regular people on that day.
B) The Squeegee was purchased at a hardware store right around the corner from the old World Trade Center.
C) The packet of letters is also being used to write a book about September 11.
D) The directors hope that displaying the purses and wallets will be a way to get personal property back to its original owners.

BLUE WRITING LESSON 5: MAIN IDEA, TOPIC SENTENCES, AND SUPPORT
Diving into the Deep End

PRACTICE EXERCISE:

Directions: Answer the questions that accompany the following passage.

Guinea's Battle Against Ebola

{1} Ebola has broken out periodically in Africa since it first appeared in 1976 in what were then Zaire and Sudan. The virus has a 90% fatality rate and is spread through contact with infected blood, bodily fluids, and tissue. There is no cure.

[1] Nobody would have thought that Gueckedou, a market town in Southern Guinea, was the front line in West Africa's battle against the deadly Ebola virus. [2] It was business as usual on the dusty streets. Traders set up their stalls, shoppers negotiated prices.

[3] Below the surface, though, lay a simmering tension. [4] Nobody shook hands, and those who could afford it bought gloves and face masks to avoid the gruesome disease that killed well over 100 people in Guinea and Liberia in a mere three months. {2, 3}

1. Which choice most effectively establishes the main topic of the paragraph?

   A) Ebola has been restricted to Zaire and Sudan.
   B) Ebola is an extremely serious disease which has plagued parts of Africa since 1976.
   C) Ebola kills almost everyone who gets it.
   D) Scientists have not yet worked out a cure for Ebola.

2. Which choice most effectively functions as the topic sentence of the previous paragraph?

   A) Sentence 1
   B) Sentence 2
   C) Sentence 3
   D) Sentence 4

3. Which choice best supports the main idea of the previous paragraph?

   A) The traders were selling fruit and vegetables.
   B) Guinea is one of the poorest countries in Africa.
   C) Southern Guinea is roughly 6,000 kilometers away from where Ebola first struck in Zaire.
   D) A normal day in Guinea is different from that in the United States.

[1] Guinea is one of the world's poorest countries. [2] Only 19% of the population has access to modern sanitation, and the country has the lowest number of hospital beds per capita in the world.

[3] Disease surveillance and control measures are non-existent.

[4] Poverty, bad habits, and tradition fuel the spread of Ebola.

[5] Butchers sell bush meat in the markets despite a government ban; doctors who may be infected with Ebola refuse to go into quarantine and risk spreading the disease; and traditional funerals continue despite the health warning about the cultural practices associated with them. {4, 5, 6}

4. Which choice most effectively establishes the main topic of the paragraph?

A) Many negatives factors combine to dictate that Guinea is actually a prime suspect for disease outbreaks.
B) Citizens of Guinea are primarily to blame for the Ebola outbreak.
C) The doctors in Guinea do not know how to combat Ebola.
D) Because Southern Guinea is so isolated, there is little chance that Ebola will spread from there.

5. Which choice most effectively functions as the topic sentence of the paragraph?

A) Sentence 1
B) Sentence 2
C) Sentence 5
D) Guinea as a country has many problems which mean that its public health is in a very bad way.

6. Which choice best supports the main idea of the paragraph?

A) Cultural norms in Guinea are not conducive to public health.
B) Guinea is in west Africa.
C) Guinea is in a similar situation to several other African countries around it.
D) Butchers in Guinea usually do not sell pork because there are Muslims in Guinea.

[1] Guinea can be forgiven for its slow response. [2] It was the first time that Ebola had hit the impoverished nation and the symptoms could easily be confused with those of minor infections like influenza, or of diseases endemic in the area like malaria.

[3] Still, given the release of donor funds after recent elections and the high level of foreign investment in the country, Guinea could have done more and faster. {7, 8, 9}

7. Which choice most effectively establishes the main topic of the paragraph?

   A) Guineans did not know what their symptoms indicated.
   B) Health officials initially thought the outbreak was malaria.
   C) There are several factors not in Guinea's control that have contributed to the outbreak, but more still could have been done.
   D) Foreign governments tried to help Guinea.

8. Which choice most effectively functions as the topic sentence of the paragraph?

   A) Sentence 1
   B) Despite some controllable negative factors in Guinea, there are actually several reasons why Guinea is not to blame.
   C) Sentence 2
   D) Sentence 3

9. Which choice best supports the main idea of the paragraph?

   A) Despite Guinea's poverty, money from outside sources could have enabled a better defense against the outbreak.
   B) The foreign countries that gave the money were to the south of Guinea.
   C) Malaria is a disease caused by mosquitos.
   D) Influenza is the full name for what is usually called the flu.

A reduction in government corruption and higher taxes on mining corporations could have released cash to build a better health system that could react quickly and effectively to a threatened epidemic. Better communication and more transparency would have helped win the public's trust and encouraged citizens to act together to overcome the disease. More responsible media coverage could have had an impact on public awareness; instead of informing readers about personal hygiene and disease prevention, local media chose to print a dubious April Fool's Day joke about a possible cure. {10}

[1] Instead, Guinea relies primarily on donated funds and personnel from organizations like the Centers for Disease Control. [2] Because of a lack of education and communication about the outbreak, many Guineans believe that these foreign aid workers brought Ebola to Guinea in the first place. [3] This resulted in mistrust and suspicion that prevents people from seeking prompt medical care or heeding advice about disease prevention. {11}

10. Which choice most effectively establishes the main topic of the previous paragraph?

A) The media in Guinea is primarily to blame for the outbreak.
B) A key aspect in the fight against disease is communication.
C) The April Fool's Day joke made the situation in Guinea much worse.
D) There is a lengthy list of things that Guinea could have done better to combat the outbreak.

11. Which choice most effectively functions as the topic sentence of the previous paragraph?

A) Sentence 1
B) All of the missteps in combating the disease are compounded by mistrust of essential foreign aid workers.
C) Foreign workers have contributed to the Guinean lack of trust in them.
D) Sentence 3

TEST EXERCISE:

Directions: Answer the questions that accompany the following passage.

When Coral Reefs Thrive

{1} The fish that live off the Malay Archipelago, between Southeast Asia and Australia, are among the most diverse in the world. Scientists have long wondered why this particular region is home to such a diverse marine population. Now researchers are reporting that the area owes its diversity to the **(2)** changes of coral reefs over the past three million years. The reefs have given fish a safe home, which provides the means to diversify and evolve into new species.

Using information from underwater sediment, **(3)** estimation of changes could be made by scientists in surface temperatures over time. This information was used to determine where coral reefs were, how stable they were over time, **(4)** and how long their stability lasted. This data was then compared with the current geographic distribution of more than 6,000 species of fish.

{5} [1] There was a very strong correlation between coral reefs and species diversity. [2] Areas that had stable coral reefs in ancient times are now home to a wide variety of fish. [3] As you go further from the locations of ancient reef habitats, you find fewer and fewer fish.

A correlation between coral reefs and wildlife diversity has long been established. As the foundation for complex food webs, coral reefs support an incredible diversity of marine life **(6)** . Including not only fish, but also algae, sponges, and invertebrates. A wide array of marine crustaceans, reptiles, mammals, and fish depend on reefs for food, habitat, and protection, making coral reefs some of the most complex and fragile ecosystems on earth.

1. Which choice most effectively states the main idea of the paragraph?

   A) The diversity of fish off the Malay Archipelago makes it a prime fishing location.
   B) Scientists hope to encourage tourism in the area around the Malay Archipelago to inspire support for ocean protection.
   C) The coral reefs around the Malay Archipelago are crucial for scientists to understand how the oceans work.
   D) Coral is essential to fish life.

2. A) NO CHANGE
   B) size
   C) unpredictability
   D) stability

3. A) NO CHANGE
   B) scientists were able to estimate changes
   C) changes could be estimated by scientists
   D) scientists could estimate, based on extensive research, changes

4. A) NO CHANGE
   B) and their stability.
   C) and the longevity of their stability.
   D) and the length of their stability.

5. Which choice most effectively functions as the topic sentence of the paragraph?

   A) Sentence 1
   B) Scientists discovered that coral reefs had changed a lot over time.
   C) Sentence 2
   D) Sentence 3

6. A) NO CHANGE
   B) ; including
   C) , and including
   D) , including

{7} While the relationship between reefs and fish diversity was not surprising in and of itself, the correlation between ancient coral reefs and current fish populations was unexpected. "It really drives home the fact that the past shapes the present **(8)** <u>says Dr. Peter Cowman</u>, an evolutionary biologist at Yale who authored the new study.

This new research provides additional incentive to protect coral reefs. Today, coral reefs are threatened by human factors like pollution and climate change. Recent reports **(9)** <u>claim</u> that about 75% of the world's coral reefs are threatened. Of these, most are threatened by overfishing, coastal development, and water pollution. **(10)** <u>Scientists believe endangered reefs will have a detrimental impact in the future.</u>

Threatened coral reefs have long been a rallying cry for ecologists and conservationists, but this new research suggests that the degradation of coral reefs could have far longer lasting effects **(11)** <u>than</u> previously thought. If the reefs of ancient times helped to determine today's marine life populations, what might the destruction of today's reefs mean for marine life in the centuries and millennia to come?

7. Which choice most effectively states the main idea of the paragraph?

A) Scientists learned little new information from this study of coral reefs.
B) Scientists believe that this new study proves the importance of saving coral reefs.
C) Scientists mostly learned about the way coral reefs used to function.
D) Scientists could not make firm conclusions about the history of coral reefs.

8. A) NO CHANGE
   B) , says Dr. Peter Cowman
   C) ", says Dr. Peter Cowman
   D) ," says Dr. Peter Cowman

9. A) NO CHANGE
   B) claims
   C) claimed
   D) have claimed

10. Which choice most effectively concludes the paragraph?

A) NO CHANGE
B) Delete it. It is unnecessary.
C) Scientists hope that more people will understand the urgent need to take up the cause of coral reefs.
D) The most endangered reefs are those in Southeast Asia, like the ones off the Malay Archipelago.

11. A) NO CHANGE
    B) then
    C) than they
    D) then they

BLUE WRITING LESSON 5: MAIN IDEA, TOPIC SENTENCES, AND SUPPORT
Race to the Finish

HOMEWORK EXERCISE 1:

Directions: Use the following paragraphs to answer the questions below.

{1, 2, 3} [1] In the summer of 1989, construction workers renovating a 150-year-old building in Augusta, Georgia made a disturbing discovery. [2] Deep in the building's basement, they found layers and layers of human bones. [3] Many of the bones showed the marks of dissection, while others had been labeled as specimens. [4] All together, they found close to 10,000 individual human bones and bone fragments.

1. Which choice most effectively establishes the main topic of the paragraph?

   A) Georgia has many caches of bones beneath buildings, so construction workers were unsurprised.
   B) The fact that some bones were labeled led historians to speculate that the bones were used for medical purposes.
   C) What led to bones being found in Augusta, Georgia in 1989 remains a mystery.
   D) Construction workers found thousands of human bone pieces beneath a building, but at first no one knew why they were there.

2. Which choice most effectively functions as the topic sentence of the paragraph?

   A) Sentence 1
   B) Sentence 2
   C) Sentence 3
   D) Sentence 4

3. Which choice best supports the main idea of the paragraph?

   A) The human bones did not make up full skeletons.
   B) The construction workers revealed their discovery to researchers who looked into the bones in more detail.
   C) The basement used to be a cemetery.
   D) This discovery of the bones is the largest of its kind.

{4, 5, 6} [1] The bones were a disturbing remnant from Augusta's medical history. [2] From 1835 to 1913, the building had been home to the Medical College of Georgia, where students dissected cadavers as part of their training. [3] During those years, grave robbers illegally unearthed corpses and brought them to the school's labs. [4] Afterward, the remains were dumped into the basement and covered in quicklime to hide the stench.

4. Which choice most effectively establishes the main topic of the paragraph?

   A) It turned out that bodies had been illegally taken to help medical students learn their craft.
   B) The perpetrators of this crime of stealing bodies were caught in 1913.
   C) Cadavers are bodies dissected for medicine.
   D) This practice of stealing bodies to study for science would never happen today.

5. Which choice most effectively functions as the topic sentence of the paragraph?

   A) Sentence 1
   B) Sentence 2
   C) It turned out that the bones revealed an illegal element of the Medical College of Georgia's history.
   D) Hunters tracked down the origins of the bones.

6. Which choice best supports the main idea of the paragraph?

   A) The Medical College of Georgia trained more students to become doctors than any other college in Georgia.
   B) Most of the bones found were leg bones.
   C) The directors of the Medical College did not return the bodies because they knew what they were doing was illegal.
   D) Actually, the students learned little from the dissections.

{7} For more than 50 years, first as a slave and then as an employee, Grandison Harris supplied the medical students of Georgia with most of their cadavers. Harris was purchased on a Charleston, South Carolina, auction block in 1852, and owned jointly by all seven members of the school's medical faculty.

{8,9} [1] Harris was taught to read and write so that he could monitor the local funeral announcements and seek out fresh bodies. [2] He preferred to work in Cedar Grove cemetery, reserved for Augusta's impoverished and black residents, where there was no fence. [3] Harris became a de facto teaching assistant who helped out during dissections, and students often liked him more than their professors.

7. Which choice most effectively establishes the main topic of the paragraph?

   A) Because Harris was from another state, he could not get in trouble for stealing the bodies.
   B) Harris was able to train as a doctor.
   C) Grandison Harris was a criminal who was never brought to justice.
   D) Ironically, the discovery of the bones led to a key discovery about slavery in Augusta, GA.

8. Which choice most effectively functions as the topic sentence of the paragraph?

   A) Sentence 1
   B) Harris excelled in his position of medical graverobber and gained skills because of it.
   C) Sentence 2
   D) Sentence 3

9. Which choice best supports the main idea of the paragraph?

   A) Technically, slaves were not allowed to be literate, so Harris is an exception.
   B) Harris preferred to read the Bible.
   C) Harris taught other slaves to read.
   D) Harris kept a diary that historians have used to study slave life.

{10} This friendly relationship soured somewhat in later years. Following the Civil War, a newly freed Harris moved to Hamburg, South Carolina, where he used his education to become a judge. But when Jim Crow became the law of the South, Harris returned to the dissection labs as a full-time employee amid race riots in Hamburg. The students saw his position in a carpetbagger regime as disloyal to the South, and thereafter, derisively called him "judge" to remind him of his ill-fated attempt to rise to a professional class.

{11} [1] Harris died in 1911 and was buried in Cedar Grove. [2] No one knows where his body lies because all of the cemetery records were destroyed when the Savannah River overflowed in 1929.

[3] Similar to Harris' anonymous demise, the bones found in the basement were finally buried in Cedar Grove beneath a monument that says: "Known but to God."

10. Which choice most effectively establishes the main topic of the paragraph?

   A) Harris was the first black judge in the South.
   B) Harris used his medical knowledge to decide cases as a judge.
   C) Jim Crow was oppressive to Southern blacks.
   D) Harris' background working for the College helped him gain temporary success in his life.

11. Which choice most effectively functions as the topic sentence of the paragraph?

   A) Sentence 1
   B) Sentence 2
   C) The destruction of the cemetery records ends the story of Harris and the bones.
   D) Sentence 3

HOMEWORK EXERCISE 2:

Directions: Answer the questions that accompany the following passage.

Artifacts with a Life All Their Own

What magic do museum artifacts wield? What gives these objects, documents, books, recordings, and images such **(1)** ability? They aren't pieces of art but are often encased in humidity-controlled vitrines. They aren't amusements but are often offered up for visitor's pleasure.

{2} Artifacts bear the weight of history, allowing us to encounter a trace of the past in the present. These traces have a powerful effect in part because we know they are authentic. Reproductions, even if expertly made, would disappoint.

(3) Consider, for example, a calling card left by John Wilkes Booth when he tried to visit Vice President Andrew Johnson, just hours before assassinating Lincoln. "Don't wish to disturb you," it reads, with Booth adding a flourish under his signature. This artifact is on display at the National Archives, offering us a small glimpse into a little-known moment in history. **(4)** This is the most-visited artifact at the National Archives.

Why should this be so? Most artifacts aren't artworks with subtleties lying far beyond the reach of reproductions. Many are simple, ordinary objects. It is their origins that fascinate us. When we are engrossed by an exhibition, **(5)** they are not just looking at an object or reading a text. We are engaged with the **(6)** artifacts' origins, living — just for a moment — in the past. To gaze upon a dish created thousands of years ago, to see the finger marks of the person who created it, and to know that this one dish has outlived generation after generation of people is to realize the fragility of life and the endurance of the past.

1. A) NO CHANGE
   B) accessibility
   C) control
   D) power

2. Which choice most effectively establishes the main topic of the paragraph?

   A) Artifacts are the best way for students to learn about history because they are genuine.
   B) Copies of historical artifacts allow more people to experience history than would be the case if only originals were used.
   C) Because historical artifacts are actual pieces of history, we are captivated by them in a way we never would be with copies.
   D) Artifacts, even when not originals, allow the observer to vicariously visit the past.

3. A) NO CHANGE
   B) What about the example,
   C) For example,
   D) Consider

4. Which choice most effectively concludes the paragraph?

   A) NO CHANGE
   B) Delete this sentence. It is unnecessary.
   C) If the calling card were a laser printed copy, we might be less entranced.
   D) Without artifacts like this, no one would visit the National Archives.

5. A) NO CHANGE
   B) they is
   C) we is
   D) we are

6. A) NO CHANGE
   B) artifact's
   C) artifact
   D) artifacts

{7} Artifacts become fruit for the imagination, showing history as something lived, and thus as a result of choices made. We become more alert to the way things are, and how different **(8)** <u>they might yet be.</u> The calling card that John Wilkes Booth left behind represents a moment that defined history. What might have happened if Andrew Johnson had been home to receive John Wilkes Booth that night? Would President Lincoln have lived to serve out his term **(9)** <u>, and would the fact that he lived out his term</u> have made a difference to the course our nation would follow?

{10} [1] Museum artifacts have great value to our society **(11)** <u>because</u> they allow us to better understand our place in history and our role in the future, to put our own existence in the context of time itself. [2] Their power is not a mystery but a testament to the ever-lasting impact of the present and the inescapable impacts of the past. [3] Yet without artifacts, that power of the past would be forgotten.

7. Which choice most effectively establishes the main topic of the paragraph?

   A) John Wilkes Booth left one of the more famous artifacts of American history.
   B) Another name for artifacts are primary sources.
   C) Artifacts are more helpful than secondary sources for how they inspire people to imagine the past.
   D) Americans want to know more about President Lincoln, and artifacts help greatly with this.

8. A) NO CHANGE
   B) they were.
   C) it was.
   D) it could be.

9. A) NO CHANGE
   B) , and would his living out his term
   C) , and would he
   D) , and would that

10. Which choice most effectively functions as the topic sentence of the paragraph?

   A) Sentence 1
   B) Sentence 2
   C) Sentence 3
   D) Artifacts are indispensable.

11. A) NO CHANGE
    B) :
    C) ,
    D) ?

BLUE WRITING LESSON 6: PRONOUN ERRORS
Getting Your Feet Wet

Directions: The questions below are intended as a short diagnostic exam:

1. For members of the admissions board, no personal feelings affect their <u>decision; it considers</u> each application objectively, based on merit.

   A) NO CHANGE
   B) decision, it considers
   C) decision; they consider
   D) decision, they consider

2. When considering which colleges one wishes to <u>attend, we must</u> take into account not only the prestige of the college in question but also the cost of tuition and availability of scholarships.

   A) NO CHANGE
   B) attend; we must
   C) attend, we should
   D) attend, one must

BLUE WRITING LESSON 6: PRONOUN ERRORS
Wading In

TOPIC OVERVIEW: PRONOUN ERRORS

Pronouns are words which take the place of nouns (antecedents) and make writing less repetitive. In this lesson, we'll discuss some of the **pronoun errors** tested on the SAT.

TOPIC OVERVIEW: PRONOUN AGREEMENT

Pronouns must agree with their antecedents, or the words that they have replaced. When a pronoun takes the place of a singular noun, the pronoun must be singular. Similarly, when it takes the place of a plural noun, it must be a plural pronoun. This is called number agreement, and can be a little confusing in certain sentences.

Example 1: Each high school student chooses a book to read over the summer; he or she may write a book report or take a test when school begins in August.

In this example, the pronoun *he or she* in the second clause is referring back to the subject *Each student*. Because the subject is singular, a singular pronoun must be used to refer to it.

A common conversational tactic is to use the pronoun *they* because it doesn't specify gender. In academic writing, however, *they* is only used for plural nouns; if *they* is used in Example 1, the pronoun would no longer agree with its antecedent.

TOPIC OVERVIEW: PRONOUN CASE

When we discuss the **case** of a pronoun, we are referring to whether it is being used as the subject or the object in a sentence. The table below summarizes the information about pronoun case:

Subject

	Singular	Plural
1st person	I	We
2nd person	Uou	You
3rd person	He/She/It/One	They

Object

	Singular	Plural
1st person	Me	Us
2nd person	You	You
3rd person	Him/Her/It/One	Them

Bearing the above chart in mind, for a given question involving pronouns we need to determine if a pronoun is being used as a subject or an object, and then make sure that the correct version of the pronoun is in the sentence. Remember the basic definitions: the subject of a sentence performs the action, while the object of a sentence has the action performed on it.

Example 2: On our trip to the Grand Canyon, my sister and I played card games in the car.

We use the pronoun *I* (and not *me*) in the sentence because the phrase *my sister and I* acts as the subject of the sentence.

Example 3: After that trip, my father decided to leave my sister and me with our aunt and uncle in Phoenix while he and my mother returned home.

Because the phrase *my sister and me* is the object of the verb *leave*, we need to use the object pronoun *me* and not *I*.

This topic tends to confuse people because well-intentioned teachers or relatives may have insisted that they use *my sister and I* all the time, without taking case into account. One simple test is to take apart the compound sentence or object and use the pronoun by itself — you wouldn't say *my father left I with my aunt and uncle*, so it would be inappropriate to use *I* in this example.

TOPIC OVERVIEW: AMBIGUOUS REFERENCE

An **ambiguous** pronoun is a pronoun for which the antecedent is unclear. Take this sentence, for example:

Example 4: When we went rock climbing, our guide told my uncle that his son was the best climber in our group.

In this sentence, it's not completely clear whether *his* refers to the guide's son or my uncle's son. If there is any ambiguity as to who or what a pronoun in a sentence is referring, the sentence must be rewritten. A better way to write the sentence in Example 4 would be:

Our guide told my uncle that my cousin was the best climber in our group.

Example 5: If you want to be a rock-climbing guide, they look very closely at your employment history and your experience with adventure athletics.

In this sentence, while it may seem implied that *they* refers to the people who would be hiring you, the sentence does not actually state who *they* are — thus the pronoun has no antecedent. A better way to write this would be:

When you apply to be a rock-climbing guide, the management looks very closely at your employment history and your experience with adventure athletics.

<u>Example 6</u>: Although many people are athletic, it doesn't translate directly into skill at rock-climbing.

In this last example, *it* is an ambiguous pronoun. The noun to which it is referring is athletic ability, but this is not mentioned in the sentence so the pronoun is ambiguous. A better way to write this would be:

Athletic skill doesn't necessarily translate directly into skill at rock-climbing.

TOPIC OVERVIEW: RELATIVE PRONOUNS

Relative pronouns introduce certain types of dependent clauses. Like all pronouns, relative pronouns must agree with their antecedent.

The two types of relative clauses are **restrictive** (defining the antecedent and giving necessary information) and **non-restrictive** (giving extra, unnecessary information).

When choosing relative pronouns, a distinction is made between human and non-human antecedents. For people (and other beings that can think like people), you use the pronoun *who*, and for everything else you should use the pronoun *which*. Examples of antecedents that you might replace with *who* are Kiera Knightley (a person), Thor (a deity), Mickey Mouse (a fictional character), or Chewbacca (an alien).

In <u>restrictive</u> clauses, the pronoun *that* can be used for all nouns. You can also use *who* for people (or characters as described above), but you cannot use *which* to refer to non-human antecedents.

In <u>non-restrictive</u> clauses, use *which* for objects and *who* for people (or characters).

<u>Example 7</u>: The instructor, <u>*who* taught our class</u>, was well-spoken.

In this example, the relative pronoun *who* is used because the subject of the sentence (*instructor*) is human. The underlined clause is non-restrictive.

<u>Example 8</u>: After we got done climbing, we went out for ice cream with the youth group <u>*that* was climbing with us</u>.

In Example 8, the pronoun *that* is used because the clause is restrictive (it defines the youth group) and its antecedent is not a person.

BLUE WRITING LESSON 6: PRONOUN ERRORS
Learning to Swim

CONCEPT EXERCISE:

Directions: Find and correct any errors in the following sentences. Some sentences may not have any errors.

1. Gillian and me are going to the mall later if you want to come along.

2. The mayor almost introduced Abed and I as "Mr. and Mrs. Nadir" before realizing that we weren't married.

3. James and Grandpa were pleased that his impressive tomato garden would be featured on the newspaper's front page.

4. I don't know if I'll have Mr. Henshaw or Ms. Perry for Algebra I next year, but I hope they don't assign too much homework.

5. Each member of the class managed to finish their homework just as the bell rang.

6. Rural doctors in the early 18th century didn't have an easy job; you often saw diseases that couldn't be treated effectively without expensive equipment.

7. My older brother said he would drive we band members to our first gig on Saturday night.

8. When one considers the butterfly, one cannot help but be impressed with the transformation it has undergone.

9. I heard an interesting fact the other day: it is impossible for babies to choke until he or she is almost four months old.

10. An infant's larynx is high in their throats when they are born, allowing the infant to nurse and breathe at the same time.

11. The larynx's descent allows for a longer vocal tract, meaning it can make a wider variety of sounds.

12. As a result of laryngeal descent, people have to beware of food or liquid accidently entering the vocal tract for the rest of our lives.

13. My grandmother had eight children, all of which became doctors or nurses.

14. In this article, they argue for the inclusion of graphic novels into curriculum designed to encourage reluctant readers to improve their skills.

15. Many of the words that we use in academic English come from Greek or Latin roots; some students choose to take it as a foreign language specifically for that reason.

16. On Field Day, students should beware challenging we teachers to tug-of-war; we are more massive and therefore harder to pull over the line.

17. One should never take one's eyes off of the Simpson triplets; they love playing tricks on their babysitters.

18. They say that high school students are lazy, but I don't believe it.

19. She told the boys to be careful on their trip, reminding each scout to pack their first-aid kit.

20. Her library contained thousands of books, who she considered to be some of her best friends.

BLUE WRITING LESSON 6: PRONOUN ERRORS
Diving into the Deep End

PRACTICE EXERCISE:

Directions: Answer the questions that accompany the following passage.

What Do We Know About Pain?

We may experience pain as a prick, tingle, sting, burn, or ache somewhere in or on **(1)** <u>one's</u> body. Receptors on the skin trigger a series of events, beginning with an electrical impulse that travels from **(2)** <u>it</u> to the spinal cord. The spinal cord acts as a sort of relay center where the pain signal can be blocked, enhanced, or otherwise modified before **(3)** <u>they are</u> relayed to the brain. One area of the spinal cord in particular, called the dorsal horn, is important in the reception of pain signals.

The most common destination in the brain for pain signals is the thalamus and from there to the cortex, where **(4)** <u>it is</u> translated into more complicated thought. The thalamus also serves as the brain's storage area for images of the body and plays a key role in relaying messages between the brain and various parts of the body. In people who undergo amputation, the representation of the amputated limb is stored in **(5)** <u>their</u> thalamus as well.

Pain is a complicated process that involves intricate interplay and reactions between a number of important chemicals, called neurotransmitters, found naturally in the brain and spinal cord. In general, **(6)** <u>they help</u> transmit nerve impulses in between cells to another.

There are many different neurotransmitters in the human body; some play a role in human disease and, in the case of pain, act in various combinations to produce painful sensations in the body. Some chemicals govern mild pain sensations; others control intense or severe pain.

1. A) NO CHANGE
   B) our
   C) ones'
   D) ones's

2. A) NO CHANGE
   B) them
   C) the skin
   D) the pain

3. A) NO CHANGE
   B) their
   C) its
   D) it is

4. A) NO CHANGE
   B) they are
   C) the cortex is
   D) the thalamus is

5. A) NO CHANGE
   B) they're
   C) its
   D) his or her

6. A) NO CHANGE
   B) it helps
   C) neurotransmitters help
   D) the brain and spinal cord help

The chemicals act in the transmission of pain messages by stimulating neurotransmitter receptors found on the surface of cells. Each receptor corresponds to **(7)** <u>it</u>. Receptors function much like gates or ports and enable pain messages to pass through and on to neighboring cells. One brain chemical of particular interest to neuroscientists is glutamate. During experiments, mice with blocked glutamate receptors show a reduction in **(8)** <u>their</u> responses to pain. Other important receptors in pain transmission include opiate-like receptors. Morphine and other opioid drugs work by locking on to **(9)** <u>them</u>, switching on pain-inhibiting pathways or circuits, and thereby blocking pain.

Another type of receptor that responds to painful stimuli is called a nociceptor. Nociceptors are thin nerve fibers in the skin, muscle, and other body tissues, that, when stimulated, carry pain signals to the spinal cord and brain. Normally, nociceptors only respond to strong stimuli such as a pinch. However, when tissues become injured or inflamed, as with a sunburn or infection, **(10)** <u>they</u> release chemicals that make nociceptors much more sensitive and cause **(11)** <u>their</u> to transmit pain signals in response to even gentle stimuli such as breeze or a caress. This condition is called allodynia — a state in which pain is produced by innocuous stimuli.

7. A) NO CHANGE
   B) a single pain message
   C) a single neurotransmitter
   D) a cell

8. A) NO CHANGE
   B) his or her
   C) its
   D) they're

9. A) NO CHANGE
   B) pain transmission
   C) opioid receptors
   D) pain-inhibiting pathways

10. A) NO CHANGE
    B) it
    C) nociceptors
    D) stimuli

11. A) NO CHANGE
    B) its
    C) they're
    D) them

TEST EXERCISE:

Directions: Answer the questions that accompany the following passage.

Von Braun Joins the Americans

By early 1945, the Soviet Army was moving in on Peenemunde, the base where Werner von Braun and his rocket scientist colleagues were stationed, and nobody had the slightest doubt that Germany would soon be completely defeated. Von Braun organized a meeting of his colleagues at a hotel to determine what to do. They agreed that the group should flee west so **(1)** they could be captured by the Americans, instead of the Soviets. The scientists knew that they couldn't bring any of their equipment with them; they had to flee immediately. Peenemunde was evacuated in mid-February. The technical staff, along with their families, **(2)** were evacuated to Nordhausen.

United States Third Army **(3)** advance units entered Nordhausen on 11 April 1945. Von Braun and his colleagues surrendered to the Americans on 2 May 1945. Although the soldiers who captured Von Braun and his rocket scientists didn't know who they had caught, in fact Army officials were already looking for **(4)** them. In February 1945, Captain Robert B. Staver of the Ordnance Corps, who had worked closely with Jet Propulsion Laboratory officials, was sent to Europe **(5)** ensuring that the U.S. got as many German rocket scientists as possible. He welcomed von Braun and his associates with seemingly open arms. {6}

1. A) NO CHANGE
   B) it
   C) them
   D) their

2. A) NO CHANGE
   B) will be
   C) was
   D) have been

3. A) NO CHANGE
   B) advanced
   C) advances
   D) advancing

4. A) NO CHANGE
   B) the soldiers
   C) the rocket scientists
   D) the Americans

5. A) NO CHANGE
   B) ensures
   C) to ensure
   D) ensured

6. Which of the following pieces of information best supports the claims made in the previous sentence?

   A) The U.S. Army kept von Braun and the other rocket scientists on an Air Force base for three weeks to debrief them.
   B) The scientists were brought to a military base, but their families were not allowed to join them.
   C) The scientists were offered jobs in either military or civilian industries, and the U.S. government helped to relocate them and their families.
   D) Many of the scientists wanted to leave the United States, and they were allowed to do so without being debriefed.

As far as von Braun and his colleagues went, they played a cautious game, being cooperative, but not too cooperative, with their captors. Von Braun was no fool, and he wanted to get the best deal he could out of the Americans for him and his fellows. **(7)** As a technical evaluation of his worth, von Braun wrote a detailed document titled "The Development of Liquid Rockets in Germany and Their Future Prospects." It combined pragmatic detail with far-reaching but disciplined imagination in a shrewd sales pitch that would appeal to both the hard realists and visionaries among **(8)** their captors. However, the Americans didn't need much of a sales pitch. Only two months later, Operation OVERCAST was put into motion to bring 350 top-ranked German researchers, including about 100 of von Braun's people, to the United States for a year. The war in the Pacific was still in progress at that time, and many American officials believed **(9)** it would take much more time and blood to end **(10)** it. The Japanese surrendered before any of von Braun's people crossed the Atlantic, but they were still brought over as officials were becoming increasingly fearful of Josef Stalin's intentions. Although the Cold War had not quite begun, the temperature was falling rapidly.

It would still be another sixteen years before Werner von Braun proposed the idea that a manned mission to the Moon would help win the Space Race for the Americans. {**11**}

7. A) NO CHANGE
   B) To provide
   C) Being
   D) Looking at

8. A) NO CHANGE
   B) its
   C) they're
   D) his

9. A) NO CHANGE
   B) the Japanese
   C) the rocket scientists
   D) the officials

10. A) NO CHANGE
    B) the war
    C) progress
    D) the Pacific

11. In the context of the passage as a whole, what is the purpose of the final paragraph?

    A) It serves to identify the main reason why the rocket scientists were welcomed to the United States.
    B) It suggests that the relationship between the United States and von Braun yielded long-lasting results.
    C) It indicates that von Braun's first priority was a manned mission to the moon.
    D) It further develops the idea suggested in the last sentence of the previous paragraph.

BLUE WRITING LESSON 6: PRONOUN ERRORS
Race to the Finish

HOMEWORK EXERCISE 1:

Directions: Find and correct any errors in the following sentences. Some sentences may have no errors.

1. They say that comic books do not qualify as literature and should not be allowed in language arts classes; I believe that superhero comics encourage students to read for fun.

2. My favorite superhero team formed when six teenagers realized that their parents were actually supervillains.

3. Each member of the Runaways goes on to discover a secret power inherited from their parents.

4. Old Lace is a psychic dinosaur from the future, which communicates telepathically with Gertrude Stein.

5. Chase is the only team member capable of driving the getaway car, which looks like a giant robotic frog.

6. Alex is the leader of the group; fitting, since his parents seem to be the leaders of the supervillain gang who controls Los Angeles.

7. Nico's mother and father are magic users; in the first battle, she steals her magic staff.

8. A colossally strong mutant, who name is Molly, dreams of one day joining the X-Men.

9. Karolina discovers that she is actually an alien; the medical alert bracelet she has worn since she was a child actually suppresses them.

10. The robotic son of Ultron joins the group after a cryptic message from a time-traveler, saying that he will one day destroy the Avengers.

11. Nico and Karolina had a very awkward conversation before she was abducted by an alien.

12. The Runaways often work with other heroes of the Marvel Universe, though sometimes they try to convince them to give up the heroic life.

13. We have been reading this series since we were in high school; the struggles of these heroes really resonated with my friends and I.

14. Cloak, a New York hero with a cloak who concealed a portal to another dimension, was accused of attacking his partner Dagger.

15. Because of the varied nature of the powers inherited from their parents, this team can find themselves in many different kinds of storylines.

16. They do not currently have an ongoing title as a team, but they still occasionally show up as part of other events.

17. Nico and Chase were forced to participate in Avengers Arena, a Hunger Games-style competition where young superheroes were forced to battle for their survival.

18. Molly has appeared as a fringe character in several X-Men titles, in which she maintains her love of pink hats; however, they have yet to put her on a regular team.

19. Karolina and Xavin's species, the Majesdanians and the Skrull, are both featured to some extent in the wider galactic Marvel Universe; they even infiltrated Earth and impersonated well-known heroes.

20. It is extremely unlikely that audiences will see them in the upcoming move Guardians of the Galaxy, except perhaps in the obligatory post-credits scene.

HOMEWORK EXERCISE 2:

Directions: Answer the questions that accompany the following passage.

Do Bike Lanes Make New Bikers?

Many cities have been making their streets more bike-friendly in recent years, but how exactly they have done this varies greatly. A line in the pavement dividing cars from cyclists **(1)** are nice, but it doesn't offer the security of a protected bike lane **(2)** which is a track completely separated from vehicle traffic. Cyclists who use protected lanes say they feel **(3)** safer, and some studies show they truly are safer, with their risk of injury cut in half.

That's great for committed riders and public health more broadly. But what about city residents who don't already ride a bike, perhaps due to safety fears **(4)** . City officials didn't create separated bike lanes just for those who are already committed to biking; **(5)** it is hoping that these separated lanes will incentivize city biking.

A study team led by Christopher Monsere of Portland State University analyzed new protected bike lanes in five major U.S. cities. The researchers videotaped the new lanes, conducted local surveys, and collected data on cycling trends **(6)** in order to assemble enough data about these bike lanes. They found that ridership increased anywhere from 21 to 171 percent, with about 10 percent of new riders drawn from other modes.

The analysis focused on new bike **(7)** locations along eight city streets: Barton Springs, Bluebonnet, and Rio Grande in Austin; Dearborn and Milwaukee in Chicago; Multnomah in Portland, Oregon; Oak and Fell (a street couplet) in San Francisco; and L Street in Washington, D.C.

1. \A) NO CHANGE
   B) be
   C) is
   D) will be

2. A) NO CHANGE
   B) , this is a track completely separated from vehicle traffic
   C) : which is a track completely separated from vehicle traffic
   D) : a track completely separated from vehicle traffic

3. A) NO CHANGE
   B) safest
   C) more safer
   D) the most safest

4. A) NO CHANGE
   B) ?
   C) !
   D) Delete it. It is unnecessary.

5. A) NO CHANGE
   B) they is
   C) they are
   D) it are

6. A) NO CHANGE
   B) in hope that they would then have enough data to draw conclusions
   C) so that they could have enough data about the bike lanes to draw conclusions
   D) to gather comprehensive data about these bike lanes

7. A) NO CHANGE
   B) facilities
   C) stores
   D) destinations

{8} Some of the corridors (Rio Grande to Milwaukee) had an unprotected bike lane before the study; others had nothing at all (Dearborn to Barton Springs). Cycling rates rose on all of the new lanes. {9} As expected, the biggest gains — with ridership more than doubling — occurred on two streets converted into two-way lanes. But even streets with an existing bike lane saw a spike in ridership.

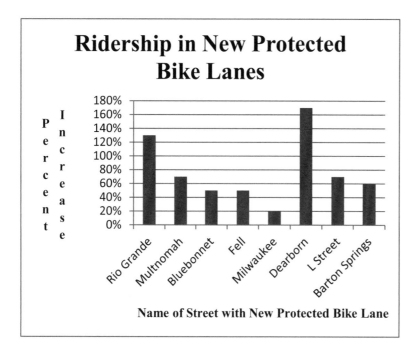

Ridership in New Protected Bike Lanes

Percent Increase

Name of Street with New Protected Bike Lane

(10) <u>Even if</u> the fact that ridership is generally rising is taken into account, comparing ridership in the new corridors against general trends across the city still shows that ridership in the new lanes beat the city average along all but one street — and on that street (Milwaukee) it matched the average.

8. Based on the evidence in the graph, what conclusion can you draw about city bike lanes in this study?

   A) Even before the new protected bike lanes, cities were more likely to have bike lanes than not have bike lanes.
   B) The new protected bike lanes had a uniform impact across the city streets.
   C) Ridership increased more where there already were bike lanes of some kind than where there were none.
   D) Ridership did not increase because of the new protected bike lanes.

9. Based on the evidence in the graph, to which two streets is this sentence referring?

   A) L Street and Barton Springs
   B) Rio Grande and Dearborn
   C) Rio Grande and Multnomah
   D) Dearborn and L Street

10. A) NO CHANGE
    B) If
    C) Delete it. It is unnecessary.
    D) When

Ultimately, the key is not just whether the protected lanes attract more riders, but whether they attract new riders. **{11}** The surveys showed that 65 percent would have already biked on that street, 24 percent would have biked but on another street, and, critically, 10 percent of the new riders would have taken another (unspecified) mode — a share that reached 21 percent along the Dearborn corridor in Chicago. Clearly, protected bike lanes do serve the double purpose of improving rider safety while also inspiring people to ride in the first place.

11. Which of the following statements about the relationship between the sentence and the graph is true?

A) The graph confirms all of the information in the sentence.

B) The graph shows the information about the Dearborn corridor but not the rest.

C) The graph does not show any of this information.

D) The graph shows the information about the 10% of new riders, but not the rest.

BLUE WRITING LESSON 7: POSSESSION ERRORS
Getting Your Feet Wet

Directions: The questions below are intended as a short diagnostic exam.

1. Even though they may have differing ways of execution, <u>at there core</u>, all Communist states obey similar principles.

   A) NO CHANGE
   B) at their core
   C) at they're core
   D) in there core

2. <u>Your opinion of Communism and it's</u> principles may be a product of the negative image it received during the mid- to late-twentieth century.

   A) NO CHANGE
   B) You're opinion of Communism and it's
   C) Your opinion of Communism and its'
   D) Your opinion of Communism and its

3. Whether you agree with the principles of Communism or not, <u>their is no denying its</u> failure in the Soviet Union.

   A) NO CHANGE
   B) there is no denying it's
   C) there is no denying its
   D) there cannot ever be a denying of its

4. Unfortunately, <u>the individuals basic human rights</u> seemed to be unimportant under Soviet Communism.

   A) NO CHANGE
   B) the individual's basic human rights
   C) the individuals' basic human rights
   D) the individual's basic human right's

BLUE WRITING LESSON 7: POSSESSION ERRORS
Wading In

TOPIC OVERVIEW: POSSESSION ERRORS

The SAT will test your ability to form **possessives** and **plurals**, and to tell the difference between the two. Additionally, some plural or possessive words are often confused with certain contractions or adverbs, and your skill in detecting these errors may also be tested

TOPIC OVERVIEW: THERE/THEY'RE/THEIR

Three words that are often mixed up are *their*, *there*, and *they're*. Clearly these words are confused because they sound the same, but when you're writing, it's important to know the difference. Here are the uses of each:

They're: A contraction for "They are." This is always used this way, no exceptions.

Example 1: Although many people believe in the precepts of Communism, they're not convinced that it is practical to execute in the real world.

Their: A possessive pronoun for the third person. This is always used this way, no exceptions.

Example 2: Karl Marx and Vladimir Lenin developed the fundamental ideas of Communism, and their ideas sparked other forms as well, including Stalinism, Trotskyism, and Maoism.

There: An adverb which describes the place, position, or existence of something. This word can also be used to show emphasis or as an interjection, but it is unlikely that you'll see this use on the SAT.

Example 3: The earliest forms of Communism can be found in ancient Greece, which is odd, because most people believe that democracy originated there.

TOPIC OVERVIEW: YOU'RE/YOUR

Another pair of commonly confused words is *your* and *you're*. As with *they're* and *their*, the word with the apostrophe is a contraction and can always be expanded to make two words, while the other is a possessive pronoun:

Example 4: If you're not sure about the history of Communism, your school library should have plenty of material you can use to research the subject.

TOPIC OVERVIEW: ITS/IT'S/ITS'

The possessive pronoun *its* is very frequently confused with the contraction *it's*, which is a shortening of the words *it is*. As we saw above, one easy way to tell if the contraction is appropriate is to expand it into the two words and see if the sentence still makes sense.

<u>Example 5</u>: The idea of communal ownership of property appeals to some, but to others it's antithetical to their desire for individuality.

<u>Example 5 (again)</u>: The idea of communal ownership of property appeals to some, but to others it is antithetical to their desire for individuality.

Because both of these make sense, you can be confident that you've used the correct version of this word.

The pronoun *its* is used to indicate possession of something. The word *its'* is never correct – avoid using it.

<u>Example 6</u>: Its application in the real world has never quite matched up to the ideals set forth in *The Communist Manifesto*, the modern-day bible for Communists.

TOPIC OVERVIEW: POSSESSIVE NOUNS

In English, nouns are made **possessive** by adding an *'s* to the end of it – just adding an *s* makes it plural. The one exception is when a noun ends with an *s*, in which case an apostrophe is added *after* the *s*. This happens when a singular noun ends with an *s* (like *Charles*) or the noun is plural already (like *students*). It is unlikely that you will be asked to make this distinction on the SAT, but in order to avoid possibly choosing the incorrect error in the writing section, it is good to know the difference.

<u>Example 7</u>: The Chinese Communist Party's membership is the largest in the world, totaling almost 80 million members.

<u>Example 8</u>: Although he was a major contributor to it, Friedrich Engels' contribution to Marxist theory often goes underappreciated.

<u>Example 9</u>: The workers' ownership of the means of production is largely theoretical, but it is a major component of Communist doctrine.

BLUE WRITING LESSON 7: POSSESSION ERRORS
Learning to Swim

CONCEPT EXERCISE:

Directions: Find and correct any errors in the following sentences. Some sentences may not have any errors.

1. Some students left there lunchboxes, sweatshirts, and homework at the bus stop again today.

2. English is a pluricentric language, which means that their are many different varieties that can all be considered correct.

3. British English differs from American English in a few significant ways, including it's treatment of collective nouns.

4. Canadian, Australian, and Indian English are all based on British English, but contain significant difference's of their own.

5. Most of these differences are limited to vocabulary, pronunciation, and spelling; educated speakers and writers are mutually intelligible, but they're dialects can make conversation difficult.

6. German is another pluricentric language, with three distinct and equally correct varieties governed by there own rules and regulations.

7. Strong Austrian German dialects can be incomprehensible to speakers of Northern German, but there much more intelligible to the people of Bavaria.

8. Most languages have prestige dialects, or varieties who's users have high social status among the general populace; academic English is one such dialect.

9. Writing research papers and other pieces of non-fiction is a situation in which students must use academic English.

10. The English that you speak with you're friends is conversational, and may follow rules that are significantly different from those of academic English.

11. Many features of Southern American English are not appropriate in academic English, such as the use of *y'all* as a pronoun; if your caught using it in a paper, your teacher will probably mark it wrong.

12. Despite users of academic English lacking a distinct second person plural pronoun, there not keen to allow features of a non-prestige dialect to be used in formal situations.

13. Each person must decide for him or herself whether the situation calls for conversational or academic English.

14. If a person is comfortable using both forms of the language, he or she is more likely to be successful in determining the form demanded by a wide range of situation's.

15. You are unlikely, for example, to use academic English on a camping trip with you're family; by the same token, you would not use conversational English when explaining the design specifications a fuel-efficient engine.

16. Clarity and specificity are essential components of academic English because its designed to be written; unlike in conversation, the user is not always going to be there to explain themselves.

17. Therefore writers of academic English must be very careful to word their sentences precisely and carefully, so that they're meanings cannot be misunderstood or misinterpreted.

18. Academic English carries it's own jargon, though, and writers must also be aware of their audience; if you use terms that your readers aren't familiar with, you run the risk of losing their attention or confusing them.

19. You may be surprised at how much thought must go in to a piece of academic writing — you're probably already making most of these decisions unconsciously.

20. During the editing stage, however, it can be important to step back and look at your writing from the viewpoint of your reader's and take all of these factors into consideration.

BLUE WRITING LESSON 7: POSSESSION ERRORS
Diving into the Deep End

PRACTICE EXERCISE:

Directions: Answer the questions that accompany the following passage.

Belief of the Ancients

All primitive **(1)** <u>peoples</u> thought of the earth's surface as a flat, level plain; it was roughened, **(2)** <u>its</u> true, by hills and mountains and indented by valleys and ravines, but still in its larger aspects a level, horizontal expanse of land and sea. Indeed, is not this **(3)** <u>its</u> obvious appearance? From any single post of observation, even if it be a mountain-top or the ocean with its unimpeded view, who would doubt the fact that the earth is level. Who would infer that it slopes away in the form of a curve? Even today there are some persons, and we need not go beyond Boston to find them, who still proclaim **(4)** <u>there</u> belief in the flatness of the earth. We may charge them with being crassly ignorant.

But how should we set about to refute them? The simple testimony of the **(5)** <u>sense's</u> seems to say that the earth is level. You may ride for a thousand miles in a railroad train from Boston to Chicago and except for the slight upgrades and downgrades due to intervening mountain slopes; you shall certainly think that **(6)** <u>your</u> following a dead level line. Or I may cross the Atlantic in an ocean liner and in that long journey of three thousand miles never once realize that the **(7)** <u>ship's</u> passengers and I are being borne around the surface of a sphere. Whether on land or sea, the earth seems a plain, and if I trust only to first appearances, I shall pronounce it such. Therein lies the rub; the appearance is a deceptive one as it obscures our **(8)** <u>spheres</u> circular nature.

1. A) NO CHANGE
   B) people's
   C) peoples'
   D) people

2. A) NO CHANGE
   B) it's
   C) its'
   D) it

3. A) NO CHANGE
   B) it
   C) it's
   D) its'

4. A) NO CHANGE
   B) theirs
   C) they're
   D) their

5. A) NO CHANGE
   B) senses'
   C) senses
   D) sense

6. A) NO CHANGE
   B) you're
   C) yours
   D) yore

7. A) NO CHANGE
   B) ships
   C) ships'
   D) ship is

8. A) NO CHANGE
   B) sphere's
   C) spheres'
   D) sphere is

(9) <u>Its'</u> not surprising for us, then, to learn that in the past all men, even the wisest, conceived the earth's surface as a level plain. In the olden times, in the morning of the history of the race, people did not travel as readily as now; they had no cars or boats propelled by steam or electricity to whirl them from one place to another. Their means of travel were limited to only **(10)** <u>they're</u> limbs and beasts of burden like the camel and the horse. To voyage a hundred miles was for them a serious journey. They sojourned but little in foreign lands and among strange peoples, and similarly, few strangers came among them. And when strangers did arrive from the distance of a few hundred miles they were said to have come from afar. Afar! Today, we scoff at a few hundred miles being more than a few **(11)** <u>hours'</u> travel.

9. A) NO CHANGE
    B) It
    C) Its
    D) It's

10. A) NO CHANGE
    B) their
    C) there
    D) there's

11. A) NO CHANGE
    B) hour
    C) hours
    D) hour's

TEST EXERCISE:

Directions: Answer the questions that accompany the following passage.

The Modesty in Women's Clothing in the 1910s

Modesty, as the word is commonly understood, is a distinctly human invention. While **(1)** you're understanding of the word may involve innocence, or inexperience, or even humility, these are not the case. It means **(2)** to be aware of your appearance and its appropriateness in the presence of the opposite gender.

{3} It is one of the innumerable proofs of our peculiar psychic power to attach emotions to objects without a faintest shadow of real connection. The different levels of modesty vary most strongly not by a person's class or wealth, but by his or her gender.

Men's clothing — hats, shirts, shoes — **(4)** are most modified by physical conditions. On the other hand, the clothing that women wear is most modified by psychic conditions. As **(5)** there usually restricted to a very limited field of activity, and as **(6)** they're personal comfort was of no importance to most people, it was possible to maintain in their dress the influence of primitive conditions long considered inconsequential to men.

Over time, men have grown their scope and responsibilities in our society. We see at once why the dress of men has developed along the line of practical efficiency and general human distinction. As women are given **(7)** fewer roles, and the dress of women is still most modified by the separation of gender. Women's dresses are exactly that: labels for women to wear to seem more feminine.

1. A) NO CHANGE
   B) you are
   C) your
   D) yours

2. A) NO CHANGE
   B) being
   C) you are being
   D) you ought to be

3. Which of the following transitions, if inserted here, would most closely match the author's style and tone?

   A) A most variable thing is this modesty.
   B) Modesty a concept that many people have different opinions on.
   C) Most people agree that a woman should cover her legs when out in public.
   D) Clearly there are cultural differences that determine the suitability of dress.

4. A) NO CHANGE
   B) must be
   C) they are
   D) is

5. A) NO CHANGE
   B) theirs
   C) their
   D) they're

6. A) NO CHANGE
   B) there
   C) their
   D) they are

7. A) NO CHANGE
   B) fewer roles, the
   C) fewer roles, therefore the
   D) fewer roles, this is the reason that the

A man may run in a city's streets in scant clothes — a lack of clothes, even — women would be called grossly immodest wearing the same. He may bathe, publicly, and in company with women, so nearly bare as to shock even himself; while the women beside him are covered far more fully than in evening dress. **{8}**

Why should it be "modest" for a woman to exhibit her neck, arms, shoulders, and back, but "immodest" to go bathing without stockings? It is because we have attached sentiments of modesty to certain parts of the human frame, and not to **(9)** <u>others</u> — that is all.

These certain parts vary. In certain African tribes, women are forbidden to reveal even part of their faces. The British peasant woman is forced cover her hair, for to show **(10)** <u>it's</u> an indecency.

We need not look for a reason where there never was one. These distinctions sprang from emotion or mere caprice, and vary with them. But whatever our notions of modesty in dress may be, we apply them to women for the most part and not to men. **{11}**

8. Which of the following facts would contradict the claims made in the previous paragraph?

   A) The rules of public decency have been applied in an unfair way since the beginning of the 20th century.
   B) A woman was arrested for public exposure when she left her house wearing a shirt which exposed her shoulders.
   C) The women's liberation movement has made great strides in achieving equality for women.
   D) A man was arrested for public exposure when he was picnicking with his family and removed his shirt.

9. A) NO CHANGE
   B) other
   C) other's
   D) others'

10. A) NO CHANGE
    B) it is
    C) its'
    D) it

11. Does the final sentence of this preceding paragraph effectively conclude the passage?

    A) No, because it does not address the main question of the passage, the inequalities between men and women.
    B) No, because it is does not address the specific issue discussed in the paragraph.
    C) Yes, because it summarizes the arguments made in the passage.
    D) Yes, because it defines what the rules of modesty should be.

BLUE WRITING LESSON 7: POSSESSION ERRORS
Race to the Finish

HOMEWORK EXERCISE 1:

Directions: Find and correct any errors in the following sentences. Some sentences may not have any errors.

1. It is every countries dream for its team to participate in the World Cup.

2. Have you seen James new calculator?

3. You can hear the chorus of feral cats' cries clearly at night.

4. How many chicken's will you need to start an egg farm?

5. Sports media tends to focus on mens' professional teams, especially during March Madness and the Super Bowl.

6. How many woman's hats will disappear before the thief is caught?

7. You can't even imagine how thick the sheeps' coats will be in the autumn.

8. There are fifteen species of fish in the aquarium; each species' needs balances the needs of the others.

9. The local farmer's market is selling avocado's for less than a dollar.

10. The World Series is the culmination of thirty team's dreams for the whole season.

11. Even though Aunt Astrid takes us to Disney World in the summer, your my favorite aunt because you help us with homework after school.

12. The unpopular newspaper article predicted they're landslide win; many others thought that all six candidates would lose to entrenched incumbents.

13. High school students often don't realize how bright their future's will be.

14. Will you be attending there graduation in Seneca Falls this October?

15. It's very difficult for some students to choose "No Error" on both practice questions and the official exam.

16. Its always interesting to see which grammar mistakes students can invent in order to avoid marking a sentence correct.

17. It is important to pay attention to vocabulary not only in academic schoolwork, but also in the movies and TV shows that your watching for fun.

18. Make sure you always do you're homework before coming in to class.

19. If you don't see evidence of their arguments in the body paragraphs, you can't be sure that their organizing the essay correctly.

20. Although it's not their favorite, many students like your class more than Mr. Radley's.

HOMEWORK EXERCISE 2:

Directions: Answer the questions that accompany the following passage.

Childhood Memories

Two people feature prominently in my earliest **(1)** memories, one, my mother, and the other, a tall man with a small, dark mustache. I remember that his shoes or boots were always shiny, and that he wore a gold chain and a gold watch. He always let me play **(2)** with it when I asked. He used to come to the house in the evenings, perhaps two or three times a week; it became my appointed duty whenever he came to bring him a pair of slippers, and to put the shiny shoes in a particular corner. I was always fascinated by **(3)** they're luster as I carried them carefully.

I remember **(4)** distinctly the last time this tall man came to the little house in Georgia. That evening before I went to bed he took me up in his arms, and squeezed me very tightly while my mother stood behind his chair wiping tears from her eyes. **(5)** Laboriously, I remember how I watched him drill a hole through a ten-dollar gold piece, and then tie the coin around my neck with a string. I **(6)** wore that gold piece around my neck for the greater part of my life, and still do, but more than once I have wished that some other way had been found of attaching it to me besides putting a hole through it.

1. A) NO CHANGE
   B) memories: one,
   C) memories; and one,
   D) memories, but one,

2. A) NO CHANGE
   B) with them
   C) with they
   D) with its

3. A) NO CHANGE
   B) there
   C) their
   D) theirs

4. A) NO CHANGE
   B) noticeably
   C) evidently
   D) plainly

5. A) NO CHANGE
   B) I remember how laboriously I watched him drill
   C) I laboriously remember how I watched him drill
   D) I remember how I watched him laboriously drill

6. A) NO CHANGE
   B) had worn
   C) have worn
   D) had wore

{7} At Savannah we boarded a steamer; **(8)** <u>its</u> destination, New York. From New York we went to a town in Connecticut, which became the home of my boyhood.

7. Which of the following, if inserted here, would best transition from the previous paragraph?

   A) I found the coin to be a reassuring presence, although I never really knew the man who had given it to me.

   B) On the day after the coin was put around my neck my mother and I started on what seemed to me an endless journey.

   C) I had always been nervous on boats, and this day was no exception.

   D) My mother and I got onto a boat and headed out to begin our new life.

8. A) NO CHANGE
   B) it's
   C) it is
   D) its'

[1] My mother and I lived together in a little cottage which seemed to me to be fitted up almost luxuriously. [2] There were horse-hair covered chairs in the parlor, and a little square piano; there was a stairway with red carpet on it leading to a half second story; there were pictures on the walls, and a few books in a glass case. [3] I learned to play the piano in that small parlor, though we never used it for much else. [4] My mother dressed me very neatly, and I developed that pride which well-dressed boys generally have. [5] My mother rarely went to anyone's house, but she did sewing, and there were a great many **(9)** <u>ladies</u> coming to our cottage. [6] If I were around they would generally call me, and ask me my name and age and tell my mother what a pretty boy I was. **{10, 11}**

9. A) NO CHANGE
    B) lady's
    C) ladies'
    D) ladies's

10. Which choice most effectively establishes the main topic of the paragraph?

    A) Nowhere else but Connecticut would I have been able to find my way.
    B) My mother had inherited a large sum of money, and she put it to good use in our new home.
    C) The man I was to become found his roots in a life lived with the guidance of only a female parent.
    D) The greatest influence on my life came from music, which my mother made sure was a major part of my life.

11. Which of the following should be removed to improve the focus of the paragraph?

    A) Sentence 3
    B) Sentence 4
    C) Sentence 5
    D) Sentence 6

BLUE WRITING LESSON 8: ORGANIZATION
Getting Your Feet Wet

Directions: The following is intended as a short diagnostic exam. Use the paragraph below to answer the questions.

Do Sugar Taxes Work?

[1] Two out of three adults and one out of three children in the United States are overweight or obese, leading to an annual expenditure of about $190 billion treating obesity-related health conditions. [2] Rising consumption of sugary beverages has been a major contributor to the obesity epidemic. [3] As a result, more than 10% of U.S. daily calorie intake comes purely from sugary drinks.

[4] Before the 1950s, standard soft drink bottles were 6.5 ounces, while today, 20-ounce plastic bottles are the norm. [5] Worse yet, these sugary beverages provide empty calories with no nutritional value, thus contributing to weight increases in people of all ages.

[6] To combat soda's contribution to obesity, some regions have experimented with sugary beverage taxes. [7] A new study of how taxes might be used to curb consumption of sugary drinks suggests that applying a tax based on the amount of calories contained in a serving rather than its size would be more effective. [8] The study found that consumption of calories in drinks would drop 9.3% if a tax of .04 cents were added for every calorie.

1. Which of the following changes would create the most logical and coherent paragraph?

   A) Delete Sentence 1
   B) Switch Sentences 1 and 2
   C) Switch Sentences 3 and 4
   D) Delete Sentence 4

2. The author of the passage is considering adding the following sentence to the passage:

   "The same study found that consumption would fall by just 8.6% under a tax of .5 cents per ounce."

   Where should it be placed to add most effectively add support to her argument?

   A) Before Sentence 6
   B) Between Sentences 7 and 8
   C) After Sentence 8
   D) The sentence should not be added.

3. After making the addition above, the author is considering switching Sentences 6 and 7. Should the author make this change?

   A) Yes, because doing so moves all the information about the study together.
   B) Yes, because doing so creates a better transition from the first paragraph to the second.
   C) No, because doing so interrupts the flow of information regarding the study.
   D) No, because doing so creates a contradiction to information provided in the previous paragraph.

BLUE WRITING LESSON 8: ORGANIZATION
Wading In

TOPIC OVERVIEW: ORGANIZATION

The SAT's focus on context-based questions means that there will be fewer questions that simply require you to find grammatical errors. A topic that will get increased attention is **organization**. Organization questions test your ability to put ideas in logical order, whether that means rearranging sentences within a paragraph or paragraphs within a passage.

TOPIC OVERVIEW: SENTENCE ORGANIZATION

Sentence organization questions deal with the presentation of ideas in the most logical sequence possible. The best order can usually be determined by the content of the sentences. The flow of information should be natural, with concepts that relate to each other appearing close to each other in the paragraph. Also, if there are any cause/effect relationships, it is better to put the cause first.

An example of poor logical flow appears in the sample passage on the previous page. The second question asks you to insert a sentence in the most logical place in a paragraph, giving you four options as to where to place it. Choice A would put the sentence at the beginning of the paragraph. Because the sentence you are inserting references a study that is mentioned later in the paragraph, you can't put it at the beginning — the words "The same study" don't make any sense without the study being introduced already.

TOPIC OVERVIEW: PARAGRAPH ORGANIZATION

Paragraph organization questions require you to use similar skills as the sentence organization questions do, but at a wider scale. The first paragraph of a passage should be summative, introducing basic ideas or people that will be discussed in the passage. It should introduce the main point that will be made in the passage (sometimes called the thesis). The middle paragraphs should be supporting information for the thesis, and should flow logically from one to the other. The last paragraph should be a "wrap-up" where the connections between the supporting ideas and the main idea are restated. Looking for these basic organizational markers will help you determine which answer is correct.

BLUE WRITING LESSON 8: ORGANIZATION
Learning to Swim

CONCEPT EXERCISE:

Directions: For each paragraph below, list the order of the sentences that would create the most logical and coherent flow of ideas.

1. [1] The most remarkable quality of the possum is the pouch found under the belly of the female, in which it carries its young ones when they are small. [2] The head is mostly white and the body is covered with long black-and-white hair. [3] Possums typically have around fifty teeth. [4] If the little creatures are frightened when absent from their mother, they scamper to this haven as soon as possible. [5] It climbs up trees with great skill, hides itself in the leaves to catch birds, or hangs itself by the tail from a branch. [6] It is nocturnal, living on fruit, insects, and birds' eggs. [7] The Possum is an American animal, having large eyes and a head like the fox.

_____ _____ _____ _____ _____ _____ _____

2. [1] Hares are remarkably quick, and no dog but a greyhound could overtake one in a race. [2] It feeds upon clover, apples, and other fruits, and will often sit for hours in some snug covered place quietly chewing its cud. [3] It is a harmless and innocent creature, such that few have the heart to do it injury. [4] There is another kind of rabbit, commonly referred to as a hare, which runs wild in the woods and fields. [5] This is just as well, since rabbits do not have much in the way of defense and prefer to run away from threats. [6] The Rabbit is a very pretty animal that lives around houses and barns in a state of friendship with all around it.

_____ _____ _____ _____ _____ _____

[1] A small piece of lawn, well made and well kept, will give more satisfaction than a larger plot of inferior turf. [2] If well made, a lawn will be a delight as long as the proprietor lives, but if the soil is thin and poor, or if coarse grass and clovers are allowed to grow, he or she will be discouraged. [3] In this case, the lawn-tender will very likely try some expensive experiments, and at last plow everything up and begin over again. [4] "A smooth, closely shaven surface of grass is by far the most essential element of beauty on the grounds of a suburban home." [5] This will increase both the cost and annoyance of the project, especially since well-established weeds will have filled the soil as much as they were able. [6] A good lawn then is worth working for, and if it has a substantial foundation, it will endure for generations, and improve with age. [7] This is the language of Mr. F. J. Scott, and it is equally true of other than suburban grounds.

_____ _____ _____ _____ _____ _____ _____

3. [1] The confederacy existed at least as early as 1540, and included the Muskogee, the Alabama, and others of the Muskogean stock. [2] They were brave fighters, but during the 18th century only had one struggle, of little importance, with the settlers. [3] In the Civil War, the Creeks were divided in their allegiance and suffered heavily in the campaigns. [4] The so-called Creek nation is now settled in Oklahoma, but independent government virtually ceased in 1906. [5] The Muskogee Confederacy was a confederacy of North American Indians, who formerly occupied most of Alabama and Georgia. [6] The confederacy was completely defeated in three hard-fought battles, and the peace treaty which followed involved the cession to the United States government of most of the Creek country. [7] The Creek War of 1813-14 was, however, serious. [8] The Muskogee are also known as the Creek, for the large number of creeks and small rivers running through their land.

_____ _____ _____ _____ _____ _____ _____ _____

4. [1] How does the child of a poet get involved with computers? [2] Sadly, Ada died of cancer only a few years after publication of the article, and never saw the legacy of her early work. [3] Luckily, Ada enjoyed her studies and showed an early aptitude for numbers. [4] At 17 she was introduced to Charles Babbage, the inventor of the first computer. [5] Few are familiar with his mathematician daughter, Ada Lovelace, the first computer programmer. [6] Many fans of English literature are familiar with Lord Byron, a poet and influential figure in the Romantic period. [7] When Ada translated an article on Babbage's Analytical Enginge, she added her own commentary and several early computer programs, signing her name with only her initials, A.L.L. [8] Ada's mother, fearing that Ada might inherit her father's moodiness and "poetic" personality, insisted that Ada's tutors train her in logic, science, and mathematical thinking.

— — — — — — — —

5. [1] The tunnels, often as large as a lead pencil, extend usually in a longitudinal direction and follow a very irregular, tangled course. [2] The mollusks' food consists of protozoa and is not obtained from the wood substance. [3] They attack the exposed surface of the wood and immediately begin to bore. [4] Almost invariably they are confined to salt water, and all the woods commonly used for piling are subject to their attacks. [5] There are two genera of mollusks that do serious damage to wood in many places along both the Atlantic and Pacific coasts. [6] Vast amounts of timber used for piles in wharves and other marine structures are constantly being destroyed or seriously injured by marine borers. [7] The sole object of boring into the wood is to obtain shelter.[8] Hard woods are apparently penetrated as readily as soft woods, though in the same timber the softer parts are preferred. [9] The mollusks, which are popularly known as "shipworms," are much alike in structure and mode of life.

— — — — — — — — —

6. [1] This happened once in the 19th century, when Pedro Carolino wrote a New Guide of the Conversation in Portuguese and English. [2] Throughout history, from at least the time of Shakespeare through to today, linguists and comedians have amused themselves and the public at the expense of students learning a new language. [3] It is less common, however, for amateur linguists to make jokes of themselves by publishing guides to languages which they clearly do not speak. [4] The result was, as you can imagine, hilarious to native English speakers. [5] However, Carolino did not himself speak any English, and wrote his guide with the help of a Portuguese to French dictionary and a French to English phrasebook. [6] It was written seriously, for the purpose of instructing Portuguese students in English grammar and phrasing.

— — — — — — —

7. [1] It practically sounded the death-knell of the conservative doctrine of non-expansion beyond our own natural physical boundaries. [2] Hawaii marks our first advance into foreign lands, and ranges America for the first time among the nations whose policy is that of expansion, by territorial extensions, over the globe. [3] The fact, however, that it was a republic is the only circumstance which makes its case analogous to that of Hawaii. [4] The Louisiana Territory, Florida, and Alaska were acquired by purchase; California, New Mexico, and a part of Colorado were obtained by cession from Mexico; Oregon, Washington, Montana, and Idaho by treaty with Great Britain--Texas alone was annexed. [5] The only precedent approaching this act, in our history, is the annexation of Texas. [6] Texas lay between two large nations, and was obliged to seek union with one of them; it was within our own continent and inhabited largely by our own people. [7] The annexation of the Hawaiian Islands to the United States, by a joint vote of Congress, July 7, 1898, marks a new era in the history of our country.

— — — — — — —

8. [1] They prescribe certain rules for wiring a house, and they insist that their agent inspect and pass such wiring before current is turned on. [2] Insurance companies recognize that a large percentage of farm fires comes from the use of kerosene; for this reason, they are willing to give special rates for farm homes lighted by electricity. [3] Once the wiring is passed, the advantage is all in favor of the farmer with electricity over the farmer with kerosene. [4] Additionally, the added value a water-power electric plant adds to the selling price of a farm. [5] The National Board of Fire Underwriters is sufficiently logical in its demands, and powerful enough, so that manufacturers who produce the necessary fittings find it profitable to conform to insurance standards. [6] Therefore it is difficult to go wrong in undertaking to wire a house.

— — — — — —

9. [1] There is no specific treatment for smallpox disease, and the only prevention is vaccination. [2] Variola major is the severe and most common form of smallpox, with a more extensive rash and higher fever. [3] There are four types of variola major smallpox: ordinary, modified, flat, and hemorrhagic. [4] Smallpox is a serious, contagious, and sometimes fatal infectious disease. [5] Historically, variola major has an overall fatality rate of about 30%; however, flat and hemorrhagic smallpox usually are fatal. [6] There are two clinical forms of smallpox, variola major and variola minor. [7] Variola minor is a less common presentation of smallpox, and a much less severe disease, with death rates historically of 1% or less.

— — — — — —

BLUE WRITING LESSON 8: ORGANIZATION
Diving into the Deep End

PRACTICE EXERCISE:

Directions: Answer the questions that accompany the following passages.

PASSAGE 1

Bringing an Artist to Light

[1]

[1] Though many early wordless novels focused on oppression, capitalism, and the general plight of humanity, *From My Childhood* was an impressionistic narrative of sheltered, middle-class lives that resembled the artist's own. [2] Inspired by Masreel, Bochořáková-Dittrichová began creating woodcuts of her own, publishing the gorgeous, light-filled *Z Mého Dětství (From My Childhood)* in 1929. [3] Her subsequent work further expanded the genre's scope, focusing on history, religion, and impressions of other cultures. [4] Here's what we know: Bochořáková-Dittrichová first discovered woodcut novels while studying in Paris, where she came across the work of Belgian artist Frans Masereel, who created some 20 wordless, woodcut novels throughout his career. [5] As a result, Bochořáková-Dittrichová quietly strengthened the case for topics such as domestic life, allowing them be seen as legitimate art subjects rather than as easily dismissed "female-only" fodder. {1}

1. Which of the following orders would produce the most logical and coherent version of Paragraph 1?

   A) NO CHANGE
   B) 4, 2, 5, 3, 1
   C) 4, 1, 5, 3, 2
   D) 4, 2, 1, 5, 3

[2]

[1] Tucked away above the main gallery halls, the library at the National Museum of Women in the Arts (NMWA) is filled with its own variety of treasures: rare books, research texts, and yes, even artwork. [2] Recently, the library hosted an exhibit on Helena Bochořáková-Dittrichová (1894-1980), a Czech painter, illustrator, and graphic artist who was the first woman to create a wordless novel. [3] This genre that emerged in 1920s Europe and presaged the contemporary graphic novel.**{2}**

[3]

Bochořáková-Dittrichová will occasionally receive a brief mention in books about printmaking, but her existence is often reduced to such footnotes. The exhibit is designed to help bring her work out of the footnotes and into the art world's consciousness.

[4]

[1] Although her work is in the collections of a number of Czech museums, Bochořáková-Dittrichová remains relatively unknown in the United States. [2] It was only a matter of chance that she came to the attention of Heather Slania, the director of NMWA's library and research center. [3] The 52-woodcut manuscript, called *Malířka Na Cestách* (*The Artist on Her Journey*), tells the story of a young woman who moves to Paris to study art on a government scholarship—a trajectory Bochořáková-Dittrichová herself followed. [4] Several of the woodcuts are on display as part of the exhibition. [5] When a rare book dealer approached Slania with an unpublished manuscript with original woodcuts by Bochořáková-Dittrichová, Slania knew she had stumbled upon a hidden gem.**{3}**

2. Which of the following orders would produce the most logical and coherent version of Paragraph 2?

A) NO CHANGE
B) 1, 3, 2
C) 3, 2, 1
D) 3, 1, 2

3. For the sake of the coherence of Paragraph 4, Sentence 5 should be placed

A) after Sentence 1.
B) after Sentence 2.
C) after Sentence 3.
D) where it is now.

[5]

Even though wordless novels never became a mainstream medium, Bochořáková-Dittrichová's pioneering place within the art form is still noteworthy. Without Bochořáková-Dittrichová, it is unlikely that the graphic novel would exist as the diverse and fascinating art form that it is today. **{4}**

4. The author is considering adding the following sentence to Paragraph 5:

    Her influence bears testament to the power of women to shape a developing genre.

    To produce the most coherent paragraph, where the author should place the sentence?

    A) Before Sentence 1
    B) Between Sentences 1 and 2
    C) After Sentence 2
    D) Do not add the sentence.

5. Which of the following lists the most logical order for the paragraphs in the passage?

    A) 1, 3, 2, 4, 5
    B) 4, 2, 1, 5, 3
    C) 2, 4, 1, 3, 5
    D) 2, 3, 1, 5, 4

PASSAGE 2

Learning by Doing

[1]

{6}There are so many praiseworthy aspects of the IntelliZeum. Each specialized learning area within the IntelliZeum has different clothing, tools, and unique things to do. Children may enter a "space center," where they dress in space suits. They may visit a pretend doctor's office where they don white coats and stethoscopes. When the children travel to the "Arctic room," it's freezing cold; in the "rainforest room," it's hot and muggy. In the "electricity and water center," they discover how water makes power and learn about water conservation.

[2]

[1] Before each visit, children are prepared with vocabulary and background knowledge so they can get the most out of the experience. [2] The IntelliZeum sets high expectations for what children can learn. [3] After the visit, learning is reinforced by incorporating the concepts and rich oral language into classroom activities. [4] There, children learn about parts of the solar system, types of dinosaurs, and even tools used for building construction. {7}

[3]

I recently visited a great hands-on, experiential learning site for young children. The IntelliZeum, founded 10 years ago in El Paso, Texas, is a one-of-a-kind interactive learning environment. This stimulating learning center provides enriching experiences for the lucky area children who get to visit it.

6. Which paragraph would be the most logical choice to start the passage?

A) Paragraph 1
B) Paragraph 2
C) Paragraph 3
D) Paragraph 4

7. Which of the following is the most logical order for the sentences in Paragraph 2?

A) 1, 2, 4, 3
B) 1, 3, 4, 2
C) 3, 4, 1, 2
D) 2, 4, 1, 3

[4]

The learning environments at the museum are sophisticated and designed to stretch children's minds, encouraging them—even at age 3 and 4—to start thinking about interesting and important future careers. I know children leave dreaming of becoming doctors, architects, engineers, pilots, or reporters.{8}

[5]

[1] The underwater "ocean," an area enclosed by three giant aquariums, is also handicapped accessible, so a child in a wheelchair can wheel right in while the other children scramble under one of the aquariums. [2] Another positive is the intentional inclusion of children with disabilities. [3] A child in a wheelchair can get inside the time capsule for traveling to the age of the dinosaurs. {9}

[6]

[1] I wish engaging learning centers like the IntelliZeum could be available to all children. [2] However, all parents can help their children engage in rich learning experiences at home and during daily activities. [3] For example, instead of watching television, families can take a trip to the airport, visit a train station, or observe a construction site in the neighborhood and take advantage of teachable moments within these experiences. [4] Even errands to the store can be turned into solid learning experiences by exposing children to vocabulary words, letting the children participate by picking out and weighing fruits and vegetables, taking photos of something they like, or talking to a person at the store. [5] We need to get back to experiential learning that is real, exciting, and meaningful. {10}

8. Which choice is the best topic sentence for Paragraph 4?

A) Many other museums have similar exhibits and activities that are equivalent to those at the Intellizeum.
B) A singular characteristic of the Intellizeum is the thought that went into the design of the exhibits.
C) One distinctive feature of the Intellizeum is how forward-thinking its designers are.
D) The Intellizeum doesn't treat children like miniature adults–it treats them like children.

9. Which of the following is the most logical order for the sentences in Paragraph 5?

A) NO CHANGE
B) 2, 3, 1
C) 1, 3, 2
D) 2, 1, 3

10. The author is considering adding the following sentence to Paragraph 6:

A regular medical checkup can turn into a chance to learn about the tools doctors and nurses use.

After which sentence would it most logically be placed?

A) Sentence 1
B) Sentence 2
C) Sentence 3
D) Sentence 4

TEST EXERCISE:

Directions: Answer the questions that accompany the following passage.

Blighted Detroit

[1]

{1} [1] The once great Motor City has become a shadow of its former self. [2] This remarkably swift exodus has resulted in a city marred by blight [3] Home to 1.8 million residents in 1950, Detroit's population has shrunk to a mere 700,000 people. [4] Back in 1950, Detroit was the center of car production in the world, but since that year, other countries and other regions of the U.S. provided successful competition. [5] Of Detroit's 380,000 parcels of land, nearly one in four properties **(2)** <u>are</u> damaged, vacant, or uninhabitable.

[2]

Blight spreads like an infectious disease. A single vacant residence can bring down home values along an entire street, placing homeowners in **(3)** <u>an impossible</u> situation in which they owe more than their homes are worth. In recent years, high unemployment has forced many to simply abandon these properties in order to seek better opportunities elsewhere.

[3]

[1] Along his block of Hazelridge Street on the East Side of Detroit, Karl Baker is the only remaining resident. [2] Most of the houses nearby are standing but abandoned **(4)** <u>, and</u> visitors have clearly passed through. [3] Empty bottles lie along debris-covered floors near broken windows and doors, every memory of a metal appliance or gutter is gone from some homes, and two old couches that were dumped along a lawn are now covered in snow. [4] Just two blocks away, most of the homes along Hazelridge are still occupied. [5] Residents wonder, "How long before that block slips away, too **(5)** <u>."</u> **{6}**

1. Which of the following changes would improve the logical progression of ideas in Paragraph 1?

   A) Move Sentence 1 to the end of the paragraph
   B) Move Sentence 2 so that it follows Sentence 3
   C) Move Sentence 2 to the beginning of the paragraph
   D) Move Sentence 4 to follow Sentence 1

2. A) NO CHANGE
   B) is
   C) being
   D) been

3. A) NO CHANGE
   B) an atrocious
   C) a grim
   D) a dire

4. A) NO CHANGE
   B) ; and
   C) ,
   D) and

5. A) NO CHANGE
   B) ?"
   C) ?
   D) !"

6. Which of the following changes would create a more logical flow of ideas in Paragraph 3?

   A) NO CHANGE
   B) Move Sentence 2 to the beginning of the paragraph
   C) Exchange the positions of Sentences 4 and 5
   D) Remove Sentence 4

[4]

{7} It will likely cost the bankrupt city a staggering $1.85 billion to raze and clean up the tens of thousands of abandoned properties, almost four times the amount the city has allotted for the task. This is probably one of the cruelest realities of a shrinking city: It costs a tremendous amount of money merely to demolish and recycle what others have left behind. Beneath this cost is the lost tax revenue that each of the blighted properties **(8)** represent, making it all the more difficult to gather the resources to stop the problem.

[5]

Thus Detroit faces a Catch-22: It cannot solve urban blight without financial resources, it cannot gain financial resources without increased tax revenue, and it cannot increase tax revenue while beset with blight. {9}

[6]

Identifying the problem, unfortunately, does little to **(10)** fathom it. Once the blighted properties are cleared — a huge hurdle in and of itself — Detroit must find a way to use the resulting empty land. Some non-profit organizations have suggested turning cleared lots into urban community gardens as a means of turning dead space into usable space. Other plans call for completely reorganizing the city, consolidating the dwindling population and turning unused areas into green space. **(11)** But it all costs money, and a bankrupt Detroit is sorely lacking in resources.

7. Which choice best summarizes the main idea of Paragraph 4?

A) Detroit will use its savings to restructure the city, which will take time.
B) Detroit has planned well for what will be a very tough task of renewing the city.
C) The task of renewing the city is extremely challenging.
D) Detroit needs a lot of money to renew the city but tax revenues will pay for it.

8. A) NO CHANGE
   B) represents
   C) has represented
   D) will represent

9. Which of the following changes should be made to improve the logical flow of the passage?

A) NO CHANGE
B) Move Paragraph 3 to follow Paragraph 5
C) Move Paragraph 5 to follow paragraph 3
D) Move Paragraph 5 to the end of the passage.

10. A) NO CHANGE
    B) explain
    C) decipher
    D) solve

11. A) NO CHANGE
    B) It
    C) However it,
    D) Although it

BLUE WRITING LESSON 8: ORGANIZATION
Race to the Finish

HOMEWORK EXERCISE 1:

Directions: Answer the questions that accompany the following passage.

The Angel with Bent Legs

[1] For the past six decades, the Brazilian national soccer team **(1)** boasts many of the greatest individual talents in the sport. [2] Many of those who watched Garrincha swear that, at his peak, no one could match him—not even his teammate, the great Pelé. [3] One player, however, has held the hearts of some Brazilian fans for more than 50 years: Manuel Francisco dos Santos, more commonly known as "Garrincha" ("little bird" in Portuguese). {2}

[1] He was born with several birth **(3)** defects; a deformed spine, a right leg that bent outward, and a left leg six inches shorter than the right. [2] Somehow, despite these issues, Garrincha could not only play soccer but also play it dazzlingly well. [3] His flawed body and awe-inspiring skills combined to give him the nickname "The Angel with Bent Legs." {4}

1. A) NO CHANGE
   B) boasted
   C) boasting
   D) has boasted

2. In order to create a more logical paragraph, where should Sentence 3 be placed?

   A) Where it is now.
   B) Before Sentence 1
   C) Between Sentences 1 and 2
   D) Delete Sentence 3

3. A) NO CHANGE
   B) defects: a
   C) defects, "a
   D) defects a

4. The author is considering adding the following sentence to the second paragraph:

   Looking at Garrincha, you would never expect him to play soccer at a high level.

   In order to maintain the logic and coherence of the paragraph, where would this sentence best be placed?

   A) Before Sentence 1
   B) Between Sentences 1 and 2
   C) Between Sentences 2 and 3
   D) After Sentence 3

[1] Due largely to his unusual legs, Garrincha did not receive as many opportunities as **(5)** <u>them</u>. [2] However, when he finally got a chance to play for the professional club Botafogo, he took advantage. [3] He scored three goals in his first game and quickly became a **(6)** <u>fixture</u> in the club; he spent the next 12 years with Botafogo, scoring 232 goals in all. {7}

Garrincha finally played in the World Cup for the first time in 1958. His coaches were still distrustful of Garrincha's bent legs; he did not play until the third game. **(8)** <u>He helped</u> Brazil beat the tournament-favorite Russian team, however, Garrincha was quickly recognized as a star. Brazil went on to win the World Cup.

5. A) NO CHANGE
   B) those others
   C) they
   D) other players

6. Which of the following words fits best in the context of the passage?

   A) NO CHANGE
   B) fixation
   C) prefix
   D) fiction

7. Which of the following is the most logical order for the sentences in the preceding paragraph?

   A) NO CHANGE
   B) 1, 3, 2
   C) 2, 1, 3
   D) 3, 1, 2

8. A) NO CHANGE
   B) After helping
   C) He was one of those who helped
   D) He was helping

(9) <u>Remembered as one of the greatest players to have ever lived,</u> Pelé was injured in the first game, forcing Garrincha to step up. After scoring four goals and leading his team to another championship, **(10)** <u>voters named Garrincha</u> the best player in the tournament.

[1] Throughout his career, Garrincha dazzled fans with his ability to dribble around opposing players and change direction quickly. [2] He had finally overcome his bent legs to become a superstar. [3] Opponents were also in awe of Garrincha; one called him "a phenomenon... capable of sheer magic." {11}

9. Which option offers the best transition between the previous paragraph and this one?

    A) NO CHANGE
    B) Feeling jealous of his rival,
    C) In the next World Cup in 1962,
    D) Remembered today as the greater player,

10. A) NO CHANGE
    B) Garrincha was named
    C) a vote was held, naming Garrincha
    D) Garrincha's votes made him

11. The author is considering adding the following sentence to the second paragraph:

    Even fans of opposing teams often cheered as Garrincha baffled their own players.

    In order to maintain the logic and coherence of the paragraph, where would this sentence best be placed?

    A) Before Sentence 1
    B) Between Sentences 1 and 2
    C) Between Sentences 2 and 3
    D) After Sentence 3

HOMEWORK EXERCISE 2:

Directions: Answer the questions that accompany the following passage.

{1}

[1] Teachers work in a noble profession and deserve our respect — or do they? [2] In a recent case, Vergara vs. California, Californian teachers' unions suffered a **(1)** <u>withering</u> blow when the judge struck down the "teacher tenure" statute. [3] Teachers' unions across the nation are protesting this decision, arguing that the ruling allows bureaucracy complete impunity in **(2)** <u>their decisions</u> regarding the educators of our children. [4] As disastrous as this may seem for teachers, it's arguably a step in the right direction for the profession as a whole. **(3)**

1. Within the context of the passage, which of the following is the best replacement for the underlined word?

   A) NO CHANGE
   B) scornful
   C) disabling
   D) insulting

2. A) NO CHANGE
   B) its decisions
   C) the bureaucracy's decisions
   D) it's decisions

3. The author is considering adding the following phrase to Paragraph 1:

   "*Not according to a California superior court judge.*"

   To preserve the logic and coherence of the paragraph, where would this sentence best be placed?

   A) After Sentence 1
   B) After Sentence 2
   C) After Sentence 3
   D) After Sentence 4

C2 education
be smarter

{2}

California's employment laws for teachers are among the most relaxed in the country. As it stands, California teachers can be granted permanent employment **(4)** <u>status, known as tenure, after</u> 18 months regardless of teaching quality {5}. When schools must cut staff, they are required by law to do so on a first-hired, first-fired basis. Such practices can easily result in a system that protects weaker, tenured teachers over more skilled, newer teachers. {6}

4. A) NO CHANGE
   B) status known as tenure after
   C) status, known as tenure after
   D) status — known as tenure, after

5. Which of the following, if added here, would best support the ideas presented in the previous sentence?

   A) , but most other states require at least three years of employment for teachers to be considered for tenure
   B) , and teaching quality suffers as a result
   C) , a practice that is common in many other states
   D) , which is something that teacher unions have long fought for

6. In order to improve the logic and coherence of the passage as a whole, which of the following is the best position for Paragraph 2?

   A) Where it is now
   B) Before Paragraph 1
   C) After Paragraph 3
   D) After Paragraph 4

{3}

{7} As with all professions, there are different skill levels. There are great teachers, **(8)** teachers who inspire their students and challenge them, and teachers who do the minimum required of them in order to maintain their positions. Teaching, when done right, is a challenging profession, **(9)** not every potential educator is suited to the task. While most teachers are passionate and dedicated to their students, there are many who lack the temperament and skills necessary to create a positive and productive classroom experience.

{4}

Teachers who fail to measure up to standards set by the state will now be accountable for their failures. Though many teachers' unions are dismayed by a ruling that they believe **(10)** dismantles necessary protections for educators, this move may well result in a far stronger workforce overall. By holding ineffective teachers accountable regardless of their time in the profession, such rules have the potential to encourage a new generation of educators to improve the state of education in public schools.

{5}

Many teachers' **(11)** unions are arguing tenure is necessary to protect educators from the whims of an overly bureaucratic administrative system, and they are right to highlight the problems inherent in overly complex, budget-strapped school systems. Yet these voices should remember that in the end, the right of students to receive a useful education is paramount.

7. Which choice most effectively establishes the main idea of the paragraph?

   A) Most teachers are ineffective in the classroom and should not be protected by tenure laws.
   B) Despite the media's focus on so-called "bad teachers," the entire profession should not be dismissed as lazy or ineffective.
   C) Talented and passionate teachers should be protected by teacher tenure laws.
   D) Far too many teachers are simply lazy and unwilling to go above and beyond to help students

8. A) NO CHANGE
   B) those who inspire and challenge their students
   C) those who inspire their students to do well and provide them with intellectual challenges
   D) teachers who students find to be inspiring and challenging

9. A) NO CHANGE
   B) but not
   C) and not
   D) yet not

10. A) NO CHANGE
   B) augments
   C) injures
   D) belies

11. A) NO CHANGE
   B) unions argues that
   C) union argues that
   D) unions argue that

BLUE WRITING LESSON 9: QUANTITATIVE INFORMATION
Getting Your Feet Wet

Directions: The following is intended as a short diagnostic exam.

In essence, Monsanto has created a system that tells farmers which seeds to plant and how to cultivate them. This prescriptive-planting system, called FieldScripts, can be used to run machines made by Precision Planting, a company Monsanto bought in 2012, which makes devices pulled behind tractors to plant seeds. The result is a machine that can plant a field with different varieties at different depths and spacings, varying all of this according to the weather.

{1} The benefits are clear. Farmers who have tried this system say it has improved yields by roughly 5% over two years, a feat no other single intervention could match. The seed companies think that utilizing data in this way could increase the national food supply by as much as 25%, giving a terrific boost to farmers' meager margins.

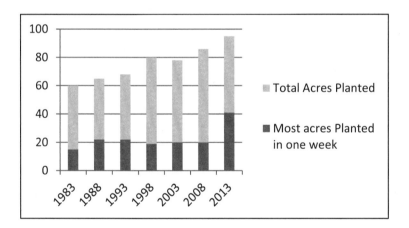

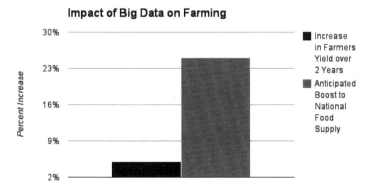

Impact of Big Data on Farming

1. Based on the passage and graphics below, what will the impact of the new system be on farmers?

   A) Because 5% is so much less than 25%, the impact will be negligible.
   B) No one knows what the impact on farmers will be.
   C) The impact on farmers will be so great that more Americans will once again become farmers.
   D) While 5% may seem small comparatively, this could be a significant boost to individual farmers.

2. Based on the passage and the graphics, which of the following is most likely true about the new planting technique?

   A) It has increased efficiency, giving farmers the ability to plant crops more quickly than ever before.
   B) It has decreased efficiency, resulting in a decrease in acres planted per week.
   C) It has resulted in an increase in the number of total acres planted.
   D) It has resulted in a decrease in the number of total acres planted.

BLUE WRITING LESSON 9: QUANTITATIVE INFORMATION
Wading In

TOPIC OVERVIEW: QUANTITATIVE ANALYSIS

A new feature of the SAT is the inclusion of graphics with the passages. To answer some of the questions that accompany these passages, you will need to use the information in both the passage and graphic — this skill is called *synthesis*.

RECOGNIZING QUANTITATIVE ANALYSIS QUESTIONS

Questions that require the use of a graphic will always indicate this in the question statement. They will have phrases like "According to the graphic and the passage…" or "The passage and the graphic imply that…" Remember that these questions are testing your ability to synthesize information from both the text and the graphic, and will likely require the use of both to find the answer.

ANSWERING QUANTITATIVE ANALYSIS QUESTIONS

One of the best methods for answering questions like these is elimination. It's often easy to quickly find answers that do not agree with the information in the graphic. Here is an outline of a strategy to use:

1) Read the question and examine the graph carefully, paying close attention to the scale and labels on each axis (if the graph is a line or bar graph).
2) Eliminate any choices that provide information that does not agree with the graphic.
3) If two or more choices remain, use the passage to eliminate the answers until there is only one. Look for synonyms or words in the answer choices that appear in the passage to locate the relevant part.

Below is a short passage and a graphic, followed by two questions and explanations of their answers:

The Greenland ice sheet is the second-largest ice body in the world (behind Antarctica's). It experiences annual melting at low elevations near the coastline, but melting at the surface is rare in the dry snow region at higher elevations in its center. In mid-July 2012, however, nearly the entire ice sheet experienced surface melt, the first widespread melt during the era of satellite observation. {1}

Even the area around Summit Station in central Greenland, which at 2 miles (3.2 kilometers) above sea level is near the highest point of the ice sheet, showed signs of melting. Such pronounced melting at Summit and across the ice sheet has not occurred since 1889, according to ice cores analyzed by Kaitlin Keegan at Dartmouth College in Hanover, N.H. A National Oceanic and Atmospheric Administration weather station at Summit confirmed air temperatures hovered above or within a degree of freezing for several hours July 11 to 12. {2}

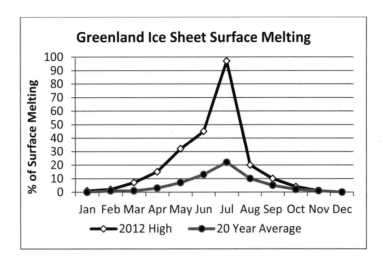

1. Which statement, if added here, would provide the most accurate and appropriate data, based on the graph at the end of the passage?

   A) In 2012, the surface melt peaked at slightly above 20%.
   B) The historical surface melt rate typically rises in the summer months before peaking in September and October.
   C) In a month, the surface melt rate rose from 45% (already well above historical levels) to an unprecedented 97%.
   D) The rise in surface melt rate came during months when the ice sheet's melt rate is usually decreasing, not increasing.

   1. Notice that on our graph, the horizontal axis is in months, and the vertical axis is in percent of surface melt.
   2. Start with Choice A. The peak level of surface melt in 2012 was close to 100%, not 20% as the answer choice implies (the 20% is for the average, not for 2012). Choice B is incorrect because the historical (or average) rate appears to peak in July, not September and October. Choice C looks good, because if you compare the numbers in the answer choice to the numbers in the graphic, you can see that they match. Choice D is incorrect because the average rate and the rate for 2012 match as far as when they are increasing or decreasing, just not in the extent to which that is happening.
   3. The only remaining answer is Choice C, so this is the correct answer.

2. Based on information in both the passage and the graphic, which of the following is true about the relationship between ice sheet melting and temperature?

   A) The level of ice sheet melt is not related to temperature.
   B) There is an inverse correlation between temperature and ice sheet melt.
   C) Temperatures just above freezing will result in ice sheet melt.
   D) The temperatures in 2012 and the temperatures in 1889 were the same, resulting in the same level of ice sheet melting.

1. We've already examined the graph closely. Note that this question will require the use of information in both the graphic and the passage.

2. There is no data provided about the temperature in Greenland in 1889, so Choice D is incorrect. To eliminate any other answer choices, we'll need to use the passage.

3. The relevant portion of the passage for this question is at the end of the second paragraph: *confirmed air temperatures hovered above or within a degree of freezing for several hours July 11 to 12*. This tells you that during the period of high levels of melting (mid-July), the temperatures were very close to freezing, making Choice C the correct answer. This same part of the passage makes Choice A incorrect, there is no evidence to support Choice B; in fact, using the graphic, it seems as if the opposite is true.

WRAP-UP: QUANTITATIVE INFORMATION

Use this strategy to answer questions that are accompanied by graphics in the writing section:

1) Read the question and examine the graph carefully, paying close attention to the scale and labels on each axis (if the graph is a line or bar graph).

2) Eliminate any choices that provide information that does not agree with the graphic.

3) If two or more choices remain, use the passage to eliminate the answers until there is only one. Look for words or synonyms or words in the answer choices that appear in the passage to locate the relevant part.

BLUE WRITING LESSON 9: QUANTITATIVE INFORMATION
Learning to Swim

CONCEPT EXERCISE:

Directions: Answer the following questions using the graphs and the passage below.

Making Way for Alternative Transportation

In 1991, the Intermodal Surface Transportation Efficiency Act (ISTEA) created the Transportation Enhancement (TE), Recreational Trails (RTP) and Congestion Mitigation and Air Quality programs (CMAQ), all of which have become major sources of funding for bicycling and walking projects. Before ISTEA, states had the option of spending up to $4.5 million of their highway funds each year on independent bicycling and walking projects (up to a national cap of $45 million), and the funds required NO state matching funds. In the 18 years before 1991, a total of $40 million was spent by all 50 states combined – approximately $2 million a year. Most states spent nothing between 1988 and 1991.

The chart below shows how spending on bicycling and walking projects and programs has increased since 1991 – and there are very noticeable dips in spending as each transportation bill has neared expiration. While this may partly be explained by the general level of uncertainty caused by numerous short-term funding fixes, there is also a strong possibility that States are hoping these programs will go away in the new bills.

1. Based on the information provided in the passage and the graphics, which of the following is most likely true?

   A) The ISTEA had no effect on the levels of spending by states on bicycle and pedestrian funding.
   B) The overall effect of ISTEA has been to increase state spending on bicycle and pedestrian projects.
   C) The most important component of the ISTEA was the Recreational Trails Program.
   D) The increase in bicycle commuting over the past 20 years has been due exclusively to the provisions of the ISTEA.

2. What provides the best evidence to answer the previous question?

   A) The first graphic.
   B) The second graphic.
   C) Both graphics
   D) Only information in the passage is required to answer the question.

3. If the author provided data indicating where the most was spent to develop bicycle and pedestrian trails in their cities, which of the following cities would be expected to spend the most?

   A) Washington, D.C.
   B) Baltimore. MD
   C) Cleveland, OH
   D) St. Louis, MO

		% Bike Commuters		
City	Population	1990	2013	% Growth
Chicago, IL	2,714,844	0.3%	1.6%	459.7%
Philadelphia, PA	1,547,607	.23%	0.6%	300.6%
San Francisco, CA	825,863	.31%	1.0%	292.2%
Detroit, MI	701, 524	0.1%	0.6%	464.4%
Baltimore, MD	621,342	.09%	0.2%	320.8%
Washington, D.C.	632,323	0.8%	4.1%	445.4%
Portland, OR	603,650	1.2%	6.1%	430.3%
Cleveland, OH	390,923	0.6%	1.9%	385.0%
St. Louis, MO	318,172	1.2%	3.1%	332.8%

State Use of Federal Funds for Bicycle and Pedestrian Projects

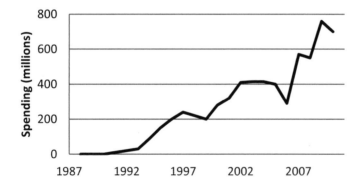

4. Given the information in the passage and the graphics, it can be inferred that the transportation bills neared expiration in which of the following years?

A) 1993
B) 1997
C) 2001
D) 2007

5. Based on information in the passage and the graphics, which of the following is most likely true?

A) Given the choice, states will spend more on pedestrian projects than bicycle projects.
B) Given the choice, states will spend more on bicycle projects than pedestrian projects.
C) Given the choice, states will not spend any money on either pedestrian or bicycle projects.
D) Given the choice, most commuters would drive to work rather than bike to work.

6. Which graphic (or graphics) provides the best evidence for the answer to the previous question?

A) The first graphic only.
B) The second graphic only.
C) Both graphics provide evidence for this question.
D) Neither graphic provides evidence for this question.

Just watch our travel export growth numbers drop as people around the world see the uncontrolled activities of the TSA's new aggressive and invasive personal searches. This week I was repeatedly poked, prodded, groped, frisked, and fondled, about which I have blogged and tweeted extensively. Just as Congressmen were reluctant to oppose J. Edgar Hoover's FBI in the 1950s for fear of being thought soft on Communism, so it is with Congress and John Pistole's TSA, lest they be thought to be soft on terrorism.

The Department of Commerce should recognize that these TSA policies do not improve passenger safety in any way and that they are bad for American businesses. Fewer Americans will travel, fewer foreigners will visit, and tourist-dependent businesses will be affected. I'm not sure why the airlines, hotel chains, convention centers, and theme park operators haven't objected to the TSA's assault on civil liberties, but it may be simply that they are still benefiting from the reservations made before the TSA's escalation of searches.

I'm sure that it is difficult for one government agency to oppose another agency, but I hope that the Department of Commerce will carefully monitor the negative reactions to the TSA's procedures, and be among the first to raise an alarm when American travel-related businesses are hurt by these procedures. I hope that Secretary Locke is not among those who are intimidated by the TSA.

Note: The Transportation Safety Administration (TSA) was founded after the terrorist attacks on September 11, 2001 to strengthen the security of America's transportation systems.

7. Based on the information provided in the passage and the graphics, which of the following is most likely true?

A) The TSA is responsible for the decrease in tourism exports in the United States during 2009-2010.
B) The fears brought up by the author of the editorial are evidenced by the information in the graphics.
C) The TSA has had no consistent effect on the number of aircraft hijackings in recent years.
D) Despite people's beliefs, the TSA has had the effect of reducing the number of aircraft hijackings since 2001.

8. What provides the best evidence to answer the previous question?

A) The passage and the first graphic
B) The passage and the second graphic
C) The passage and both graphics
D) The passage only

9. Based on the concerns raised in the passage and the information presented in the first graphic, which of the following conclusions can be drawn?

A) The measures enacted by the TSA have not had a negative effect on the economy.
B) The measures enacted by the TSA have had no effect on travel and travel exports in the United States.
C) The measures enacted by the TSA did not have a negative effect on travel and travel exports in the United States during 2010.
D) No conclusion can be drawn.

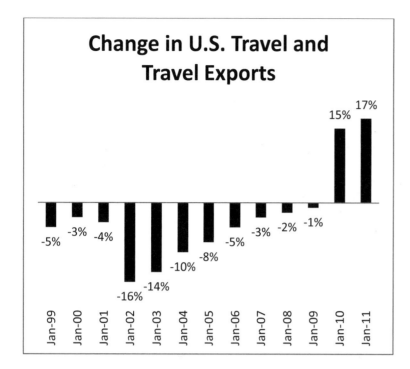

Change in U.S. Travel and Travel Exports

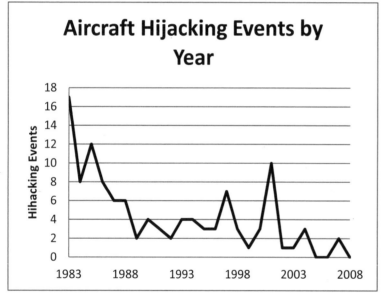

Aircraft Hijacking Events by Year

10. If the information provided in the second paragraph of the passage is true, what trend would be expected in the first graphic as time progressed?

   A) The percent change would remain the same.
   B) The percent change would begin to decrease.
   C) The percent change would begin to increase.
   D) There is no connection between the second paragraph and the graphic.

11. Based on information in the passage and the graphics, which of the following is most likely true?

   A) The terrorist attacks on September 11, 2001 were responsible for the large drop in travel exports seen in 2002.
   B) John Pistole believes that the measures enacted by the TSA are necessary for the continued success of American travel exports.
   C) There is a direct correlation between Travel exports and aircraft hijackings.
   D) The TSA is a sub-agency of the U.S. Department of Commerce.

12. Which graphic (or graphics) provides the best evidence for the answer to the previous question?

   A) The first graphic only
   B) The second graphic only
   C) Both graphics provide evidence for this question
   D) Neither graphic provides evidence for this question

BLUE WRITING LESSON 9: QUANTITATIVE INFORMATION
Diving into the Deep End

PRACTICE EXERCISE:

Directions: Answer the following questions using the graphs and the passage below.

The Long Shadow of an Inner City Childhood

(1) Our society holds sacred the popular ethos that we are the makers of our own fortune. (2) In America, hard work and dedication can lead to success, regardless of a person's background. A groundbreaking study, in which Johns Hopkins University researchers followed 800 inner city school children for more than 25 years, provides a far different picture, suggesting that a person's ultimate fate is largely determined by the family (3) he or she is born into.

Starting in 1982, Johns Hopkins sociologist Karl Alexander (4) lead a study of 800 Baltimore school children. Through repeated interviews with the children and their parents and teachers, the research team observed the group as its members made their way through elementary, middle and high school, joined the work force and started families.

1. Based on the context of the passage as a whole, which of the following is the most contextually accurate?

   A) NO CHANGE
   B) American
   C) This
   D) Global

2. Based on the context of the passage as a whole, which of the following is the most contextually accurate?

   A) NO CHANGE
   B) Based on evidence, in America
   C) Supposedly, in America
   D) Delete it.

3. A) NO CHANGE
   B) they are
   C) we are
   D) you are

4. A) NO CHANGE
   B) led
   C) has led
   D) leads

(5) <u>The project was supposed to end after three years.</u> Researchers had hoped to better understand how early home life helped some children successfully acclimate to first grade. Before the three years were up, Alexander and his team realized that they had established the foundation for something much bigger — to watch the children's life trajectories unfold.

In most cases, the children's life trajectories unfolded exactly as their parents' had. At nearly 30 years old, almost half the sample found themselves in the same socio-economic status as that of their parents. The poor remained poor; the better off remained better off. Only 33 children from families in the low-income bracket moved to the high-income bracket as young adults; if family had no bearing on children's mobility prospects, data suggest that 70 children should have made this transition.

5. Based on the graphs below, which of the following must be true about this sentence?

A) What initially was a project to monitor children for 3 years turned into a foundation for a crucial longitudinal study that lasted at least until participants turned 28.
B) This study is one of the most important studies of young children that has ever been produced.
C) Young children provide an excellent model to study the way that children develop.
D) Once the researchers saw what happened with the children, they were able to predict what would happen to them as they grew older.

One finding in particular helps to explain this conclusion.

(6) <u>Among children from low-income families, only 3.8 percent had obtained a college degree by the age of 28,</u> **(7)** <u>compared to roughly 50 percent of children from higher-income backgrounds.</u>

Pecentage of Students from Each Class

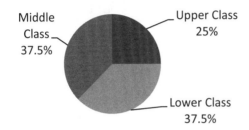

Percentage College Graduates by Age 28

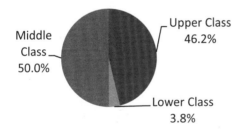

6. Which of the following is true based on the first half of the sentence and the two graphs below?

   A) Only the first graph is needed to visualize this statistic.
   B) Both graphs are needed to visualize this statistic.
   C) Only the second graph is needed to visualize this statistic.
   D) Neither graph gives further visualization of this statistic.

7. Which of the following is true based on the second half of the sentence and the two graphs below?

   A) If the age were less than 28, the graduation rates of those in "higher-income backgrounds" would be closer to those of the lower class.
   B) If the age were extended beyond 28, lower class graduation rates would equal those of "higher-income backgrounds."
   C) The first graph would lead you to the conclusion that the second graph shows.
   D) "Higher-income backgrounds" must mean both middle and upper class.

(8) <u>This is all the more galling to many who argue that the most concern should be given to lower class students because they make up a greater percentage of students than those from the upper class.</u> **(9)** <u>This data is in line with other studies that have found that children from low-income backgrounds are far less likely to graduate from college than their higher-income peers.</u>

8. Assuming the data from the study is representative of the nation as a whole, which of the following is a legitimate disagreement, based on the graphs, with the sentiment expressed in this sentence?

    A) The first graph shows that the number of upper class students is actually higher than that of lower class students.
    B) The first graph shows that the number of middle class students is just as high as that of lower class students, so no special concern should be given to the lower class.
    C) The second graph shows that lower class students are still succeeding at graduating from college, so they do not need extra help.
    D) The two graphs conflict; one shows that lower class students are the largest percentage of students and the other shows the opposite.

9. Based on the sentence and the two graphs, which of the following proves how the idea in the sentence occurs?

    A) Only the first graph is needed to prove this sentence.
    B) Both graphs are needed to prove this sentence.
    C) Only the second graph is needed to prove this sentence.
    D) Neither graph gives further proof of this sentence.

Children from low-income backgrounds face many obstacles in obtaining a college degree, from a lack of resources during high school to an inability to afford tuition at many higher education institutions. As a result, such children are far less likely to obtain a college degree, thus **(10)** <u>resulting</u> them to a lifetime of lower-income jobs. **(11)** <u>The cycle then repeats itself in future generations.</u>

10. A) NO CHANGE
 B) delegating
 C) relegating
 D) assimilating

11. Which of the following is most likely based on the sentence and the two graphs?

 A) Students from the lower class can defy the statistics in the graphs and go on to graduate from college.
 B) The percentage of students in the lower class bracket will not decrease in future generations.
 C) The middle class are actually doing quite well in that their percentage is only 37.5% (graph 1) but their college graduation rate is 50% (graph 2).
 D) As shown by graph one, each class grows at a constant rate, so the lower class will continue at 37.5%.

TEST EXERCISE:

Directions: Answer the following questions using the graphs and the passage below.

The Measle Resurgence

Today, more than 1 in 20 children nationwide enter kindergarten without the recommended vaccines. The risks of going without vaccinations **(1)** <u>are not isolated to unvaccinated children</u>; as the number of unvaccinated children grows, the potential for disease outbreaks increases dramatically. **(2)** <u>This is proven by facts.</u> In 2000, it appeared that the U.S. had nearly eliminated the measles. Since then, we have experienced numerous troubling outbreaks. In 2008, **(3)** <u>nearly 250 measles cases were confirmed</u> in the U.S., the largest outbreak since 1997. That record was **(4)** <u>beat in 2009 and again in 2010.</u> In 2014, **(5)** <u>more than 800 confirmed measles cases were reported</u>, the highest number in more than 20 years. According to the CDC, the spread of these outbreaks was attributable to "pockets of persons unvaccinated because of philosophical or religious beliefs."

Measles Occurrence in the U.S.

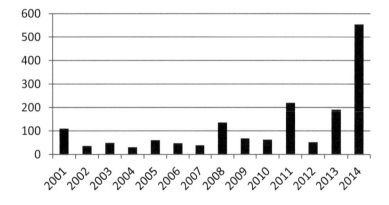

1. A) NO CHANGE
   B) is not isolated to unvaccinated children
   C) are not isolated, to unvaccinated children
   D) were not isolated to unvaccinated children

2. Which of the following best fits the style and tone of the passage?

   A) NO CHANGE
   B) Don't believe it? Check this out.
   C) This is far from mere conjecture.
   D) Recent measles rates have been through the roof.

3. Which choice best completes the sentence with accurate data based on the graph provided?

   A) NO CHANGE
   B) nearly 550 measles cases were confirmed
   C) nearly 140 measles cases were confirmed
   D) nearly 80 measles cases were confirmed

4. Which of the following best fits the data provided on the graph?

   A) NO CHANGE
   B) beat in 2011 and again in 2013
   C) beat in 2010 and again in 2012
   D) beat in 2009 and again in 2013

5. Which choice best completes the sentence with accurate data based on the graph provided?

   A) NO CHANGE
   B) more than 1000 confirmed measles cases were reported
   C) more than 260 confirmed measles cases were reported
   D) more than 550 confirmed measles cases were reported

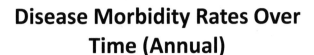

Disease Morbidity Rates Over Time (Annual)

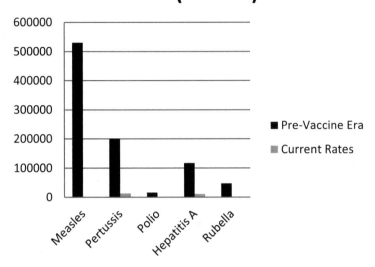

In the decades since vaccines were introduced, millions of lives have been saved. Vaccines are responsible for the elimination of several deadly diseases, including polio. While many other vaccine-preventable diseases have not yet been eliminated, morbidity rates have dropped drastically since the introduction of vaccines. Measles, despite recent outbreaks, **(6)** is a far lesser threat than it once was. Prior to the widespread use of the measles vaccine, **(7)** nearly one hundred thousand people were infected each year. Today, even the most alarming outbreak seems minor by comparison. Pertussis (or whooping cough), another all-but-eliminated disease that has been making a slow resurgence as a result of the anti-vaccine movement, **(8)** once affected more than 700,000 Americans each year. Today that number is just 13,500, a 93% decrease. {**9**}

6. A) NO CHANGE
   B) are a far lesser threat
   C) is far less than a threat
   D) is less than a threat than

7. Which choice best completes the sentence with accurate data based on the graph provided?

   A) NO CHANGE
   B) over one million
   C) more than half a million
   D) almost two hundred thousand

8. Which choice best completes the sentence with accurate data based on the graph provided?

   A) NO CHANGE
   B) once affected approximately 13,500 Americans each year.
   C) once affected 200,000 Americans every year.
   D) once affected more than 550,000 Americans every year.

9. Which of the following, if added to this paragraph, would add additional accurate data to the passage?

   A) Measles has been a greater threat than other diseases such as pertussis.
   B) This has not been the case for other diseases, such as rubella and hepatitis A.
   C) Vaccines have helped reduce measles as well as other diseases.
   D) Other diseases, such as hepatitis A and rubella, have seen similar declines thanks to vaccines.

If vaccines are so important for public health, why are so many parents choosing not to vaccinate their children?

The modern anti-vaccine movement stems, in large part, from a **(10)** paper which was deceitful and improperly vetted, by Andrew Wakefield in 1998. The paper claimed to have found that Measles-Mumps-Rubella (MMR) vaccines contributed to a spike in autism cases between 1988 and 1993. The media seized the story, inciting public fear of the MMR and of vaccines in general. In 2010, the paper was fully retracted after reviews by the CDC, the Institute of Medicine, the U.K. National Health Service, and others found absolutely no link between vaccines and autism, but by then, the damage had been done.

All efforts to negate the misconception about the link between vaccines and autism have proved ineffective. If public education is **(11)** deficient to address the growing problem of unvaccinated children, perhaps the only alternative is through public policy. In some states, opting out of vaccination requires little more than a onetime signature on a form. Tightening these policies may be considerably more helpful than trying to win the hearts and minds of skeptical parents.

10. A) NO CHANGE
    B) paper from 1998, written by Andrew Wakefield, who was deceitful and improperly vetted
    C) deceitful, improperly vetted paper written by Andrew Wakefield in 1998
    D) paper which was written by Andrew Wakefield, deceptive and improperly vetted, in 1998

11. Which of the following is the most precise replacement for the underlined word?

    A) NO CHANGE
    B) inefficient
    C) defiant
    D) insufficient

BLUE WRITING LESSON 9: QUANTITATIVE INFORMATION
Race to the Finish

HOMEWORK EXERCISE 1:

Directions: Answer the following questions using the graphs and the passage below.

Spinal Cord Injury

Until World War II broke out, a serious spinal cord injury (SCI) **(1)** usually meaning certain death. Anyone who survived such injury relied on a wheelchair for mobility in a world with few accommodations and faced an ongoing struggle to survive **(2)** the many various other secondary complications such as breathing problems, blood clots, kidney failure, and pressure sores. By the middle of the twentieth century, new antibiotics and novel approaches to preventing and treating bed sores and urinary tract infections **(3)** had revolutionized care after spinal cord injury. This greatly expanded life expectancy and required new strategies to maintain the health of people living with chronic paralysis. Now there are more than a quarter of a million Americans currently living with spinal cord injury of some kind. Though most are caused by vehicular accidents, **(4)** fewer people are injured in sports or violence related incidents than most would expect. {5}

1. A) NO CHANGE
   B) usually meant
   C) usually means
   D) could mean

2. Which of the following changes would create the most concise version of this sentence?

   A) NO CHANGE
   B) the many other
   C) the various other
   D) Remove this phrase

3. A) NO CHANGE
   B) have revolutionized
   C) revolutionizing
   D) revolutionize

4. A) NO CHANGE
   B) fewer persons suffer in sports and violence related incidents
   C) less people are injured in sports or violence related incidents
   D) fewer injuries are caused by sports or violence related incidents

5. Based on the graph, what fact should be added into the above paragraph?

   A) "Other" causes of spinal cord injury occur more often than sports-related causes.
   B) The second most common cause of spinal cord injury is falling, not sports or violence.
   C) Sports-caused injuries happen fewer times than violence related injuries.
   D) The most common cause of spinal cord injury is vehicular accidents.

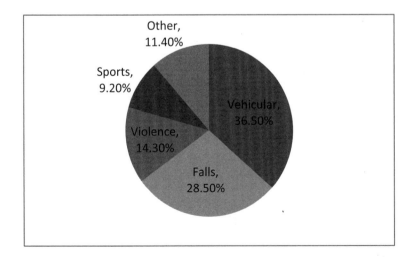

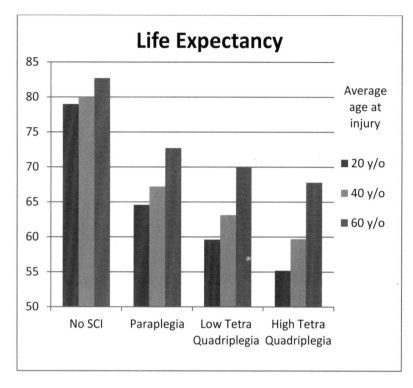

Note: In the figure above, there were 100 people surveyed in each age group

Today, **(6)** improved emergency care by people with spinal cord injuries, antibiotics to treat infections, and aggressive rehabilitation can minimize damage to the nervous system and restore function to varying degrees. Thanks to these modern innovations, **(7)** patients with paralysis regularly live pretty long; some of these patients are still able to find employment after their injuries {**8**}.

6. A) NO CHANGE
   B) improved emergency care for people with spinal cord injuries
   C) improved emergency care with people with spinal cord injuries
   D) improved emergency care from people with spinal cord injuries

7. Using the above graph, what is the best way to improve this sentence?

   A) patients with paraplegia regularly live longer than patients with quadriplegia
   B) patients with quadriplegia regularly live to at least 55
   C) patients with paraplegia and quadriplegia regularly live an average of 30 additional years after injury
   D) patients without spinal cord injury regularly live over 75

8. Given the context of the passage, which of the following facts would best support the claim made in this sentence?

   A) More than half of the patients with SCI were employed at the time of their injury.
   B) 80% of all SCI patients are men.
   C) 34.9% of patients eventually find employment
   D) 87.1% of patients discharged from the hospital go back to regular life.

Current advances in spinal cord injury research **(9)** <u>is giving</u> doctors and people living with SCI **(10)** <u>hope</u> that these injuries will eventually be repairable. With new surgical techniques and developments in spinal nerve regeneration in mind, **(11)** <u>the future for spinal cord injury survivors looks brighter than ever.</u>

9. A) NO CHANGE
    B) is given
    C) has given
    D) are giving

10. A) NO CHANGE
    B) hopes
    C) are hoping
    D) hoping

11. A) NO CHANGE
    B) the future for spinal cord injury survivors looks bright.
    C) spinal cord injury survivors have a brighter future to look forward to than ever.
    D) spinal cord injury survivors have a brighter future than ever.

HOMEWORK EXERCISE 2:

Directions: Answer the questions that accompany the following passage.

Horrible Bosses

[1]

[1]If the laws of economics were enforced as **(1)** strictly as the laws of physics, America would be a workers' paradise. [2] The supply of most kinds of labor are low, relative to the demand, so one would think each worker was treated as a cherished asset. [3] Unfortunately, despite the substantial increase in corporate productivity over the past several decades there have been only grudging gains in wages, especially over the past 10 years, **(2)** and in the realm of dignity and autonomy, a palpable decline. [4] Fortunately, the Federal government has been steadily increasing the minimum wage in an attempt to make up for the discrepancies created by some employers. {**3, 4**}

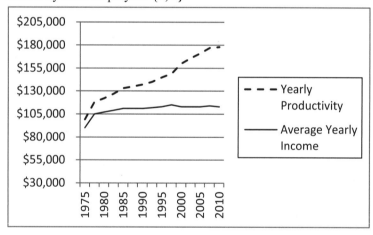

1. A) NO CHANGE
   B) authoritatively
   C) harshly
   D) punctually

2. A) NO CHANGE
   B) and in the realm of dignity and autonomy: a palpable decline.
   C) and in the realm of dignity and autonomy, a palpable, decline.
   D) and in the realm of dignity and autonomy a palpable decline.

3. Which of the following sentences should be eliminated in order to improve the focus of this paragraph?

   A) Sentence 1
   B) Sentence 2
   C) Sentence 3
   D) Sentence 4

4. Based on the data in the chart, which of the following effectively establishes the main idea of the paragraph?

   A) There has been a steady increase in both productivity and wages over the past 30 years.
   B) There has been an increasing disparity between employee productivity and wages, especially in the past decade.
   C) While productivity has increased, wages have decreased steadily.
   D) Increases in minimum wages have effectively bridged the gap between wages and productivity.

[2]

Similar trends have developed between employment and corporate productivity. This, of course, is mainly a consequence of the boom in technological advances over the past two decades. **(5)** <u>Where technology becomes more complex fewer employees are needed to complete certain tasks.</u> These tasks range from something as simple as restaurant labor to more specialized procedures like financial analysis for large corporations. Thus, American companies' productivity has experienced an overall increase, while employment itself has remained stagnant. **{6}**

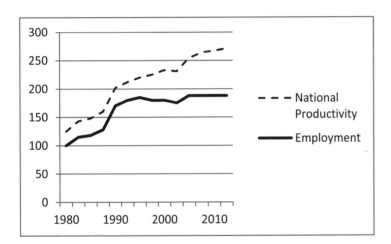

5. A) NO CHANGE
   B) Although technology becomes more complex, fewer employees are needed to complete certain tasks.
   C) As technology becomes more complex, fewer employees are needed to complete certain tasks.
   D) Fewer employees are needed, when technology becomes more complex.

6. Which of the following statements could serve as supporting evidence for the information provided by the paragraph and the graph?

   A) Since the inventions of certain technologies, the common person has more time to devote to work.
   B) The invention of computers required specialized technicians and has, therefore, created jobs.
   C) Many parts assemblers at automobile plants are being replaced by the latest robot technology.
   D) Many workers cannot afford the technology needed to maintain office jobs.

[3]

{7} In 1996, a grocery store worker in Dallas was fired for wearing a Green Bay Packers T-shirt to work on the day before a Cowboys-Packers game. While this may have been an insensitive gesture, it certainly could not have influenced his ability in the workplace. That being said, it might come as a surprise to some that his firing was entirely legal. While employees have the right to express their religion at work, some other forms of "self-expression" are not protected. {8}

[4]

It could also be argued that employers have the ability to take some basic American rights. One such right is the right to assemble. On a recent journalistic foray into a series of low-wage jobs, it was revealed that management often regarded the most innocent conversation between employees as potentially insubordinate. One restaurant prohibited "gossip," and a manager would hastily disperse any gathering of two or more employees.

7. Which of the following sentences effectively transitions from the second to third paragraph?

A) In addition to the difficulties gaining employment, maintaining employment can prove to be just as difficult, especially when employers have an incredible amount of freedom in hiring and firing.
B) One way that employers breach employees' trust is by monitoring their every move.
C) Certain laws have been formulated to limit the powers of employers.
D) However, most of these practices are considered illegal and do not reflect the opinions of lawmakers.

8. Which of the following facts would support the claims made in this paragraph?

A) A man was fired from his job for wearing a necklace with a cross on it.
B) An employer fired a man for wearing a shirt that advertised his political beliefs.
C) An employer punished employees who were caught gossiping.
D) An employee was fired for no apparent reason.

(9) <u>By keeping the employees separated, they are unable to gather into groups and make any demands on workplace conditions and environment.</u>

[5]

The mystery is why American workers have so meekly surrendered their rights. **(10)** <u>Sure, individual workers find ways to outwit the electronic surveillance and sneak in a bit of "gossip" here and there, but these petty acts of defiance seldom add up to concerted resistance.</u> *This is in part because of the weakness of American unions: it is not easy to organize your fellow workers if you cannot communicate freely with them on the job.*

[6]

{11} Gossip raids, however, are relatively innocuous compared with the sophisticated chemical and electronic forms of snooping adopted by many companies in the 90's. The American Management Association reports that in 1999 a record two-thirds of major American companies have monitored their employees electronically: videotaping them; reviewing their e-mail and voice-mail messages; and even monitoring any Web sites they may visit on their lunch breaks.

9. A) NO CHANGE
   B) By keeping the employees separated, the employers keep workers from gathering into groups and making any demands on workplace conditions and environment.
   C) By keeping the employees separated, the employers keep them from gathering into groups and make any demands on workplace conditions and environment.
   D) By keeping the employees separated, they keep them from gathering into groups and making any demands on workplace conditions and environment

10. A) NO CHANGE
    B) Sure, individual workers find ways to outwit the electronic surveillance and sneak in a bit of "gossip" here and there, these petty acts of defiance seldom add up to concerted resistance.
    C) Sure, individual workers find ways to outwit the electronic surveillance and sneak in a bit of "gossip" here and there, and these petty acts of defiance seldom add up to concerted resistance.
    D) Sure, individual workers find ways to outwit the electronic surveillance and sneak in a bit of "gossip" here and there; but these petty acts of defiance seldom add up to concerted resistance.

11. For the sake of the logical progression of the passage, where in the passage should this paragraph be placed?

    A) NO CHANGE
    B) After Paragraph 2
    C) After Paragraph 3
    D) After Paragraph 4

BLUE WRITING LESSON 10: EFFECTIVE LANGUAGE USE: STYLE/TONE AND SYNTAX
Getting Your Feet Wet

Directions: The following is intended as a short diagnostic exam. Use the paragraph below to answer the questions.

H. Sebastian Seung is a neuroscientist whose work focuses on the connectome, the wiring diagram of the brain. By wiring, Dr. Seung means the connections from one brain cell to another, seen at the level of the electron microscope. For a human, that would be 85 billion brain cells, with up to 10,000 connections for each one. The amount of information in a three-dimensional representation of the whole connectome at that level of detail would equal a zettabyte, a term recently invented to encompass the huge amount of digital data accumulating in the world. **(1)** <u>A zettabyte is such a monstrous number it's hard to even say how big it is, but 75 billion 16-GB iPads is close.</u>

Dr. Seung is an optimist who predicts that this ultimate map of the human brain could be achieved within 20 to 30 years if computer technology continues to progress at its current pace. For every piece of known data that exists about the human brain, there is a world of

(2) <u>unknowns. Neuroscientists have found it largely difficult, if not impossible, for</u> neuroscientists to test theories about the brain. As a result, there is a huge gap between what the public wants scientists to know about the brain, and what scientists **(3)** <u>actually know. That gap is where Dr. Seung's work lies.</u>

1. Which choice best matches the style and tone of the rest of the paragraph?

   A) NO CHANGE
   B) A zettabyte equals about a trillion gigabytes, or 75 billion 16-GB iPads
   C) A zettabyte is an absolutely enormous number, almost as much 75 billion iPads.
   D) A zettabyte is about 75 billion 16-GB iPads.

2. A) NO CHANGE
   B) unknowns. It is largely impossible for
   C) unknowns, but it is difficult, if not impossible, for
   D) unknowns, largely because it is difficult, if not impossible, for

3. A) NO CHANGE
   B) actually know, and this is where Dr. Seung's work lies.
   C) actually know, and that gap is where Dr. Seung's work lies.
   D) actually know, so there lies Dr. Seung's work.

2/3

BLUE WRITING LESSON 10: EFFECTIVE LANGUAGE USE: STYLE/TONE AND SYNTAX
Wading In

TOPIC OVERVIEW: STYLE/TONE AND SYNTAX

When an author writes something, he or she uses a certain tone in order to convey his or her meaning. If the point of the work is to convince someone of something, to inform someone of something, or just to tell a story, the author's tone will most likely be different. Certain questions on the SAT will ask us to choose a sentence which most closely matches the author's tone.

RECOGNIZING STYLE/TONE AND SYNTAX QUESTIONS

Syntax, as tested by the SAT, is the effective use of different sentence structures in order to fulfill the author's purpose. For example, an author may use short, repetitive sentences to emphasize a point or imply a recurring action. In general, having varied sentence structure makes written work easier to read — many short sentences can seem choppy. A question that asks us to rewrite a sentence or to combine two sentences may be asking about syntax. Any question that specifically asks about matching the author's tone is clearly a question about tone.

ANSWERING STYLE/TONE AND SYNTAX QUESTIONS

In order to match the tone of the author or choose a sentence structure that best fits the author's purpose, it's helpful to know what the author's tone (or purpose) is. Some possibilities are persuasion, exposition, or narration. Another important part of determining tone is ascertaining how formal the text is intended to be. Is the author speaking from a place of knowledge, or is the author pointing out something unknown? Does the author employ first- and second-person pronouns? Are the adjectives and adverbs colorful or bland? Answer all of these questions and you'll be able to decide which of the answer choices most closely matches the tone of the passage.

Here is a checklist of things to look for:

1) What is the author's purpose? To convince the reader of something, to explain a concept to the reader, or to narrate a story?
2) Does the author refer directly to him/herself or directly to the reader? This is an indication of a somewhat informal tone.
3) Is the writing straightforward or metaphorical?
4) Are the adjectives and adverbs used vibrant or dull?

Below you'll find a short passage and some questions, with explanations of their answers:

Dr. Seung's most recent study is **(1)** <u>hardly earth-shattering. Dr. Seung</u> <u>focused his research</u> on the mouse retina, which is a part of the central nervous system and is composed of brain tissue. Previous research had found that the starbust amacrine cell of the retina was involved in detecting motion, but it was not clear exactly how. Dr. Seung and his colleagues analyzed the structure of the starburst amacrine cell and its connections, considering previous work on physiology and the workings of neurons, and ultimately proposing a mechanism for how the cell responds to motion. Their theory suggests that a pair of cells must send a signal to the starburst cell simultaneously. The starburst cell then sends its own signal, which carries the news that something is moving in a particular direction on to ganglion cells and then to the brain itself.

The proposed system **(2)** <u>is just the same as</u> the motion detection circuit in the fruit fly. If Dr. Seung's theory is correct, it raises questions about how evolution produced such similar systems in such different animals with such different brains and vision systems. More importantly, if Dr. Seung's findings are proved correct, then this research represents a significant step toward understanding exactly how information is coded and travels through circuits of neurons to allow perceptions to be formed, actions to be taken, and decisions to be made.

1. A) NO CHANGE
    B) hardly earth-shattering. He focused his research
    C) hardly earth-shattering, because Dr. Seung focused his research
    D) hardly earth-shattering, only in the sense that Dr. Seung focused his research

This question requires us to determine which sentence structure best fits into the passage as a whole. Notice that Choices A and B separate these ideas into two sentences, while Choices C and D combine them into one sentence. In this case, separating the idea into two sentences is the better option because the idea in the first sentence gains emphasis if it is stated by itself. In order to choose between Choices A and B, we'll try each one in turn. Choice A repeats the name *Dr. Seung*, while Choice B does not. Because the name was mentioned so recently in the passage, there is no ambiguity as to the antecedent of the pronoun. Therefore, Choice B is the best choice.

2. Which of the following choices provides a tone that is most consistent with that of the passage?

A) NO CHANGE
B) is similar to
C) is a lot like
D) is more alike than you might think to

This question requires us to identify the tone of the passage. The passage is an explanation of a scientific process, and because Choice D addresses the reader directly, it does not fit with the somewhat formal tone of the rest of the passage. Choice C has a conversational tone, and is therefore also inconsistent. Finally, because the author mentions that the two systems are similar in the next sentence, and not "just the same as," Choice B fits better than Choice A.

WRAP-UP: STYLE/TONE AND SYNTAX

Use these questions determine the tone of the passage:

1) What is the author's purpose? To convince the reader of something, to explain a concept to the reader, or to narrate a story?
2) Does the author refer directly to him/herself or directly to the reader? This is an indication of a somewhat informal tone.
3) Is the writing straightforward or metaphorical?
4) Are the adjectives and adverbs used vibrant or dull?

BLUE WRITING LESSON 10: EFFECTIVE LANGUAGE USE: STYLE/TONE AND SYNTAX
Learning to Swim

CONCEPT EXERCISE:

Directions: Answer the questions that accompany the following passages.

Passage 1

The Greatest Pirate

In the early 1800s, the most successful pirate sailing the South China Sea was Ching Shih, captain of the Red Flag fleet. She was not born into **(1)** that life, but became one after marrying Zheng Yi, a pirate who had gained control of the Red Flag fleet after the death of his cousin. The Red Flag fleet had been powerful but not particularly notable until Ching Shih came aboard — and its power grew even more after the death of Zheng Yi, when Ching Shih took complete control.

At its peak the Fleet had as many as a thousand ships **(2)** manned by practically 80,000, and Ching Shih instituted a very strict code of behavior among her crewmen. Pirates were not allowed to disobey or countermand orders from their superiors, nor withhold treasure from **(3)** their fellows. A common punishment was immediate death. Thanks to the code her crews became widely known for the ferocity of their attacks, **(4)** the desperation of their defenses, and their unwillingness to yield even to forces larger than their own.

Ching Shih is also notable for being one of the few successful pirates known to retire. The Chinese **(5)** government, resulting from the failure of attempts by their navy and the navies of Portugal and Britain to subdue the Red Flag Fleet, offered the pirates amnesty in 1810. **(6)** Through skillful negotiation, Ching Shih was able to keep her fortune and her life. She retired from piracy in her mid-thirties, opened up a gambling house, and ran it successfully until her death at the age of 69.

1. A) NO CHANGE
   B) it, instead becoming one
   C) that life, yet she became one
   D) a life of piracy, but entered the profession

2. A) NO ERROR
   B) crewed by almost 80,000 people;
   C) crewed by nearly 80,000 pirates,
   D) manned with almost 80 times as many pirates,

3. A) NO CHANGE
   B) their fellow sailors. If they did, most often their
   C) their fellows; a common
   D) their fellows, because the

4. A) NO CHANGE
   B) the desperation with which they defended their prizes,
   C) how desperately they defended their ships,
   D) their desperate defenses,

5. A) NO CHANGE
   B) government, as a result of their navy
   C) government, when failing with their navy
   D) government, after failed attempts by their navy

6. A) NO CHANGE
   B) After weeks of frustrating negotiation with government representatives,
   C) As a result of tough negotiations,
   D) Luckily,

Passage 2

A Borrowed Language

How many words do you think English has? Ten thousand? One hundred thousand? According to some estimates, the English language contains **(7)** more than 500,000 words. When compared to related languages like German (150,000 words) and French (100,000 words), even half a million seems like a lot. **(8)** Why is the English vocabulary so large?

One reason could be the enthusiasm with which English borrows words from other languages. Many of our scientific terms come **(9)** from Latin, our medical vocabulary from Greek, not to mention the endless foods and animals for which we have always used the foreign names. French and German are known for their periodic translation and purging of loan words from other languages, but English adopts and uses foreign loan words **(10)** without caring one whit about rules or regulations.

Often, English borrows words and phrases for concepts that are already **(11)** found in our language, and begins using the loanwords to convey more subtle shades of meaning. For example, we use the Germanic *hen* for a chicken on the farm, but the French-derived *poultry* for the same creature on our dinner plates. We borrowed *jungle* from Hindi to refer to a specific kind of forest, *safari* from Swahili to refer to a specific kind of travel, and *canoe* from Taino for a specific kind of boat. **(12)** Perhaps our vocabulary isn't actually bigger, just more willing to borrow from others.

7. A) NO CHANGE
   B) an estimated more than 500,000 words.
   C) somewhere between 500,000 and 750,000, and potentially as many as 1,000,000 words.
   D) about five times that many.

8. A) NO CHANGE
   B) How did it come to pass that English developed such an enormous lexicon?
   C) There are several explanations as to why this over-inflated vocabulary developed in our language.
   D) As a matter of fact, English has more than three times as many words as its nearest competitor.

9. A) NO CHANGE
   B) from Latin or our medical ones
   C) from Latin and our medical terms
   D) from Latin or

10. A) NO CHANGE
    B) with cheerful abandonment of rules and regulations regarding their usage.
    C) without any of that fussiness.
    D) without hesitation.

11. A) NO CHANGE
    B) present, then begins using
    C) found in our language and begins using
    D) found in our language. It then begins using

12. A) NO CHANGE
    B) Can we truly say that our vocabulary is bigger, or are we just more willing to borrow from others?
    C) No one knows exactly how many English words actually began in other languages.
    D) Because of this, English users are able to use specific words to convey precisely what they mean.

BLUE WRITING LESSON 10: EFFECTIVE LANGUAGE USE: STYLE/TONE AND SYNTAX
Diving into the Deep End

PRACTICE EXERCISE:

Directions: Answer the questions that accompany the following passage.

Zoroastrianism's Effects

(1) <u>Although</u> adherents of one religion or ideology encounter those of other faiths, as well as new political, social, or philosophical realities, changes will occur. This paper proposes that while the people of Israel lived under the domination of the Babylonian and then the Persian empires, their society and their religion underwent changes. (2) <u>In truth</u>, as the Jewish people encountered the religion of Zoroastrianism, the faith of their Persian masters which contained many similarities with Judaism, many of them adopted and adapted Zoroastrian tenets in order to make their religion suit their present needs. Over the centuries following the exile, a new branch of Jewish theology (3) <u>arose: which</u> in turn gave rise to Christianity,

(4) <u>demonstrating the flexibility that ideologies have in adapting to shifting historical circumstances.</u>

(5) <u>For understanding how</u> Zoroastrianism infiltrated Judaism, and thus later Christianity, one must first understand the person and religion of Zoroaster. Zoroastrianism is the religion of Zoroaster or Zarathustra. Zoroaster is the Greek form of Zarathustra which meant, "he who can manage camels." Zoroaster lived on the central Asian steppes of Iran at the beginning of the Iron Age, (6) <u>somewhere between 1400 and 1000 B.C.E.</u>

1. A) NO CHANGE
   B) As
   C) Before
   D) While

2. A) NO CHANGE
   B) Meanwhile
   C) Mainly
   D) Over time

3. A) NO CHANGE
   B) arose, that
   C) arose, which
   D) arose, for example, in which

4. Which of the following would best develop the main idea of the paragraph?

   A) NO CHANGE
   B) a change that many historians seem unable to account for.
   C) in which guise the ideology would remain permanent.
   D) thus ushering in centuries of civil strife

5. A) NO CHANGE
   B) By understanding that
   C) To understand how
   D) If he understands that

6. A) NO CHANGE
   B) for some time between 1400 and 1000 B.C.E.
   C) in the time between 1400 and 1000 B.C.E.
   D) at some point between 1400 and 1000 B.C.E.

Iran, during this period, was connected to Vedic India.

(7) Vedic theology centered around polytheism. It viewed the gods as benevolent cosmic beings and focused on the universal principle of Asha "that which ought to be." The adherents believed that the gods formed the world **(8)** in seven stages (sky, water, earth, plants, animals, man, and fire). **(9)** Fire stood as the vital life force which gives warmth and existence to all.

7. Which of the following choices most effectively combines the two underlined sentences?

A) NO CHANGE
B) Vedic theology centered around polytheism, viewing the gods as benevolent cosmic beings and focusing on the universal principle of Asha "that which ought to be."
C) Vedic theology centered around polytheism to view the gods as benevolent cosmic beings and focus on the universal principle of Asha "that which ought to be."
D) Vedic theology centered around polytheism, viewing the gods as benevolent cosmic beings and focused on the universal principle of Asha "that which ought to be."

8. A) NO CHANGE
B) in seven stages, like sky, water, earth, plants, animals, man, and fire
C) in seven stages such as sky, water, earth, plants, animals, man, and fire
D) in seven stages, namely: sky, water, earth, plants, animals, man, and fire

9. Which of the following additions to the underlined sentence would best develop the ideas of the paragraph?

A) , and therefore the Zoroastrians prized it as the highest of the elements.
B) , because fire is the hottest of the elements.
C) , for fire is known to evaporate water, generate steam, and melt metal
D) , yet many other religions have prized fire as a spiritual element

The Iron Age brought the iron war chariots to the Iranian steppes and allowed roving bands of warriors to create havoc and mayhem. **(10)** These chaotic times caused a young priest named Zoroaster to contemplate good and evil and the purpose of life. During a religious ceremony near a river, Zoroaster beheld a shining entity named Vohu Manah (Good Purpose). This being led Zoroaster into the presence of the supreme being, Ahura Mazda (Wise Lord), and other radiant personages. Ahura Mazda instructed the young priest to move away from polytheism and into the way of righteousness. **(11)** Zoroaster became convinced that this being was "uncreated, existing eternally, and Creator of all else that is good, including all other beneficent divinities."

10. Which of the following alternatives to the underlined sentence most nearly matches the tone of the passage?

A) NO CHANGE
B) These chaotic times caused a young priest named Zoroaster to think about good and evil and the purpose of life
C) These chaotic times caused a young priest named Zoroaster to muse longingly over good and evil and the purpose of life
D) These chaotic times caused a young priest named Zoroaster to meditate with good and evil and the purpose of life

11. A) NO CHANGE
B) Zoroaster became convinced that this being was "uncreated God, existing eternally, and Creator of all else that is good, including all other beneficent divinities."
C) Zoroaster became convinced that this being was "uncreated God, existing eternal, and Creator of all else that is good, including all other beneficent divinities."
D) Zoroaster became convinced that this being was "uncreated God, existed eternally, and Creator of all else that is good, including all other beneficent divinities."

TEST EXERCISE:

Directions: Answer the questions that accompany the following passage.

Our First $1 Bill

The relationship between Salmon P. Chase and President Abraham Lincoln had been a strange one from the start. They had been rivals for the presidency in the 1860 election, **(1)** <u>which Lincoln won with some clever political maneuvering</u>. Chase had been a **(2)** <u>terrible</u> opponent: he was staunchly anti-slavery, and **(3)** <u>both holding a Senate seat and the Ohio governorship</u>. Yet he lacked something that Lincoln possessed in abundance: a personality that would win over the average man. **{4}**

1. A) NO CHANGE
   B) which was won by Lincoln with some clever political maneuvering
   C) which, with some clever political maneuvering, was won by Lincoln
   D) won by Lincoln following clever political maneuvering

2. Within the context of the passage, which of the following is the best replacement for the underlined word?

   A) NO CHANGE
   B) formidable
   C) impossible
   D) unlikely

3. A) NO CHANGE
   B) both a Senate seat and the Ohio governorship he had held
   C) having the jobs of a Senator and the Governor of Ohio
   D) had held both a Senate seat and the Ohio governorship

4. Which of the following provides the best evidence to support the previous sentence?

   A) Chase had few friends, lived a life shaped by routine, and had no sense of humor.
   B) Chase was well-liked by the other senators.
   C) Chase looked "exactly as you'd expect a statesman to look," according to one of his fellow senators.
   D) Chase's anti-slavery stance made him some enemies.

[1] Three of Lincoln's competitors for the presidency became part of his cabinet: **(5)**William H. Seward was named Secretary of State, and also Edward Bates was named Attorney General, and finally Chase was offered the post of Secretary of the Treasury.

[2] Chase felt that Lincoln had failed "to tender me the Treasury Department with the same considerate respect which was manifested toward Mr. Seward and Mr. Bates," and initially declined. [3] He finally accepted in March 1861. {**6**}

(7) That he was the ablest man in the Cabinet he was convinced, Chase also believed he was Lincoln's superior as both an administrator and statesman. He dreamed of taking the White House back from Lincoln in 1864; these dreams often resulted in **(8)** awkward standoffs between himself and the president. While ably handling his duties as Secretary of the Treasury, financing four years of hard fighting against the Confederacy, he still sought to further his ambitions. {**9**}

5. A) NO CHANGE
   B) William H. Seward was named Secretary of State, Edward Bates was named Attorney General
   C) William H. Seward was named Secretary of State and Edward Bates Attorney General
   D) William H. Seward being named Secretary of State as well as Edward Bates's placement as Attorney General

6. To improve the logical flow of the paragraph, Sentence 3 should be relocated

   A) NO CHANGE
   B) before Sentence 1.
   C) before Sentence 2.
   D) to the beginning of the next paragraph.

7. A) NO CHANGE
   B) Convinced that the ablest man in the Cabinet was he,
   C) In the Cabinet, he was convinced, he was the most capable man,
   D) Convinced he was the ablest man in the Cabinet,

8. A) NO CHANGE
   B) obstinate quarrels
   C) intolerable feuds
   D) anxious disputations

9. Which of the following, if inserted here, would provide the best support for the previous sentence?

   A) Chase got along well with Seward and Bates.
   B) He gathered revenue to support the troops in battle by means of various taxes.
   C) Having designed paper currency, he put his face on the $1 bill to keep his face in the mind of the public.
   D) He frequently questioned Lincoln's decisions to Lincoln's face.

A personal dispute ended Chase's career in Lincoln's cabinet. During previous clashes, Chase had offered to resign from his post — knowing that during wartime, Lincoln would be hesitant to accept his offers. However, when the two clashed on the subject of the Union's top general in the war — and Chase publicly aired his disagreement with the president's stance — Lincoln had had enough. Out of patience, Lincoln ended **(10)** his tenure with the observation that "you and I have reached a point of mutual embarrassment in our official relation which it seems cannot be overcome, or longer sustained."

Chase's downfall proved short-lived. In December Lincoln appointed him to the Supreme Court to succeed Chief Justice Roger **(11)** Taney, having died three months earlier. In a letter to his fiancée, Lincoln's other secretary, John Nicolay, wrote that "no other man than Lincoln would have had ... the degree of magnanimity to thus forgive and exalt a rival who had so deeply and unjustifiably intrigued against him. It is," he continued, "only another ... illustration of the greatness of the President, in this age of little men."

10.A) NO CHANGE
B) the
C) Chase's
D) their

11. A) NO CHANGE
B) Taney, who had died three months earlier
C) Taney, dying three months earlier
D) Taney, three months earlier who had died

BLUE WRITING LESSON 10: EFFECTIVE LANGUAGE USE: STYLE/TONE AND SYNTAX
Race to the Finish

HOMEWORK EXERCISE 1:

Directions: Answer the questions that accompany the following passage.

Old Against New

From the vantage point of hindsight, that which came before so often looks quaint, at least with respect to technology: The switchboard operators crisscrossing the wires into the right slots; Dad settling into his luxury automobile, all fins and chrome; Junior ringing the bell on his bike as he heads off on his paper route.

(1) Such scenes being viewed in a movie or television show, we almost have trouble imagining that the users weren't at some level aware of the absurdity of what they were doing. The attitude of the present to the past is mutable. The older you are, the more likely it is that your regard will be benign — indulgent, even nostalgic. Youth, by contrast, quickly become derisive, preening themselves on knowing better, oblivious to the fact that their toys will be found **(2)** no less preposterous by the next wave of the young.

Knowing this, I can easily envision a world — in the not so distant future — in which bookstores and print media are viewed with that same sense of strangeness, **(3)** a world of quaintness and silliness regarding books and newspapers. You can pretty much extrapolate this view from the habits and behaviors of **(4)** kids in their teens and 20s, who navigate their lives with little or no recourse to paper. **(5)** In class they sit with their laptops open on the table in front of them, and I pretend to believe they are taking course-related notes. These students have every answer at their fingertips, and from where they stand, books and newspapers are already an archaic remnant of a sepia-toned era.

1. A) NO CHANGE
    B) Viewed in a movie or television show
    C) Viewing such scenes in a movie or television show
    D) In movies and television shows

2. A) NO CHANGE
    B) preposterous by an equal amount
    C) preposterous no less
    D) no more preposterous

3. A) NO CHANGE
    B) a world in which books and newspapers are regarded as quaint and slightly silly
    C) a world of quaint and silly books and newspapers
    D) a world that regards books and newspapers as being quaint and slightly silly.

4. A) NO CHANGE
    B) teens and 20s
    C) today's youth
    D) kids who are in their teens and 20s

5. A) NO CHANGE
    B) They are sitting in class
    C) Sitting in class
    D) They sit in class

C2 education
be smarter

(6) <u>This is no mere medium shift</u>. If the printed word were simply replaced by those same words in a digitized format, **(7)** <u>less worrisome would be the transition from print to digital</u>. On the contrary, this is a shift in content, since the Internet presents information and ideas **(8)** <u>different</u> than traditional books and newspapers have done. And as the media theorist Marshall McLuhan pointed out in the 1960s, media are not just passive channels of information — they supply the stuff of thought, but they also shape the process of thought. Thus this shift from print to digital is more than a change of format — it is **(9)** <u>thought changing</u>.

The Internet presents information in aggregate, valuing quantity over quality. As our reading habits digitize, I worry that our thought processes will devolve to reflect **(10)** <u>the digital world with its shallow depths</u>. Does the digital world allow for reflection, imaginative projection, or a contextual understanding of information? Will our digitized brains remain capable of contemplation, or will they grow ever hungrier for simple information?

6. A) NO CHANGE
   B) This is no mere shift in medium.
   C) Not a mere shift in medium, this is more than that.
   D) This is more than a medium shift.

7. A) NO CHANGE
   B) the transition from print to digital would be less worrisome.
   C) the transition would be less worrisome from print to digital.
   D) from print to digital the transition would be less worrisome.

8. A) NO CHANGE
   B) that are different
   C) in a different way
   D) that are done in a different way

9. A) NO CHANGE
   B) thought provoking
   C) changing the ways in which we think
   D) a change of thought

10. A) NO CHANGE
    B) the shallow depths of the digital world
    C) how shallow the digital world is
    D) the ways in which the digital world is shallow

HOMEWORK EXERCISE 2:

Directions: Answer the questions that accompany the following passage.

Walking Softly

At this moment our country is passing through **(1)** <u>a period of great unrest</u> — social, political, and industrial unrest. It is of the utmost importance for our future that this should prove to be not the unrest of mere rebelliousness against **(2)** <u>life, but the</u> unrest of a resolute and eager ambition to secure the betterment of the individual and the nation.

So far as **(3)** <u>this plague of depression and dissatisfaction</u> takes the form of a fierce discontent with evil, of a determination to punish the **(4)** <u>authors of evil, whether in industry or politics,</u> the feeling is to be **(5)** <u>considered worthy and proper.</u>

If, on the other hand, it turns into **(6)** <u>a senseless war of ideas</u>, of a contest between the brutal greed of the "have nots" and the brutal greed of the "haves," then it has no significance for good, but only for evil.

1. Which of the following best fits the style of the rest of the paragraph?

   A) NO CHANGE
   B) a time of strife and depression
   C) a dangerous and uncertain period
   D) a challenge the likes of which we have never seen

2. A) NO CHANGE
   B) life. This must be the
   C) life. There will be no
   D) life. This must not be the

3. Which best maintains the tone of the paragraph?

   A) this plague of dissatisfaction
   B) this catastrophic movement
   C) the unwieldy attitude
   D) this movement of turmoil throughout the country

4. A) NO CHANGE
   B) authors of evil, even if they are in industry or politics,
   C) authors of evil, though they may be in industry or politics,
   D) authors of evil. Only if they are in industry or politics,

5. Which best expresses the tone of the paragraph?

   A) considered worthy and proper
   B) heartily welcomed as a sign of healthy life
   C) embraced before we discard it
   D) resisted as a danger to our nation

6. Which wording best sets the tone of the paragraph?
   A) NO CHANGE
   B) a grievous expression of American exceptionalism
   C) a mere crusade of rich against poor
   D) a petty battle between ignorant neighbors

(7) <u>He who seeks to establish a line of cleavage,</u> not along the line which divides good men from bad, but along that other line, running at right angles thereto, which divides those who are well off from those who are less well off, then it will be fraught with immeasurable harm to the body politic.

(8) <u>We can no more and no less</u> afford to condone evil in the man of capital than evil in the man of no capital. The wealthy man who exults because there is a failure of justice in the effort to bring some trust magnate to account for his misdeeds is as bad as, and no worse than, the so-called labor leader who clamorously strives to excite a foul class feeling on behalf of some other labor leader who is implicated in murder. One attitude is as bad as the other, **(9)** <u>and no worse. In each case the accused is entitled to exact justice. In neither</u> case is there need of action by others which can be construed into an expression of sympathy for crime.

It is important to this people to grapple with the problems connected with the amassing of enormous **(10)** <u>fortunes, and the use of those fortunes,</u> both corporate and individual, in business. We should discriminate in the sharpest way **(11)** <u>between fortunes of greatness and fortunes of evil;</u> between those gained as an incident to performing great services to the community as a whole and those gained in evil fashion by keeping just within the limits of mere law honesty. Of course, no amount of charity in spending such fortunes in any way compensates for misconduct in making them.

7. A) NO CHANGE
    B) If it seeks to establish a line of cleavage,
    C) If it is used to cleave,
    D) He who chooses to divide by cleaving,

8. Which best fits with the tone and style of the rest of the paragraph?

    A) We can no more and no less
    B) We will be unable to
    C) There is no way we can
    D) Our values do not let us

9. Which best connects the thoughts at the underlined portion?

    A) and no worse, in each case the accused is entitled to exact justice. In neither
    B) and no worse; in each case the accused is entitled to exact justice, in neither
    C) and no worse, in each case the accused is entitled to exact justice, in neither
    D) and no worse; in each case the accused is entitled to exact justice; in neither

10. Which of the following is the best way to express the underlined portion?

    A) NO CHANGE
    B) fortunes. One must use those fortunes,
    C) fortunes. We must understand the need for those fortunes,
    D) fortunes, and how to make the best usage of these fortunes,

11. Which of the following best fits with the style of the passage?

    A) fortunes of greatness and fortunes of evil;
    B) fortunes well won and fortunes ill won;
    C) fortunes amassed in righteousness and those ripped from the hands of the poor;
    D) fortunes used for good and ones used to do harm;

BLUE WRITING LESSON 11: ADVANCED PUNCTUATION
Getting Your Feet Wet

Directions: The following is intended as a short diagnostic exam. Use the paragraphs below to answer the questions.

Every day, millions of Americans climb into their cars to go to work, to school, or any number of other places. Transportation is a vital part of the American economy and employs hundreds of thousands of American workers. Not only do auto **(1)** <u>manufacturers such as Ford Chrysler and GM need</u> labor and skills, many smaller industries are inextricably entwined with the auto industry, including those that manufacture car components and the machinery used in auto manufacturing **(2)** <u>facilities. To</u> say that automobile manufacturing and construction is vital to the American job market is no understatement.

This industry, however, is at a crossroads. The CO2 vented by these vehicles has had a catastrophic effect on Earth's climate, and this climate change has led to many surprising and devastating environmental impacts. While carbon emissions from cars, trucks, and other vehicles are not the sole instigator of climate change, the automobile industry **(3)** <u>can, and should, alter</u> its processes to help curb the impact of auto emissions on Earth's climate. In 2012, President Obama's administration established new regulations requiring that gas mileage increase to 54.5 miles per **(4)** <u>gallon–up from an average of 29.3, by</u> 2025. These regulations may not only help to limit carbon emissions, but may also prove to be a boon to the American job market.

1. A) NO CHANGE
   B) manufacturers, such as Ford, Chrysler, and GM need
   C) manufacturers, such as Ford, Chrysler, and GM, need
   D) manufacturers — such as Ford, Chrysler, and GM — need

2. A) NO CHANGE
   B) facilities; to
   C) facilities: to
   D) facilities, to

3. A) NO CHANGE
   B) can — and should — alter
   C) can, and should alter
   D) can and should alter

4. A) NO CHANGE
   B) gallon, up from an average of 29.3, by
   C) gallon up from an average of 29.3 by
   D) gallon (up from an average of 29.3), by

BLUE WRITING LESSON 11: ADVANCED PUNCTUATION
Wading In

TOPIC OVERVIEW: ADVANCED PUNCTUATION

In addition to commas and semicolons, the SAT will test your knowledge of less commonly used punctuation marks, including dashes and colons. Because these are less common in writing, many students don't know the appropriate way to employ them. This lesson will help to clarify exactly how these punctuation marks are used.

RECOGNIZING ADVANCED PUNCTUATION QUESTIONS

The **advanced punctuation** questions usually deal with interrupting clauses and how you can best integrate them into a sentence. If an underlined portion of a writing passage (or an answer choice) has dashes in it, it's an advanced punctuation question. If you see items in parentheses, that may be an advanced punctuation question as well. Arguably the most difficult type of question like this deals with parenthetical and non-restrictive clauses, which are usually clauses set off from the sentence by commas (see question 4 above). These errors were discussed in Lesson 1, but we will review the concepts here.

ANSWERING ADVANCED PUNCTUATION QUESTIONS

Let's look at the different types of punctuation marks and their uses in the context of this type of question:

Colons have two major uses:
1. to begin a list of items
2. to introduce an independent clause which clarifies, illustrates, or otherwise expands on the independent clause which immediately precedes it.

Example 1: There are three teams recruiting LeBron James: the Miami Heat, the Cleveland Cavaliers, and the Chicago Bulls.

Example 2: LeBron worked hard to get where he is: he truly embodies the spirit of diligence.

Dashes are used when an interrupting clause requires emphasis or if there is an abrupt change in the thought from what surrounds it. Note the slight difference in meaning between the two sentences below:

Example 3: Dwayne Wade (the veteran on the team) didn't get enough credit for his work.

Example 4: Dwayne Wade–the veteran on the team–didn't get enough credit for his work.

In Example 3, the expression *the veteran on the team* gets less emphasis because it's in parentheses, but in Example 4, it gets *more* emphasis because it's between dashes. The dashes add significance to the phrase that comes after or between them.

Parenthetical and non-restrictive elements are clauses which interrupt a sentence, but do not change (or restrict) the subject of the sentence. They should be set off from the sentence using commas. On the other hand, a restrictive clause should not have commas separating it from the rest of the sentence. A fairly easy way to tell if a clause is restrictive is to see if the removal of the clause would lead you to ask about the subject. To clarify, look at the example sentences below:

Example 5: The Cleveland Cavaliers, who often wear blue uniforms when playing at home, have never won an NBA championship.

Example 6: The Cleveland Cavaliers have never won an NBA championship.

Removing the clause *who often wear blue uniforms when playing at home* doesn't cause the reader to ask "Which Cleveland Cavaliers?" Therefore it is non-restrictive, and should be set off with parentheses.

Example 7: The Cleveland Cavalier who has made the most three-point shots is Mark Price.

Example 8: The Cleveland Cavalier is Mark Price.

In Example 7, the clause *who has made the most three-point shots* is restrictive, because the sentence requires it to maintain its meaning, as Example 8 shows.

WRAP-UP: ADVANCED PUNCTUATION

When a question or answer choices contain dashes, colons, or parentheses, you are looking at an advanced punctuation question. Here are some tips for answering these questions:

1) If the question asks you to differentiate between dashes and other punctuation, ask yourself if the interrupting phrase is meant to have more or less emphasis than the rest of the sentence; if it should have more emphasis, use a dash.
2) If a clause follows a colon, make sure that it expands or clarifies the statement that comes before the colon. If it does not, use a different punctuation mark.
3) A colon should be used to begin a list of items. The rules for separating the items in a list can be found in Lesson 1 of this book.
4) If a phrase is set off from a sentence using commas, it should be non-restrictive — if the meaning of the sentence depends on the clause, you should not use commas to set it off from the rest of the sentence.

BLUE WRITING LESSON 11: ADVANCED PUNCTUATION
Learning to Swim

CONCEPT EXERCISE:

Directions: Find and correct any errors in the following sentences. Some sentences may not have any errors.

1. The officer, who made the arrest, had been investigated previously for excessive use of force.

2. Many companies make sugar-free soft drinks, which are flavored by synthetic chemicals; the drinks usually contain only one or two calories per serving.

3. Pertussis — also known as whooping cough — affects far fewer people now than it did in the years before the vaccine entered widespread use.

4. I am currently taking Spanish, which I enjoy, math, which I find difficult, and psychology, which is my favorite subject.

5. Jake having forgotten to save his work lost all of his revisions when his computer crashed.

6. Some for-profit colleges will survive these regulations, many will not.

7. She enjoys outdoor sports: especially hiking, biking, and kayaking.

8. The library — the ten-story building next to the dining hall — is open at all hours during finals week.

9. I can't eat blueberries, they give me a rash.

10. The book, that my uncle gave me for my birthday, won the Edgar Award.

11. Two of her friends — Kate and Beth — are planning a trip to the beach.

12. Here are the facts: The money was there before she entered the room, it was gone right after she had left, the next day she bought an expensive pair of shoes, although she had already spent her allowance.

13. The American science fiction writer, Robert Heinlein, is best known for the novel, *Stranger in a Strange Land.*

14. Julia's true motives never surfaced, not even her husband understood why she refused a pay raise.

15. Apple Tower the recently completed office complex is a monument to modern design.

16. Your cat — watching the dog intently — walked away carefully.

17. I understand the problem, nevertheless, I can't seem to solve it.

18. Her favorite authors are: Michael Chabon, John Steinbeck, and Hermann Hesse.

19. People, who have dangerous careers, usually have interesting stories to tell.

20. Yard work, not my favorite pastime, can be a time-consuming activity.

BLUE WRITING LESSON 11: ADVANCED PUNCTUATION
Diving into the Deep End

PRACTICE EXERCISE:

Directions: Answer the questions that accompany the following passage.

Nubian Queens

Perhaps as a result of the strong influence of women figures in religion, Nubia **(1)** <u>and its Kushite</u> rulers gave way to a number of strong queens during its history. Ten sovereign ruling queens are recognized from the period. Additionally, six other queens who ruled with their husbands were considered significant to the history of Nubia. Many of these rulers were immortalized in **(2)** <u>statuary, it</u> was unheard of for non-ruling queens or princesses to be immortalized in art. These queens were called **(3)** <u>Kandake (meaning queen mother).</u> This term has been corrupted to the English form Candace. Subsequently, there has been much **(4)** <u>confusion, some</u> Western scholars muddle the actions of queens together under the general name.

The emergence of the queen as a viable player in the politics of the day has its roots in the **(5)** <u>Kushite tradition: Kushite rulers married and then passed more royal power into the hands of the queen.</u>

1. A) NO CHANGE
   B) — and its Kushite —
   C) , and its Kushite —
   D) — and its Kushite,

2. A) NO CHANGE
   B) statuary: it was
   C) statuary; indeed, it was
   D) statuary; it was

3. A) NO CHANGE
   B) Kandake - meaning queen mother
   C) Kandake, meaning queen mother
   D) Kandake meaning, queen mother

4. A) NO CHANGE
   B) confusion — some
   C) confusion; some
   D) confusion, but some

5. A) NO CHANGE
   B) Kushite tradition, according to that Kushite rulers married and then passed more royal power into the hands of the queen.
   C) Kushite tradition that Kushite rulers married and then passed more royal power into the hands of the queen.
   D) Kushite tradition with which Kushite rulers married and then passed more royal power into the hands of the queen.

The perfect example of the expanded powers of the queen is Kushite Queen Amanirenas. In 24 B.C.E., she was threatened by the Roman **(6)** Empire. Egypt was under the subjugation of Rome and the frontier of the Kushite/Nubian empire was seventy miles south of Syene (Assuan). The Nubians were constantly raiding their Egyptian neighbors. On one of these journeys, the Kandace Amanirenas went along. When confronted, she led her armies into battle and defeated three Roman cohorts. In addition, the Kandace defaced a statue of Emperor Augustus Caesar, bringing the head back to Nubia as a prize. This head was buried in the doorway of an important building as a final act of disrespect.

During battle, the Kandace lost an **(7)** eye; but this only made her more courageous. "One Eyed Candace," as then Roman governor Gaius Petronius referred to her, was chased by the Romans **(8)** far into her own territory to Pselkis — modern Dakka. After a three day truce, the Romans struck back. The Kandace and her armies made another stand at Primis (Kasr/Brim), but there were soundly defeated. Although Rome destroyed the religious capital of Napata, there was still the danger of retaliation by the Kandace's armies. At this point, the leaders negotiated a treaty that she was to break in a few years. A historian of the period remarked "This Queen had courage above her sex". On a broader level, this is a telling **(9)** example of a European civilization which is unprepared for the "fierce, unyielding resistance of a queen whose determined struggle symbolized the national pride of a people who, until then, had commanded others" .

6. Which of the following choices most effectively combines the two underlined sentences?

A) Empire because Egypt was under the subjugation of Rome, the frontier of the Kushite/Nubian empire was seventy miles south of Syene (Assuan), and the

B) Empire — Egypt was under the subjugation of Rome — and the frontier of the Kushite/Nubian empire was seventy miles south of Syene (Assuan), the

C) Empire; Egypt was under the subjugation of Rome and the frontier of the Kushite/Nubian empire was seventy miles south of Syene (Assuan); the

D) Empire when Egypt was under the subjugation of Rome and the frontier of the Kushite/Nubian empire was seventy miles south of Syene (Assuan). The

7. A) eye, — but
   B) eye: but
   C) eye; and
   D) eye, but

8. A) NO CHANGE
   B) far into her own territory to Pselkis (modern Dakka)
   C) far into her own territory: to Pselkis, modern Dakka
   D) far into her own territory, to Pselkis — which was modern Dakka

9. A) NO CHANGE
   B) example of a European civilization unprepared for the "fierce, unyielding resistance
   C) example of a European civilization that is unprepared for the "fierce, unyielding resistance
   D) example of a European civilization unprepared for — "fierce, unyielding resistance

Furthermore, these queens of the Nubian/Kushite Empire were given the special distinction of assuming a priestly role in the divine succession of kings. In other societies of the period, the divine right of the king passed from god to ruler, and there was no room for a maternal figure. However, Nubian queens are often portrayed at the event of the divine birth. A fine example of this is the representation of Queen Amanishakheto **(10)** appearing before Amun; the Queen is pictured with a goddess (possibly Hathor — a goddess of fertility) and is wearing a panther skin. This signifies her priestly role in the birth of the successor to the throne. This piece is one of a series. In the first, **(11)** the Queen is elected by god — this establishes her position as rightful ruler. Soon after, the divine child is conceived out of a meeting between the god and the Queen. Finally, the child, and heir to the empire, is delivered to the Queen by the god. This complex and important role does not seem to have an equivalent in other cultures.

10.A) NO CHANGE
  B) appearing before Amun: the Queen is pictured with a goddess (possibly Hathor — a goddess of fertility)
  C) appearing before Amun, the Queen is pictured with a goddess — possibly Hathor — a goddess of fertility
  D) appearing before Amun, the Queen is pictured with a goddess, possibly Hathor, a goddess of fertility,

11.A) NO CHANGE
  B) the Queen is elected by god that establishes her position as the rightful ruler
  C) when the Queen is elected by god, which establishes her position as rightful ruler
  D) the Queen is elected by god, thus establishing her position as rightful ruler

TEST EXERCISE:

Directions: Answer the questions that accompany the following passage.

The Surprising Secret to Happiness

Happiness has traditionally been considered an elusive and evanescent **(1)** thing, but after 40 years of research, social scientists believe they have discovered its secrets.

Psychologists and economists have studied happiness for decades. The richest data available is the University of Chicago's General Social Survey **(2)** , which is a survey that has been conducted since 1972. The numbers from this survey are **(3)** surprising and consistent. Every other year for four decades, roughly a third of Americans have said they're "very happy," and about half report being "pretty happy." Only about 10 to 15 percent say they're "not too happy." Within these averages **(4)** lies demographic trends, such as the fact that women have consistently reported being happier than men. But despite demographic trends, even demographically identical people vary in their happiness. The explanation for this phenomenon has been the crux of much of the research into happiness.

{5} The first answer involves our genes. Researchers at the University of Minnesota have tracked identical twins who were separated as infants and raised by separate families, which eliminates genetics from the equation and allows researchers to focus only on environmental differences. These researchers found that we inherit a surprising proportion of our happiness at any given moment **(6)** — around 48%.

About 40% of our happiness at any given point in time stems from milestone events **(7)** , even getting a dream job. Yet the happiness gleaned from such events is remarkably short-lived and dissipates in just a few months.

1. A) NO CHANGE
   B) feeling
   C) quality
   D) idea

2. A) NO CHANGE
   B) ; this is a survey conducted since 1972.
   C) — a survey conducted since 1972.
   D) : this is a survey conducted since 1972.

3. A) NO CHANGE
   B) surprisingly and consistent.
   C) surprising consistent.
   D) surprisingly consistent.

4. A) NO CHANGE
   B) lie
   C) lay
   D) lays

5. Which choice most effectively establishes the main topic of the paragraph?

   A) The largest factor in our happiness, according to research on twins, is genetics.
   B) Despite suspicions of researchers, genes are not a significant factor in happiness.
   C) While genes are one of the factors for happiness, there are so many other factors that it is wrong to see genetics as essential.
   D) Twins are the only way to research happiness because of their genetic similarity.

6. A) NO CHANGE
   B) Delete this, it is unnecessary.
   C) , around 48%
   D) around 48%

7. A) NO CHANGE
   B) , like getting a dream job.
   C) , such as finding a way to obtain a dream job.
   D) ; for example, obtaining a dream job.

This still leaves about 12% of our happiness, and this 12% **(8)** <u>can be</u> brought entirely under our control. Research shows that choosing to pursue the four basic values of faith, family, community, and work is the surest path to happiness. The first three are unsurprising. **(9)** <u>The fourth is even more predictable.</u>

This shouldn't shock us. Vocation is central to the American ideal. What is surprising is that being satisfied with **(10)** <u>one's</u> work has little connection to income. Economists find that money makes truly poor people happy insofar as it relieves pressure from everyday life — getting enough to eat, having a place to live, and so on. But scholars have found that once people reach a little beyond the average middle-class income level, even big financial gains don't yield increases in happiness.

Franklin D. Roosevelt had it right: "Happiness lies not in the mere possession of money **(11)** <u>, it lies</u> in the joy of achievement, in the thrill of creative effort." In other words, the secret to happiness through work is a feeling of achievement. Americans who feel they are successful at work are twice as likely to say they are very happy overall than people who don't feel that way, and these differences persist after controlling for income and other demographics.

The surprising secret to happiness? Find work that satisfies you.

8. Based on the context of the paragraph, which of the following is the most effective choice?

   A) NO CHANGE
   B) will be
   C) has to be
   D) has been

9. Which choice most effectively concludes the paragraph?

   A) NO CHANGE
   B) Delete it. It is unnecessary.
   C) Work, though, seems less intuitive.
   D) The fourth, perhaps, should not be on the list.

10. A) NO CHANGE
    B) our
    C) their
    D) his

11. A) NO CHANGE
    B) : it lies
    C) ,
    D) Delete it. It is unnecessary.

BLUE WRITING LESSON 11: ADVANCED PUNCTUATION
Race to the Finish

HOMEWORK EXERCISE 1:

Directions: Find and correct any errors in the following sentences. Some sentences may not have any errors.

1. He studied hard — therefore, he earned excellent grades.

2. I have several favorite athletes — in basketball, LeBron James, in baseball, Derek Jeter, in tennis, Anna Kournikova, and in football, Eli Manning.

3. The artist preferred to paint in oils; because he did not like watercolors.

4. West Point cadets, who break the honor code, are expelled.

5. She was (as a matter of fact) chiefly interested in becoming an American Idol winner.

6. The high school course that proved most valuable to me was keyboarding.

7. Chapter Six, pages 142-162, will help you prepare for our upcoming final exam.

8. World War I ended for the United States in a little over a year, World War II lasted almost four years.

9. A river, that is polluted, is not safe for swimming.

10. New York City is, for many, a cultural mecca, its museums, theaters, and restaurants are unsurpassed.

11. The episode which aired on Sunday drew a record number of viewers.

12. Paris the City of Light actually turns off its monument lighting after 1 a.m.

13. The mission of Students Against Drunk Driving, SADD, is to stop drunk driving.

14. Nicollette, who speaks Russian, applied for the position as translator.

15. The homeowner's association issued the following warning — "All residents, who park on the street, will be fined for each infraction."

16. People, who live in glass houses, shouldn't throw stones.

17. The beach resort has closed for the winter: The hotel, of course, remains open year-round.

18. The Mississippi River which flows south from Minnesota to the Gulf of Mexico is the major commercial river in the United States.

19. There are three vital components to any well-crafted essay; the introduction, the body paragraphs, and the conclusion.

20. This is Mayor Kim's statement, "I have never advocated such practices; I do not advocate them now; I do not approve of them; and I have no reason to believe that I will ever approve of them."

HOMEWORK EXERCISE 2:

Directions: Answer the questions that accompany the following passage.

Producer Life

When a musician (or group) records a piece of music, it's often clear who contributes what to the overall composition. **(1)** <u>The pianist playing the piano, the drummer playing the drums, and so on</u>. But a job that is frequently overlooked in the recording process is that of the music producer. Surely you've **(2)** <u>seen — in a video of a band recording its latest album — a man</u> sitting in a nearby booth fiddling with knobs and operating the soundboard. This person, just as much as any of the musicians, is responsible for the final piece of music you hear on the radio, on a CD, or in an mp3.

Music producers must understand music just as much as the people playing the instruments. **(3)** <u>If one desires to become a music producer, it often helps to be a musician.</u> Learning the dynamic ranges of many instruments and how to produce the exact sound a musician wants is **(4)** <u>good</u>. Before one starts a career as a music producer, one must know music.

1. A) NO CHANGE
   B) The pianist plays the piano, the drummer plays the drums, and so on.
   C) The pianist plays the piano, and the drummer plays the drums, and so on.
   D) The pianist plays the piano while at the same time the drummer is playing the drums, and so on.

2. A) NO CHANGE
   B) seen a man, in a video of a band, recording its latest album,
   C) seen in a video of a band recording its latest album a man
   D) seen, in a video of a band recording its latest album, a man

3. A) NO CHANGE
   B) If one desires to be a music producer, you should definitely be a musician.
   C) If you want to be a music producer, you should also be a musician.
   D) If one desires to become a music producer; it often helps to be a musician.

4. Within the context of the passage, which of the following is the best replacement for the underlined word?

   A) NO CHANGE
   B) vital
   C) unnecessary
   D) obligatory

[1] In addition, the music producer must know the ins and outs of recording music. [2] A producer doesn't want the drums or the guitar to drown out the **(5)** vocals (for example). [3] Once everything is recorded, the producer must 'mix' the recordings, blending the different sounds together to create the music that the musicians want. [4] Placement of microphones plays a key role in how the microphones record the music. {**6**}

A music producer's responsibilities don't stop outside the studio. In addition to knowing how to help a musician create that ideal sound, producers must help the musician **(7)** decide which songs to record, select the studio, sign contracts with record labels, and choose the right sound engineers. Thus, a producer must have a working knowledge of the music industry at large and have contacts within that industry to make things happen. This often requires producers to have a foot in the music industry **(8)** to begin with, making contacts with other producers, music industry executives, and musicians is a key aspect of the job. Taking on larger roles, **(9)** assumption of responsibility is given to the producers for the schedule, the budget, and the negotiations.

5. A) NO CHANGE
   B) vocals, for example.
   C) vocals — for example.
   D) vocals; for example.

6. To improve the logical flow of the paragraph, Sentence 4 should be relocated

   A) NO CHANGE
   B) before Sentence 1.
   C) before Sentence 2.
   D) before Sentence 3.

7. A) NO CHANGE
   B) decide which songs to record, select the studio; sign contracts with record labels, and choose the right sound engineers
   C) decide which songs to record, select the studio — sign contracts with record labels — and choose the right sound engineers as well
   D) decides which songs they will record, what studio to go to, which record label they should sign with, and what sound engineers to use

8. A) NO CHANGE
   B) to begin with (making contacts
   C) to begin with — making contracts
   D) to begin with making contracts

9. A) NO CHANGE
   B) producers must assume responsibility for
   C) bands must ask producers to take responsibility for
   D) artists work with producers to take responsibility for

Some music producers have **(10)** become really famous by helping some of the greatest artists achieve their sound. Brian Eno, a musician and producer who was active in the seventies, has helped bands such as Coldplay and U2 record their albums. Kerry "Krucial" Brothers is the only person that pianist/singer Alicia Keys trusts to record her sound. Kanye West has some producer credits as well. Hit-makers The Neptunes produced songs for Justin Timberlake, Christina Aguilera, Kelis, and Jay-Z. All of these major artists would not be as popular or well-known if they had not chosen the right producer for the sound that they desired for their music. {11}

10.A) NO CHANGE
B) earned renown
C) gained colossal popularity
D) become almost as well-known as their artists

11. Which of the following would best conclude this passage?

A) Producers are the real stars of the show, helping each star on their way to stardom.
B) Though they may be invisible to many listeners, music producers are a vital part of the music industry and the music that people listen to every day.
C) Without music producers, artists would not be able to create the work they are known for.
D) The next time you listen to a song, think about the producer who helped create this piece of work.

BLUE WRITING LESSON 12: EFFECTIVE LANGUAGE USE: CONCISION AND PRECISION
Getting Your Feet Wet

Directions: The following is intended as a short diagnostic exam. Use the paragraph below to answer the questions.

"The Worst Bad Time," they called it — the Great Depression, the greatest financial crisis of the 20th century. The stock market crashed, banks across the country folded, hundreds of thousands of people lost their homes, and millions of **(1)** people once employed subsequently lost their jobs. President Franklin D. Roosevelt's New Deal legislation poured millions of dollars into financial recovery, and by the end of World War II, the United States' economy was back into the black — leading into one of America's most **(2)** prodigious times, the booming 1950s.

That's the **(3)** conventional story, at least. "Franklin D. Roosevelt led the country out of the Depression," is what most American history books tell us. Yet the truth is more complex, and many historians believe that this overly simplistic version of events masks the truth of this period in history.

The New Deal, a large-scale economic program, had varying effects on the nation's faltering economy. FDR's **(4)** signature legislation raised and increased taxes on the rich and expanded the scope of government spending. If he was to halt the economy's downward spiral, FDR believed that the federal government would need to invest in public sector employment. To that end, FDR's administration created several agencies, which had a dual purpose: They generated much needed employment while also making improvements to the American infrastructure by accomplishing such goals as expanding access to electricity in rural areas and building and repairing roads.

1. A) NO CHANGE
   B) people once employed then lost
   C) people lost
   D) people who had been employed lost

2. A) NO CHANGE
   B) prosperous
   C) wonderful
   D) exceptional

3. A) NO CHANGE
   B) predictable
   C) old-fashioned
   D) conformist

4. A) NO CHANGE
   B) signature legislation raised and increased the tax burden
   C) signature legislation made higher the taxes
   D) signature legislation raised taxes

BLUE WRITING LESSON 12: EFFECTIVE LANGUAGE USE: CONCISION AND PRECISION
Wading In

TOPIC OVERVIEW: CONCISION AND PRECISION

The SAT will test your ability to recognize wordiness and redundancy; these are called concision questions. Redundancy occurs when a phrase or word in a sentence could be omitted without the sentence or passage losing any meaning — the extra word is said to be redundant. In this lesson you will also review precision questions, which test your ability to choose the most appropriate word in a given context. These questions are very similar to the words in context questions you'll encounter in the Reading section of the SAT.

RECOGNIZING CONCISION AND PRECISION QUESTIONS

A precision question is easy to recognize — only one word will be underlined and the replacements will all be one (or rarely two) words. A concision question, on the other hand, is not as easy to identify. These questions will contain phrases which are synonymous or superfluous (see questions 1 and 4 on the previous page). For example, if a passage references someone who is working, and then says that the worker is employed, that information is superfluous because the word *worker* means someone who is employed.

ANSWERING CONCISION AND PRECISION QUESTIONS

Concision questions are best answered by selecting the answer that expresses the same idea as the original in the fewest number of words. Be aware that sometimes the original is the most concise way to express the thought.

Example 1: Planning your trip to the zoo in advance can help you avoid the typical pitfalls associated with family excursions.

- A) NO CHANGE
- B) to the zoo ahead of time
- C) to the zoo
- D) before you head to the zoo

In this sentence, the phrase *in advance* is redundant because the word *planning* implies doing something in advance. That means that Choice A is incorrect. Choices B and D have the same problem — in Choice B *ahead of time* is redundant, and in Choice D *before you head* is redundant. Therefore, Choice C is the most concise answer.

Note that in the example above, you needed to read the whole sentence in order to notice the redundancy. Make sure you use the context of the underlined portion to answer the question.

Some other commonly used redundancies in English include *cooperate together, consensus opinion, exactly the same, free gift, repeat again, small/large in size,*

and *usual custom*. This list can be increased with any phrase or expression that includes superfluous description or words.

Precision questions require you to know the nuance of vocabulary, the slight difference in the meanings of words. The SAT will not test you on traditional "SAT words" anymore. Instead, the test will focus on more common words with multiple meanings. For example, the words *assert, confirm, claim*, and *allege* all have very similar meanings, but there are subtleties to their definitions that you may be required to know:

Assert means to say something clearly (same meaning as *declare*).

Confirm means to show or prove that something is correct.

Claim means to say that something is true, without specific evidence to prove it.

Allege means the same thing as *claim*, but it is used in more official contexts, like in a courtroom.

Here are some steps to follow when answering a precision question:
1. Cover up the answer choices for the question and cross the referenced word off in the passage.
2. Re-read the sentence that the word appeared in, and plug the word that you think fits best into the blank.
3. Uncover the answer choices and eliminate any choices based on the word you selected.
4. Use the context of the sentence to eliminate any remaining choices that don't fit.
5. If there is more than one answer choice remaining, use standard English conventions for prepositions to choose the best answer.

Example 2: Many economists argue, however, that the New Deal did not improve, but actually <u>degraded</u>, the Depression.

A) NO CHANGE
B) deteriorated
C) worsened
D) degenerated

Because there is only one word underlined in the passage, and each answer is a different single word, you can identify this as a precision question. First, cover up the answer choices and plug your own word into the passage. Maybe a word like *extended*. Looking at the answer choices, none of them mean extended, which is unfortunate, but luckily you have two more steps to use!

Start with the word that is underlined in the passage. *Degrade* means to have a low or inferior quality or refers to breaking something down chemically. Neither of these definitions sounds good, so try Choice B. *Deteriorate* means to slowly get worse, which sounds like it might fit, but this word is almost never used with

a direct object. Eliminate it, and move on to *worsened*. This sounds good, so skip it and move on to the next word, *degenerated*. This word means to decline or deteriorate. While that sounds like that right general idea, it doesn't mean *to get worse*, which is what we want. Choice C is the best answer.

WRAP-UP: CONCISION AND PRECISION

Precision: You can identify these questions because the underlined portion of the passage will contain only one word and the answer choices will contain a different word. You can use these steps to answer these questions:

1. Cover up the answer choices for the question and cross the referenced word off in the passage.
2. Re-read the sentence that the word appeared in, and plug the word that you think fits best into the blank.
3. Uncover the answer choices and eliminate any choices based on the word you selected.
4. Use the context of the sentence to eliminate any remaining choices that don't fit.
5. If there is more than one answer choice remaining, use standard English conventions for prepositions to choose the best answer.

Concision: These questions will contain wordy or redundant phrases. Below are some steps that can help you identify the correct answer:

1. Read the entire sentence to make sure the redundancy is not caused by an expression earlier in the sentence.
2. Find the answer choice that expresses the original idea in the fewest number of words.
3. Make sure the answer you pick does not create a new redundancy.

BLUE WRITING LESSON 12: EFFECTIVE LANGUAGE USE: CONCISION AND PRECISION
Learning to Swim

CONCEPT EXERCISE:

Directions: Re-write the following sentences to make them more concise.

1. Although his term paper had been a time-consuming task, Bernard was relieved to be completely finished with all of his assignments for the semester.

2. Before their successful victory against the reigning state champs, the relatively unknown football team was considered to be the underdogs.

3. You should be cautious of your actions because people will judge you based on the way you behave and conduct yourself.

4. The pieces of string connected together by various tiny knots were precariously holding the wet clothes as they dried.

5. The detailed instructions included in the box explained the use and implementation of every function of the new toaster.

6. After all of the presentations were completed, the CEO expressed her favorable approval of all of the recommendations of the marketing team.

7. The new accounting methods allowed many companies and businesses to benefit and profit from eliminating unnecessary expenses.

8. The advent of texting has allowed government agencies to quickly provide advanced warnings to citizens in case of an emergency.

9. In the early 90s, the design of the Nissan Quest and Mercury Villager minivans was a result of a joint collaboration between the automobile manufacturers, Nissan and Ford.

10. Bees and flowers have a mutually interdependent relationship where the bees help pollenate the flowers and the flowers provide the bees with nectar.

Directions: Choose the answer which replaces the bolded word to create the most precise version of the following sentences.

11. After handcuffing the criminals, the police officers **appropriated** the stolen goods and returned them to the rightful owner.

   A) NO CHANGE
   B) devoted
   C) confiscated
   D) allocated

12. Various conductor metals, such as copper, silver, and aluminum, are utilized within wires as the **approach** that allow for the flow of electricity.

   A) NO CHANGE
   B) pathway
   C) proposition
   D) concept

13. His **conviction** that the scientific experiment would yield conclusive results was met with disappointment when the data proved inconclusive.

   A) NO CHANGE
   B) condemnation
   C) doctrine
   D) conjecture

14. Despite the board of directors' attempts to **confer** a reasonable contract with the unionized employees, the deal fell through just hours before the strike deadline.

   A) NO CHANGE
   B) bestow
   C) advise
   D) negotiate

15. The **vital** differences between the two political candidates become more apparent as they squared off during the first debate.

   A) NO CHANGE
   B) significant
   C) vigorous
   D) indispensable

16. Even though this was her first time leading a major project, Sarah's supervisor felt confident that her leadership decisions would be **bright**.

   A) NO CHANGE
   B) astute
   C) luminous
   D) rosy

17. The defendant's expression changed from worried to relieved as the jury returned a not guilty **resolution**.

   A) NO CHANGE
   B) motion
   C) verdict
   D) analysis

18. The archeologist showed an unwavering **determination** to excavate all of the artifacts without damaging them.

   A) NO CHANGE
   B) assurance
   C) judgment
   D) fortitude

19. While working on his new comic book, Darren suffered from writer's block as he was trying to determine the first **marvelous** adventure for his superheroes.

   A) NO CHANGE
   B) pleasant
   C) singular
   D) strange

20. The building was constructed using **substantial** products that are meant to withstand the brutal effects of any natural disasters that might occur.

   A) NO CHANGE
   B) consequential
   C) valuable
   D) durable

BLUE WRITING LESSON 12: EFFECTIVE LANGUAGE USE: CONCISION AND PRECISION
Diving into the Deep End

PRACTICE EXERCISE:

Directions: Answer the questions that accompany the following passage.

The Importance of Understanding College

Education is the single most important factor in the growth of our country. **(1)** <u>Indubitably, higher education provides career opportunities for students who attend college and gives them more chances for a job.</u> But with today's dropout rate, students seem less interested in being educated at colleges. The importance of education today is **(2)** <u>multiplying</u> because the nation's future depends on the students in college today.

The role of college is **(3)** <u>misunderstood</u> by many incoming freshman. **(4)** <u>All of the television advertisements and billboards encouraging students to attend college in order to achieve success are used as bait to reel in student's tuition, and parents encourage their kids to attend college after graduating high school because they convince their children that higher education offers the best shot at success.</u>

1. A) NO CHANGE
    B) In particular, students who attend college have greater career opportunities.
    C) As a matter of fact, higher education creates great opportunities for students when they try to get jobs.
    D) Undoubtedly, career opportunities obtained from college attendance give students better chances for a job.

2. Which of the following is the most precise replacement for the underlined word?

    A) NO CHANGE
    B) budding
    C) increasing
    D) magnifying

3. Which of the following is the most precise replacement for the underlined word?

    A) NO CHANGE
    B) misconstrued
    C) mistaken
    D) misread

4. A) NO CHANGE
    B) Both parents and advertisers convince students that higher education offers the best chance at success.
    C) Students are persuaded to attend college through advertisements, and parents encourage them because they want their children to succeed.
    D) Because a college diploma can lead to success, advertisers and parents alike persuade students that they should attend college.

However, college may not be **(5)** <u>appropriate</u> for everyone. More freshmen than ever are dropping out after their first year **(6)** <u>because college can be overwhelming through everything that takes place within campus boundaries</u>. The pressures of college, whether impressing parents or maintaining high GPAs, overwhelm many students, **(7)** <u>restraining</u> their time to earn money or pursue internships. Back in the 50s and 60s when college was becoming popular, **(8)** <u>people attended college to improve their education and acquire more life experience</u>, in hopes of obtaining careers after graduation. Now, people attend college because their friends or girlfriends go there or to follow their favorite football player. The reasons for attending college can be **(9)** <u>misleading</u> for teenagers fresh out of high school, and people who feel that continuing their education isn't the most important factor in attending college should not apply.

5. Which of the following is the most precise replacement for the underlined word?

A) NO CHANGE
B) apposite
C) apt
D) seemly

6. A) NO CHANGE
B) because college can be overwhelming.
C) because the pace and activities that occur within campus boundaries overwhelm them.
D) because college, in all its various aspects that take place in on-campus life, can be very overwhelming.

7. Which of the following is the most precise replacement for the underlined word?

A) NO CHANGE
B) inhibiting
C) restricting
D) barring

8. A) NO CHANGE
B) people attended college solely to improve their education and learn by means of the college experience
C) people went to college principally because they wanted to get more life experiences during the course of their educations
D) people went to college to learn

9. Which of the following is the most precise replacement for the underlined word?

A) NO CHANGE
B) confusing
C) ambiguous
D) deceptive

(10) College matters because without a thoroughly educated society, America would fall to its knees and regress into deep depression. Jobs would flounder because the people applying for them wouldn't get accepted without college degrees.

Moreover, once students enroll in college, dropping out is the worst decision they can make. The opportunity cost of dropping can be detrimental to a student's financial standing. Dropping out also means dropping tuition, and students are often left with debt to pay off. Entering in a low-paying job, drop outs must slowly pay back student loans, which is why students must **(11)** be implacable. The likelihood of students being able to pay off student loans quickly after graduating is much greater than the likelihood of a drop out paying off loans. Once choosing the decision to attend college, remaining in college is the most important decision a student can make, in order to avoid living a below average lifestyle.

10. A) NO CHANGE
   B) College matters because the economy would implode and crumble.
   C) College matters because without a well-educated population, America would regress into deep depression.
   D) College is important because education is paramount.

11. Which of the following is the most precise replacement for the underlined words?

   A) NO CHANGE
   B) preserve
   C) obdurate
   D) persevere

TEST EXERCISE:

Directions: Answer the questions that accompany the following passage.

The Conflict

Of America's wars, the conflict in Vietnam **(1)** <u>was</u> perhaps the most controversial.   Many protested America's involvement in Southeast Asia, questioning both motive and tactics.   Though many dismissed **(2)** <u>them</u> in the early years of the war, their concerns seem quite prescient when viewed through the lens of retrospection. After all, the Vietnam War ultimately became one of America's deadliest wars {**3**}. The impact of the Vietnam War was so great that, nearly half a century later, historians still **(4)** <u>debated</u> whether American involvement in Vietnam was justified.

American involvement in Vietnam began with the assassination of Ngo Dinh Diem **(5)** <u>South Vietnam's dictator</u> in 1963.   Anarchy swept the country, and John F. Kennedy's administration sent advisers in an attempt to restore order.   North Vietnam, a Communist country **(6)** <u>under the leadership of Communist dictator Ho Chi Minh</u>, began training southern insurgents, infiltrating the South Vietnamese government, and **(7)** <u>perpetuated propaganda</u> against the U.S. The situation quickly escalated, and Kennedy's successor, Lyndon B. Johnson, reacted by scheduling bombings and committing troops to the conflict.

1. A) NO CHANGE
   B) will have been
   C) were
   D) had been

2. A) NO CHANGE
   B) the protestors
   C) the motives
   D) the tactics

3. Which of the following, if added to the end of the sentence, would best support the sentence's main idea?

   A) , with American soldiers killing almost 1,100,000 North Vietnamese soldiers
   B) , much more deadly than the Korean War
   C) , third only to the American Civil War and World War II in casualties.
   D) , leaving many homeless and disabled veterans at the end of the war

4. A) NO CHANGE
   B) debate
   C) will debate
   D) have debated

5. A) NO CHANGE
   B) — South Vietnam's dictator —
   C) (South Vietnam's dictator)
   D) , South Vietnam's dictator,

6. A) NO CHANGE
   B) under the dictatorship of Communist Ho Chi Minh
   C) under the leadership of dictator Ho Chi Minh
   D) under the leadership of a Communist dictator

7. A) NO CHANGE
   B) had perpetuated propaganda
   C) perpetuating propaganda
   D) began perpetuating propaganda

In a speech to the American people, Johnson **(8)** <u>declared</u> that "around the globe, from Berlin to Thailand, are people whose well-being rests, in part, on the belief that they can count on us if they are attacked. To leave Vietnam to its fate would shake the confidence of all these people in the value of America's commitment, the value of America's word."

[1] Supporters of the Vietnam War argued that allowing South Vietnam to fall to communist forces would have led to a 'domino effect' in which more and more nations might fall under the yoke of communism. [2] After World War II, they argued, the United States was a moral force in the world, protecting countries that could not protect themselves against the larger menace of communism. [3] Johnson's speech says much to this regard. {**9**}

Over 47,000 American soldiers died in the conflict, often as a result of being ill-trained to fight in the sweltering jungles of Vietnam against the guerilla tactics of the North Vietnamese. The financial costs were great, as well. {**10**} Had the United States stayed out of this conflict and allowed South Vietnam to surrender to the North Vietnamese, this could have been a minor passing incident in Southeast Asia's history. After all, once American troops withdrew from Vietnam in 1973, the North soon took over South Vietnam, rendering the conflict pointless. In the end, America can't act as the world's police — often it **(11)** <u>butts in</u> where it is not wanted, and besides, America has problems of its own to address before it starts sending young men five thousand miles away from home to die for an idea.

8. Within the context of the passage, which of the following is the best replacement for the underlined word?

   A) NO CHANGE.
   B) swore
   C) implied
   D) suggested

9. Which of the following sentences should be eliminated in order to improve the focus of the paragraph?

   A) Sentence 1
   B) Sentence 2
   C) Sentence 3
   D) NONE OF THE ABOVE

10. Which of the following facts, if added, would best support the previous sentence?

    A) The war was enormously unpopular at home.
    B) The war cost approximately $111 billion, which is equivalent to $700 billion today.
    C) None of the soldiers knew what they were getting into.
    D) The war was continued by Richard Nixon.

11. A) NO CHANGE
    B) interferes
    C) goes places
    D) pries

BLUE WRITING LESSON 12: EFFECTIVE LANGUAGE USE: CONCISION AND PRECISION
Race to the Finish

HOMEWORK EXERCISE 1:

Directions: Re-write each sentence to be the most precise or concise.

1. When the caterpillar finally emerged out from its cocoon, it had become a beautiful butterfly.

2. The fans were disappointed when the game was not won by the local team.

3. Never have I seen such an overabundance of birds in the trees containing apples outside my house.

4. The man was angry, so he talked loudly to the manager.

5. It was shocking to me when I heard about the accident that my friend suffered.

6. Tomorrow is the day we will move.

7. Jackson re-entered his password again, hoping it would work this time.

8. The fire engine's sirens were heard by all the students.

9. Tammy liked lying in the grass and enjoyed watching the clouds go by.

10. Peter went to home plate just in time.

11. The teacher talked to her students to find out if they had begun work on starting their essays.

12. The little boy was tempted to steal a cookie while he was alone and his mother was out of the room.

13. Lilies are beautiful; that is why they are my favorite flowers.

14. The perfume had an odor, which Poppy liked.

15. Amelia's dog was tall, heavy, and big.

16. Scrabble is a game that requires good planning and a good vocabulary.

17. The adventure tour guide explained the rules; then he explained the safety procedures.

18. Sam felt bad that he had left his brother behind.

19. Because you forgot your toothbrush on your last trip, I have packed it for you since you are forgetful.

20. If you want to be understood, use words that are not unlike what you want to say.

HOMEWORK EXERCISE 2:

Directions: Answer the questions that accompany the following passage.

Navy Man Indicted for Food Hoarding (New York Times)

WASHINGTON, May 29, 1918 — Indictments were returned by a Federal Grand Jury here today against Medical Director Francis Smith Nash, U.S.N., and his wife, Caroline Nash, charging them with violation of Section 6 of the Food Control Act in having **(1)** <u>many</u> flour, sugar, and other foodstuffs in their possession, to the value of $1,923.36.

In a statement issued by the Food Administration, it was alleged that the food hoarded was sufficient to maintain the family for more than a year and **(2)** <u>conversely</u> far in excess of the requirements for thirty days, the period recognized by Food Administrator Hoover as a "reasonable one" for residents of cities.

(3) <u>This</u> is the first indictment for individual food hoarding, it was said at the Food Administration, that has been brought since the Food Control Act was enacted.

{4}The only comment of the Food Administration was that its officers were ready at all times to proceed against hoarders, regardless of their social standing, and that the charge would be followed to the end. It is understood that bail in the case of Dr. and Mrs. Nash will be fixed at $3,000 each. They will appear in court tomorrow morning to answer to the charge, it was said tonight.

(5) <u>It was said that when</u> officials of the Food Administration visited [the Nash's home] they found conditions which seemed to indicate that it had been turned into a store-house for many foodstuffs which Food Administrator Hoover had believed might run short because of the war conditions.

1. A) NO CHANGE
   B) large amounts of
   C) much
   D) large numbers of

2. A) NO CHANGE
   B) unfortunately
   C) therefore
   D) heretofore

3. A) NO CHANGE
   B) The indictment
   C) This article
   D) The period

4. Which choice would be the best topic sentence for the paragraph?

   A) The food that Dr. and Mrs. Nash hoarded has been turned over to the police.
   B) The Food Administrator hopes the case will serve as a warning to others.
   C) Questions have been raised about the source of Nash's hoarded items.
   D) The case has attracted attention because Dr. Nash and his wife are public figures.

5. Which choice provides the best replacement for the underlined portion?

   A) When
   B) It has been rumored
   C) Last Thursday
   D) Unfortunately,

(6) The Food Administrator discussed the raid and issued an official statement which said: "The Medical Director **(7)** has admitted his violation. ...Dr. Nash endeavored to dispose of part of his hoard after reading on the front page of a Washington newspaper a warning against hoarding, issued some time ago by Local Administrator Wilson. **(8)** It is clear that he told Mr. Wilson that he had sent several barrels of flour to a Washington grocer, selling one and instructing the grocer to hold the remainder until he should give instructions to distribute it among the poor. When Mr. Wilson asked for an explanation, Dr. Nash said he was holding **(9)** it for charitable purposes. When asked if he had additional supplies in his home, Dr. Nash admitted that he had."

It is understood that Mr. Wilson was informed by a friend **(10)** that he could tell him where ten barrels of flour were being stored. Mr. Wilson demanded evidence, and Dr. Nash's name was given to him. **{11}**

6. Which choice represents the most concise way to rephrase the underlined portion?

A) Local Administrator Wilson issued an official statement which said:
B) The Food Administrator issued a statement which said:
C) The raid was discussed by the Food Administrator, who said:
D) The Food administrator, not Local Aministrator Wilson, said:

7. A) NO CHANGE
B) had admitted
C) have admitted
D) was admitting

8. Which choice would provide the most concise replacement for the underlined portion?

A) NO CHANGE
B) Clearly, he
C) It
D) He

9. A) NO CHANGE
B) the flour
C) the money
D) the barrel

10. Which change to the underlined portion most improves the clarity of the sentence?

A) NO CHANGE
B) where the barrels were being stored.
C) where Mr. Wilson could find the flour stored by Dr. Nash.
D) who was storing flour.

11. Which of the following, if added at the end of the paragraph, would best conclude the article?

A) Dr. Nash has an otherwise spotless legal record.
B) The investigation remains underway.
C) Mrs. Nash has refused to comment.
D) Several other people have been named in similar cases.

BLUE WRITING LESSON 13: MISPLACED MODIFIERS
Getting Your Feet Wet

Directions: The following is intended as a short diagnostic exam. Use the paragraphs below to answer the questions.

When handing in papers for a high school English class, **(1)** grammar is surprisingly unimportant to students. When a student writes a paper for an English class, he or she is graded on both content (the argument or point that he or she made) and mechanics (the grammar and structure used). Is one of these more important than the other? The debate rages on...

(2) Raised in America, over 60% of students believe that they should be graded on content only, with no emphasis on how the information is presented. As students proceed through high school, these numbers become even more skewed: over 70% of high school seniors voice the opinion that the appearance of their work is less important than the subject matter. Unfortunately, employers and college admissions officers disagree.

The most common reason employers give for being turned off by bad grammar in a resume or cover letter has to do with attentiveness. As one business owner said, "If a potential employee isn't going to care enough about the job to hand me a well-crafted resume, why would I assume he's going to care about the job?" This concern is echoed by members of grant-approval boards at places like NASA, the National Institutes of Health, and the National Education Association. With over twenty years of experience, **(3)** 50% of the students' essays received by one college admissions officer last year contained grammatical errors. In her words, "Because the college you attend is a strong indicator of future success, you'd think that students would take more care with the application. The way you present yourself says a lot about the kind of student you will be."

1. A) NO CHANGE
   B) students' grammar is surprisingly unimportant.
   C) students believe, surprisingly, that grammar is unimportant.
   D) students' grammar, surprisingly, is unimportant.

2. A) NO CHANGE
   B) Over 60% of American students
   C) The 60% of students raised in America
   D) Raised in America, at least 60% of the students

3. A) NO CHANGE
   B) 50% of the college admission officer's essays received from students
   C) 50% of the students' essays one college admissions officer received
   D) one college admissions officer reported that 50% of the students' essays she received

BLUE WRITING LESSON 13: MISPLACED MODIFIERS
Wading In

TOPIC OVERVIEW: MISPLACED MODIFIERS

A modifier in a sentence can be either a single word (usually an adjective) or a phrase. The SAT will test your ability to notice when a modifying phrase is out of place. The way this usually occurs is when the object being modified does not appear directly after the modifier.

RECOGNIZING MISPLACE MODIFIER QUESTIONS

In order for a question to be a **misplaced modifier** question, the sentence will have to contain a modifying word or phrase, and the underlined portion will either be the phrase itself (or part of it) or the object being modified. These modifying phrases are often followed by a comma, and they give information about the noun that follows. The most common ones have a gerund (a verb ending in –*ing*) at the beginning, so be on the lookout for this when trying to identify these questions.

ANSWERING MISPLACED MODIFIER QUESTIONS

Once you've identified the question as a misplaced modifier question, you can follow the steps below to answer it:

1. Identify the modifying phrase.
2. Find the noun being modified as the sentence is written.
3. Determine which noun *should* be modified by the phrase.
4. Choose the answer which rearranges the sentence correctly.

Example 1: By relocating the team to Los Angeles, the hearts of Brooklyn Dodger fans were broken by Walter O'Malley, the owner of the team at the time.

    A) NO CHANGE
    B) the hearts of Brooklyn Dodger fans were broken by the team's owner, Walter O'Malley
    C) Walter O'Malley, the owner of the team at the time, broke the hearts of Brooklyn Dodger fans
    D) the Brooklyn Dodger fans had their hearts broken by then team owner Walter O'Malley

1. The modifying phrase here is *By relocating the team to Los Angeles*, which can be identified by the gerund *relocating* at the beginning, and because it gives additional information about the noun that follows.
2. The noun being modified in the sentence as it is written is *the hearts of Brooklyn Dodger fans*
3. In this sentence, the person who moved the team was clearly *Walter O'Malley*, which means the modifier is in the wrong place.

4. The correct answer will place *Walter O'Malley* directly after the modifying phrase, which is done only by Choice C.

Note that if, in the previous example, there were two choices that fixed the problem with the modifier, one of them would have a different error that would allow you to eliminate it.

Example 2: By helping to coordinate the move of the New York Giants to San Francisco, O'Malley brought major league baseball to the West Coast gradually.

    A) NO CHANGE
    B) gradually brought major league baseball to the West Coast
    C) brought major league baseball gradually to the West Coast
    D) brought a gradual major league baseball to the West Coast

1. This question demonstrates how a single modifying word can be misplaced. The word *gradually*, an adverb, is modifying the verb *brought*, and therefore should be as close to it as possible in the sentence.
2. In this sentence, the modifier is *gradually*. As the sentence stands now, it is not really modifying anything.
3. The word that *gradually* needs to be modifying is *brought*.
4. Choose the answer that moves the modifier so that it is clearly modifying the word *brought*. Choice B does this.

WRAP-UP: MISPLACED MODIFIERS

Misplaced modifier questions can be answered using the following steps:

1. Identify the modifying phrase.
2. Find the noun being modified as the sentence is written.
3. Determine which noun *should* be modified by the phrase.
4. Choose the answer which rearranges the sentence correctly.

BLUE WRITING LESSON 13: MISPLACED MODIFIERS
Learning to Swim

CONCEPT EXERCISE:

Directions: Find and correct the misplaced modifier errors in each of the following sentences.

1. After being trapped in the cave for over three days without food or water, the creepy sounds of bats and other creatures became less bothersome to the group of lost campers.

2. The extravagant man's lifestyle was the result of a recent inheritance that had been bequeathed to him by his grandmother.

3. The Declaration of Independence was unanimously approved on July 2nd, which was the formal declaration of the 13 American colonies sovereignty from Great Britain.

4. Having received an official email from his mentor regarding a new dig site, excitedly the archeologist caught a red-eye flight to Egypt to join the survey group.

5. The troubled teenagers were the prime suspects in a string of grave robberies after being caught on camera committing the crime.

6. After being inducted into the Hall of Fame, the baseball player greeted his many screaming fans humbly and offered to sign their baseball cards.

7. The reticent toddler grasped the coffee table and pulled himself up to a standing position gingerly.

8. The young business man ripped up a parking ticket he found under his windshield wiper, who had illegally parked in a handicapped parking space in his haste to be on time for work.

9. Being the type of person who is obsessed with cleanliness, seeing the muddy shoes sitting in the middle of the floor made Walter cringe.

10. Domesticated animals often lose their ability to survive in the wild, such as dogs and cats.

11. Days after becoming disoriented by a tsunami wave, the dolphins attempted to use echolocation to locate their next meal fervently.

12. Harold finally located his missing sock rummaging through the laundry basket full of clean clothes.

13. One of the many aspects studied in chemistry, which is an attraction between atoms that allows for the creation of chemical substances, is the strength of chemical bonds.

14. Before constructing a new football stadium in Atlanta, the funding to pay for the various expenses related to the construction had to be secured by Arthur Blank, the owner of the Falcons.

15. Skydiving is a favorite activity, the act of parachuting from an airplane midflight, of adventure seekers.

16. By dialing the seven digits that make up a phone number cautiously, you will ensure that you do not call the wrong person.

17. People in the early stages of Alzheimer's disease have difficulty retaining the names of people they have just met often, but they may be able to easily recall events that happened many years ago.

18. During a twelve hour march across hilly terrain, sore feet and aching backs were the soldiers' common complaints.

19. Baffled by the request of the commander, the captain called the commander to clarify the orders quickly.

20. President Obama made an executive order that would help immigrant children, the 44th President of the United States, who have come into the United States illegally.

BLUE WRITING LESSON 13: MISPLACED MODIFIERS
Diving into the Deep End

PRACTICE EXERCISE:

Directions: Answer the questions that accompany the following passage.

The Brickmaker

(1) We see many strange, odd-looking water creatures and plants looking through a microscope. Look at this field of view as seen through the microscope. In the center stands a brickmaker. (2) Small, he is a weird animal, and he looks like a mere speck to the eye, but through the microscope we see how wonderfully curious and strange a creature he is. He is no idle, lazy fellow. (3) He is working busily all the time.

Making them one by one, (4) little bricks build his house. He manufactures the bricks himself, and when one is finished he lays it down carefully by the side of the last, and fastens it (5) firmly in its place with a kind of cement. The bricks are laid in regular tiers one above the other.

1. A) NO CHANGE
   B) Looking through a microscope, we see many strange, odd-looking water creatures and plants.
   C) We see looking through a microscope many strange, odd-looking water creatures and plants.
   D) We see many strange, odd-looking water creatures looking through a microscope and plants.

2. A) NO CHANGE
   B) He is a weird animal, small
   C) He is a small, weird animal
   D) He is small and he is a weird animal

3. A) NO CHANGE
   B) Busily, his work is constant.
   C) His work is busy all the time.
   D) All the time, busy is his work.

4. A) NO CHANGE
   B) he uses little bricks to
   C) the bricks are little and they
   D) his bricks are used to

5. A) NO CHANGE
   B) kindly in its place with a firm cement.
   C) in a firm place of cement of its kind.
   D) with a kind of cement in place with a firm.

(6) <u>We find these still brickmakers in water</u> where various water-plants grow, especially the water-milfoil and bladderwort. They seem to be social beings. They live in large communities, attaching their houses to the stems and leaves of the plants so thickly sometimes that they almost touch one another. They look, to the naked eye, like lines about one eighth of an inch in length. **(7)** <u>Thickly in New Jersey ponds, they are on plants sometimes.</u>

If you take some of the plants and water, and put them in a bottle, you can carry a large number of the brickmakers home, where you can watch them at your leisure. Take a glass slide which has a little cup-shaped hollow to hold a few drops of water, and fill it with some of the water from the bottle. Now cover it with a very thin piece of glass and lay it over the stage of the microscope, and it is ready to be looked at and studied.

(8) <u>Darkly, the first thing you see is a</u> brick-colored, cylinder-shaped house which looks to be about the size of a cigar. **(9)** <u>Scared of the disturbance, the little builder who lives in this house</u> has stopped work and gone within. But he is so industrious a fellow that he will not remain within very long. As soon as it is quite still he will probably come to the door of his house; **(10)** <u>thrusting out two horns, you will see him.</u> He will move these horns to the right and left, cautiously feeling all around him. **(11)** <u>Cautiously satisfied that no enemy is near, now he ventures out.</u>

6. A) NO CHANGE
    B) We find still these brickmakers in water
    C) We find these brickmakers in still water
    D) Still, we find these brickmakers in water

7. A) NO CHANGE
    B) New Jersey plants are thick on those ponds.
    C) Those ponds are thick with New Jersey plants.
    D) Sometimes they are thick on the plants in the New Jersey ponds.

8. A) NO CHANGE
    B) The first dark thing you see is a
    C) The first thing you darkly see
    D) The first thing you see is a dark,

9. A) NO CHANGE
    B) Scared of the disturbance, the house is filled with the little builder who
    C) Scared of the disturbance, we have frightened the little builder
    D) Scared of the disturbance, working on the bricks

10. A) NO CHANGE
    B) you will see him thrust out two horns.
    C) with two horns you will see him thrusting out.
    D) with a thrust you will see his two horns.

11. A) NO CHANGE
    B) Satisfied that no cautious enemy is near, now he ventures out.
    C) Satisfied that no enemy is near, now he cautiously ventures out.
    D) Satisfied that no enemy is cautiously near, now he ventures out.

TEST EXERCISE:

Directions: Answer the questions that accompany the following passage.

Galileo's Invention of the Telescope

About ten months **(1)** <u>ago; a report</u> reached my ears that a Dutchman had constructed a telescope, by the aid of which visible objects, although at a great distance from the eye of the observer, were seen distinctly as if near. Some proof of its most wonderful performances **(2)** <u>was reported,</u> which some gave credence to, but others contradicted. A few days later, I received confirmation of the report in a letter written by a noble Frenchman, Jaques Badovere, which finally convinced me to inquire into the principle of the telescope, and then to construct a similar **(3)** <u>instrument. Which</u> a little while later I succeeded in doing.

(4) <u>I prepared myself</u> a tube, at first of lead, in the ends of which I fitted two glass lenses, both plane on one side, but on the other side one spherically convex, and the other concave. Bringing my eye to the concave lens, **(5)** <u>I saw objects satisfactorily large and near</u>, for they appeared one-third of the distance off and nine times larger than when they are seen with the natural eye alone. **(6)** <u>I afterwards shortly</u> constructed another telescope with more quality, which magnified objects more than sixty times. By sparing neither labor nor expense, **(7)** <u>another telescope was constructed</u>. This new instrument was so superior that objects seen through it **(8)** <u>appeared</u> magnified nearly a thousand times, and more than thirty times nearer than if viewed by the natural powers of sight alone

I betook myself to observations of the heavenly bodies; and first of all, I viewed the Moon for a long time. After the Moon, I frequently observed other heavenly bodies, both fixed stars and planets, with

1. A) NO CHANGE
   B) ago a report
   C) ago, and a report
   D) ago; and a report

2. A) NO CHANGE
   B) were reported
   C) are reported
   D) had reported

3. A) NO CHANGE
   B) instrument; which
   C) instrument: which
   D) instrument, which

4. A) NO CHANGE
   B) I prepared
   C) After preparing myself, I made
   D) Myself, I prepared

5. A) NO CHANGE
   B) satisfactorily I saw objects large and near
   C) I saw satisfactory objects large and near
   D) I saw objects large and near and satisfactory

6. A) NO CHANGE
   B) Short, I afterwards
   C) Shortly afterwards, I
   D) I short afterwards

7. A) NO CHANGE
   B) I constructed another telescope.
   C) my telescope construction was completed.
   D) there was another telescope constructed.

8. A) NO CHANGE
   B) had appeared
   C) appearing
   D) were appearing

(9) <u>credible</u> delight. **(10)** <u>Let me speak first of the surface of the Moon, which is turned towards us.</u> The brighter part seems to surround and pervade the whole hemisphere; but the darker part, like a sort of cloud, discolors the Moon's surface and makes it appear covered with spots. These spots have never been observed by any one before me; and from my observations of them, often repeated, I have been led to the opinion that the surface of the Moon is not perfectly smooth, free from inequalities and exactly spherical, as a large school of philosophers considers with regard to the Moon and the other heavenly bodies. On the contrary, **(11)** <u>its</u> full of inequalities, uneven, full of hollows and protuberances, just like the surface of the Earth.

9. A) NO CHANGE
   B) incredulous
   C) incredible
   D) incredibly

10. A) NO CHANGE
    B) Let me turn towards us and speak of the first surface of the Moon.
    C) Of the surface of the Moon, let me speak first turned toward us.
    D) The surface of the Moon is turned toward us and is speaking to me.

11. A) NO CHANGE
    B) it's
    C) its'
    D) they're

BLUE WRITING LESSON 13: MISPLACED MODIFIERS
Race to the Finish

HOMEWORK EXERCISE 1:

Directions: Find and correct all misplaced modifier errors in each of the following sentences.

1. While I was shopping with my mother, I found an adorable skirt, but the only skirt available was too large in the store.

2. As I was walking to my car, the rain began pouring from the sky and I was drenched within minutes.

3. Churning in the Atlantic Ocean, the weather man reported that the hurricane would make landfall by Tuesday.

4. Angus had no choice but to wear his only collared shirt to the wedding, which was stained with ketchup.

5. Eagerly awaiting the guests who would be attending her birthday party, Mary's cake was tempting Mary to eat it early.

6. Brian told us before the holiday that he plans to improve his health by eating better.

7. For Halloween, Sandra handed out cookies to the children wrapped in plastic wrap.

8. Loudly slurping the last bits of smoothie from the bottom of the glass, her sister was annoyed by Jennifer's impolite behavior.

9. By keeping the gas tank from dropping below three-fourths of a tank, the car seemed to run better to George.

10. The boy could not see the whiteboard sitting in the seat in the back of the classroom.

11. Gary needed a new pencil for his test desperately, but he had not brought any additional pencils with him.

12. Dr. Walters started his lecture early, since the auditorium already almost contained 300 college students.

13. My boyfriend made it clear why we were breaking up on Thursday.

14. It satisfies an actor to be complimented on his or her work often.

15. Tired from working three sixty-hour weeks, Marshall's delight was felt when his boss finally said the major project was over and he could go back to working forty hour weeks.

16. Three cars were reported broken into by the Memphis police last week.

17. For safety, I held the key tightly in my hand that my sister gave me.

18. While watering her plants, a wasp she swatted stung Jane on the ear.

19. I can take three friends to the concert on Saturday only.

20. Greg donated a camera to the youth charity that he no longer used.

HOMEWORK EXERCISE 2:

Directions: Answer the questions that accompany the following passage.

Effects of the British taxation on the American colonies

The following passage discusses how the taxation decisions of the British government, following its expensive war with France (1754-1763), contributed to growing colonial impatience with British rule.

When the War ended in 1763, the inhabitants of British North America **(1)** <u>considered themselves thoroughly patriotic</u> and loyal British subjects, but that was before they learned that they had to help pay for security and administering the Empire and that the British expected to rule more than they had in the past. Even though the colonies had flourished and become prosperous, in large part because of the Navigation Acts, many colonials believed that they were entitled to these things and should not have to shoulder any burden, a common human attitude. A smaller minority **(2)** <u>had begun already to move away</u> from strict loyalty.

(3) <u>Grenville, being the chief minister of the young George III, faced a £145 million national debt that had only been £75 million before the war and a heavily-taxed population in the British Isles.</u> Plus he had to find the funds with which to pay the 10,000 soldiers stationed in North America. **(4)** <u>He decided and Parliament agreed that the colonials as well as the people in the British Isles should be taxed.</u> Few would have dreamed that his revenue program would cause problems.

1. A) NO CHANGE
   B) thoroughly considered themselves patriotic
   C) considered thoroughly themselves patriotic
   D) , considered thoroughly patriotic,

2. A) NO CHANGE
   B) had begun to move already away
   C) , already had begun to move away,
   D) had already begun to move away

3. A) NO CHANGE
   B) Grenville, facing a £145 million national debt (which had only been £75) and a heavily-taxed population in the British Isles, was the chief minister of the young George III.
   C) Grenville, the chief minister of the young George III, faced a £145 million national debt (which had only been £75 million before the war) and a heavily-taxed population in the British Isles
   D) Grenville was the chief minister of the young George III, for that reason faced a £145 million national debt (which was only £75 before the war) and a heavily-taxed population in the British isles.

4. A) NO CHANGE
   B) He decided, and Parliament had agreed, that the colonials should be taxed in addition to the people in the British Isles
   C) He decided, and Parliament agreed, that the colonials, as well as the people in the British Isles, should be taxed
   D) He decided and Parliament agreed with his decision that therefore the colonials as well as the people in the British Isles will be taxed.

His first taxing effort was to *reduce* the Molasses tax from 6 pence to 3 pence a gallon, thereby cutting the tax rate in half! But this Revenue Act (Sugar Act) of 1763 was, for the first time, clearly revenue and not the regulation of trade. It added more colonial products which could only be sent to Great Britain and required colonial shippers to post a bond before they shipped. Worse, it created new vice-admiralty courts, providing the machinery for enforcement. **(5)** But the British government was lax in allowing criminal activity in colonial trade in the past, it was clear that the British were going to collect the taxes and punish the criminals.

It was the Stamp Act in 1765 that stirred many colonials to protest strenuously and to engage in violence and other criminal behavior. People in Great Britain were long accustomed to stamp taxes on legal documents, playing cards, marriage licenses, newspapers, printing, and the like, so Grenville had no inkling that the colonials would object to paying lesser taxes on fewer items.

He gave them a year to find alternative ways to raise **(6)** revenue but they did not do that. Instead, they erupted in protest. **(7)** The Stamp Tax offended the most influential (and richest) colonials, even though it affected them disproportionately and affected their everyday business transactions. Moreover, the act provided for trials of offenders in admiralty **(8)** courts, which had no juries. Prominent people, no matter how guilty, would be unlikely to be convicted by a colonial jury, which is why the British government wanted to avoid such juries. The radical left group, the Sons of Liberty, organized mob riots and attacked government officials. Houses and other buildings were burned in Boston and New York. Stamp commissioners were so terrorized that they resigned for fear of their lives.

5. Which of the following choices most effectively combines the two underlined clauses?

A) NO CHANGE
B) Because the British government was lax in allowing criminal activity in colonial trade in the past, it was
C) Whereas the British government was lax in allowing criminal activity in colonial trade in the past, it was
D) Despite the British government was lax in allowing criminal activity in colonial trade in the past, it was

6. Which of the following choices most effectively combines the two underlined sentences?

A) revenue, but they did not do that; instead, they
B) revenue, but they did not do that, instead, they
C) revenue, but they did not do that but they
D) revenue, but they did not do that instead, they

7. A) NO CHANGE
B) Having offended the most influential (and richest) colonials, the Stamp Tax was most offensive to them.
C) Because it affected them and their everyday business transactions, the most influential (and richest) colonials were offended by the Stamp Tax.
D) Because it affected them and their everyday business transactions, the Stamp Tax offended the most influential (and richest) colonials.

8. A) NO CHANGE
B) courts, that
C) courts whose
D) courts which

(9) <u>Nine of the colonies sent representatives to the Stamp Act Congress in New York who signed non-importation agreements</u> (boycotts) to pressure British merchants to pressure Parliament. They had learned who had power. The Sons of Liberty and members of the Stamp Act Congress argued that Parliament did not have the right to tax them directly because, as Englishmen, **(10)** <u>they</u> should not have to bear taxation without representation. Parliament said they were represented, virtually, because the House of Commons represented all commoners in the Empire and colonials were free to come to England and run for a seat. Both sides were being disingenuous. The colonials wanted to run their own affairs and any sensible British politicians knew that a **(11)** <u>colonial in Parliament could not effectively represent</u> his colony. After all, it was a minimum four-week voyage each way, longer than it takes to go from Earth to Mars.

9. A) NO CHANGE
   B) Nine of the colonies sent representatives to the Stamp Act Congress in New York, which signed non-importation agreements
   C) Sending nine of the colonies' representatives to the Stamp Act Congress in New York, they signed non-importation agreements
   D) Sending representatives to the Stamp Act Congress in New York, nine of the colonies signed non-importation agreements

10. Which of the following is the best replacement for the underlined word?

   A) Parliament
   B) Sons of Liberty and members of the Stamp Act Congress
   C) Englishmen
   D) colonists

11. A) NO CHANGE
   B) colonial in Parliament could effectively not represent
   C) colonial in Parliament effectively could not represent
   D) colonial in Parliament could not represent effectively

BLUE WRITING LESSON 14: PARALLELISM
Getting Your Feet Wet

Directions: The following is intended as a short diagnostic exam. Use the paragraphs below to answer the questions.

Teachers' salaries, expenditures per pupil, **(1)** and how a school's quality appears (including the physical plant) significantly affect the employment prospects and wages of high school graduates. Yet unlike other nations, American schools are financed at the local rather than the federal level. If parents do not live in affluent communities … they have few ways of assuring a quality education …. And voters, many of them parents who believe they already "did their bit" by raising their own children, are becoming less and less willing to subsidize schools for "other" people's kids. School bond failures are way up in comparison with earlier decades. At the same time, the property tax cuts of the 1970s and 1980s greatly decreased the resources available to schools.

International comparisons reveal that education is simply not a national priority in the United States the way it is in many countries. We have a piecemeal, incoherent system that fails to train teachers thoroughly, **(2)** keep track of student progress in a consistent way, or ensuring equality of access. Things are no better in the work world. Only 1 percent of the funding employers devote to training goes towards raising basic skills, those most needed by young entry-level workers. Both publicly and privately funded education is heavily skewed against the apprenticeship programs and vocational training needed by youngsters whose parents cannot afford to send them to college. Government **(3)** spending on employment and training programs, in inflation- adjusted dollars, is today only one-third of what it was in 1980. At the same time, the cost of higher education has soared, while loans and scholarships have been cut back

1. A) NO CHANGE
   B) and other indicators of school quality
   C) and the way schools indicate their quality
   D) and whether the quality of a school is apparent

2. A) NO CHANGE
   B) keep track of student progress in a consistent way, or to ensure equality
   C) keep track of student progress in a consistent way, or ensures equality
   D) keep track of student progress in a consistent way, or ensure equality

3. A) NO CHANGE
   B) spending on employment and to train its employees
   C) spending on employment and training for its employees
   D) spending on employment and programs for training

BLUE WRITING LESSON 14: PARALLELISM
Wading In

TOPIC OVERVIEW: PARALLELISM

Parallelism questions on the SAT will test your skill at noticing when parts of a sentence are not in the same form.

RECOGNIZING PARALLELISM QUESTIONS

You can identify a parallelism question because it will compare words or phrases when they appear in a pair or list. In addition, the answers to these questions will contain different forms of the verbs.

ANSWERING PARALLELISM QUESTIONS

The SAT presents parallelism errors in two ways. Either the underlined portion contains both items which need to have parallel structure, or the underlined portion needs to be changed to match something elsewhere in the passage. The steps below address both of these situations:

1. Locate the items that need to contain parallel structure.
2. If they are all in the underlined portion, eliminate any answer choices that contain more than one structure.
3. If one is not in the underlined portion, eliminate and answer choices that contain a different structure from that.
4. Choose the best answer from the remaining choices.

Example 1: According to the Organization for Economic Cooperation and Development, American students ranked in the lower two-thirds of counties the <u>areas of science, mathematics, and their ability to solve problems.</u>

    A) NO CHANGE
    B) areas of science, mathematics, and how they solved problems
    C) areas of how they did science, math, and problem solving
    D) areas of science, mathematics, and problem solving.

1. The three terms in the list are *science*, *mathematics*, and *their ability to solve problems*.
2. In the given sentence, all three are in the underlined portion. We can eliminate Choices A and B because they contain different structures.
3. Because all three items are in the underlined portion, you can skip this step.
4. The difference between Choices C and D is the phrase *how they* in Choice C, which is unnecessary. The correct answer is Choice D.

Example 2: Although it's not entirely clear which is the main culprit, the problem with American <u>education either centers in elementary schools or in universities</u>.

    A) NO CHANGE
    B) education either centers with elementary school or universities
    C) education centers in either elementary schools or universities
    D) education centers in elementary schools or centers in universities.

1. The related items are *elementary schools* and *universities*. Notice that in this question, they are connected because they appear in an *either...or* structure.

2. The underlined portion of this question contains both items. We can eliminate any choices where the phrase following the *either* does not match the phrase following the *or*. This occurs in Choices A and B.

3. Because all three items are in the underlined portion, you can skip this step.

4. There is nothing technically wrong with Choice D, but because it is wordier than Choice C, the better answer is Choice C.

WRAP-UP: PARALLELISM

Parallelism questions can be answered using the following steps:

1. Identify the items that need to contain parallel structure.
2. If they are all in the underlined portion, eliminate any answer choices that contain more than one structure.
3. If one is not in the underlined portion, eliminate and answer choices that contain a different structure from that.
4. Choose the best answer from the remaining choices.

BLUE WRITING LESSON 14: PARALLELISM
Learning to Swim

CONCEPT EXERCISE:

Directions: Find and correct any errors in each of the following sentences. Some sentences may not have any errors.

1. The homeless shelter needed more volunteers, supplies, and to be roomier.

2. Honesty, loyalty, a friendly attitude, and tenaciously pursuing a goal are the requirements for this job.

3. Either he will be late to or absent from the party tonight.

4. Barry and Chester want both to be awake for the eclipse tonight.

5. We tried Indian cuisine, Korean cuisine, and Jamaican's before we settled on Chinese food for our wedding reception.

6. The SAT tests your skills in reading, writing, and math-solving skills.

7. After the baseball game, the players from the teams both waved to the fans as they walked off the field.

8. Intending to lose weight gradually, I prefer running to a strenuous workout or even an aerobics session.

9. Zach grudgingly listened to his parents, packed up his toys, and to his room he went where he changed his clothes and went to sleep right away.

10. To be a successful actor, one must be capable of portraying oneself either as realistic or one liked by many.

11. Whitney told her mother that she had left her phone either at the gym or at school as no one had returned it to her yet.

12. Sightseeing in New York City is more manageable when walking around rather than to drive around.

13. The jury had listened to the case patiently for four hours before it evaluated the evidence, had a discussion about the closing arguments, and a guilty verdict was reached.

14. To read Shakespeare is like opening your mind to culture and elegance.

15. Either Jeremy will be washing the dishes or Kevin's sister will do it.

16. Of the many jobs I have had over the years, the ones that I prefer the most are the ones that pay well, have a good retirement plan, and I enjoy the work environment there.

17. People are usually swayed by politicians who make believable promises, have winning personalities, and good speakers.

18. Tom Cruise was pursued by the paparazzi into a restaurant, a club, at the park, and the grocery store.

19. The teacher instructed us on how to speak clearly, avoiding using clichés, and an efficient way to use dictionaries.

20. It is quicker to take the bus than driving there by yourself.

BLUE WRITING LESSON 14: PARALLELISM
Diving into the Deep End

PRACTICE EXERCISE:

Directions: Answer the questions that accompany the following passage.

The More You Know

There was a time when parents of newborns were perfectly content to know only a few basic things about their babies: **(1)** their height, the baby's weight, and their apgar score*.

But a graduate student at the University of California, Davis named Razib Khan wanted to know much more about his newborn son. Kahn, a doctoral candidate studying feline genetics, **(2)** convinced his wife's doctor to provide him with a tissue sample from the placenta, bringing the sample to his university laboratory, and was able to roughly sequence his son's genome with the help of free genetic analysis software. As a result, his son became the first healthy baby in the U.S. to have had his genome sequenced before his birth.

Although doctors perform genetic testing of fetuses now, the procedure is generally reserved for diagnostic purposes. For example, such tests are currently performed **(3)** to measure the risks of birth defects, diagnosing diseases like cystic fibrosis, and when assessing the risk of disorders like Down syndrome.

1. A) NO CHANGE
    B) the baby's height, weight, and their apgar score
    C) the baby's height, weight, and apgar score.
    D) the baby's height, the baby's weight, and the baby's apgar score.

2. A) NO CHANGE
    B) convincing his wife's doctor to provide him with a tissue sample, bringing the sample to his university laboratory, and being able to roughly sequence his son's genome
    C) convincing his wife's doctor to provide him with a tissue sample from the placenta, brought the sample to his university laboratory, and was able to roughly sequence his son's genome
    D) convinced his wife's doctor to provide him with a tissue sample from the placenta, brought the sample to his university laboratory, and was able to roughly sequence his son's genome

3. A) NO CHANGE
    B) to measure the risks of birth defects, diagnose diseases like cystic fibrosis, and when assessing the risk of disorders like Down syndrome
    C) to measure the risks of birth defects, diagnose diseases like cystic fibrosis, and assess the risk of disorders like Down syndrome
    D) when measuring the risks of birth defects, diagnose diseases like cystic fibrosis, and assess the risk of disorders like Down syndrome.

Genetic sequencing of fetuses may soon become commonplace. What's not yet clear is what parents **(4)** <u>can and would</u> do with this information.

The information provided by genetic sequencing is generally **(5)** <u>predictive rather than determining the future</u>. Genetic results that suggest that a child is prone to a certain condition represent a possibility, not a diagnosis. The complex relationships **(6)** <u>between genes, behavioral and environmental factors, and diseases</u> could easily result in misunderstandings about the significance of prenatal genetic sequencing. For instance, it is possible that parents might choose to terminate the pregnancy based on the mere possibility that their child might develop a debilitating disease.

Research institutions such as the National Institutes of Health (NIH) are examining the potential implications of providing parents with a forecast of their child's biological future. Recently, NIH announced a $25 million study of the **(7)** <u>potential benefits, consequences of the practice, and applications</u> of sequencing the genome of every newborn in the U.S. Researchers from many universities and hospitals will analyze different aspects of genome sequencing. For example, researchers at Boston Children's Hospital will focus on the impact genetic data has on the medical care a child receives in its formative years, while **(8)** <u>those at the University of North Carolina, Chapel Hill will have examined the ethical, legal, and social issues</u> involved in helping doctors and parents make informed decisions based on data from genome sequencing.

4. A) NO CHANGE
   B) can and will
   C) could and will
   D) can do and will

5. A) NO CHANGE
   B) predictive rather than deterministic
   C) predicting the future rather than being deterministic
   D) predictive rather than deterministically

6. A) NO CHANGE
   B) between genes, a behavioral factor, environmental factors, and a disease
   C) between genetics, behavioral factors, the environment, and disease
   D) between genes, behavior, the environment, and a disease

7. A) NO CHANGE
   B) potential benefits of the practice, consequences of the practice, and applications
   C) potential benefits, consequences, and applications
   D) potential benefits, potential consequences, and a potential application

8. A) NO CHANGE
   B) researchers at the University of North Carolina, Chapel Hill examine the ethical, legal, and social issues
   C) those at the University of North Carolina, Chapel Hill will examine the ethical, legal, and social issues
   D) those at the University of North Carolina, Chapel Hill might examine the ethical, legal, and social

Public researchers are not the only people examining the possibility of genome sequencing for fetuses. Several companies, **(9)** including Verinata, Sequenom, Natera, and a company called Ravgen, are developing non-invasive genome sequencing tests that they believe will become a routine part of prenatal care in the near future.

If genome sequencing becomes standard practice in prenatal care, both doctors and patients will require deeper understanding of **(10)** the functions of the genome, the applications of that information when making clinical decisions, and the limitations of such information in predicting the future. Detailed genetic information without the proper context could have dire consequences: perfectly healthy pregnancies may be terminated due to a misunderstanding of the implications of genetic data; **(11)** parents being subjected to unnecessary anxiety as a result of overestimating the significance of a particular gene; and otherwise healthy babies may be subjected to needless medical tests and treatments based on improperly analyzed genetic data. Clearly the ethics and implications of fetal genetic sequencing must be further explored before such tests become commonplace.

*An apgar score is a measurement of a baby's overall condition shortly after birth.

9. A) NO CHANGE
    B) including a company called Verinata, a company called Sequenom, a company called Natera, and a company called Ravgen
    C) including a company called Verinata, Sequenom, Natera, and Ravgen
    D) including Verinata, Sequenom, Natera, and Ravgen

10. A) NO CHANGE
    B) the functioning of the genome, applying information in clinical decisions, limiting such information in predicting the future
    C) how the genome functions, applying that information when making clinical decisions, and limiting such information in predicting the future
    D) how the genome functions, how to apply that information when making clinical decisions, and how to limit such information in predicting the future

11. A) NO CHANGE
    B) parents subjected to unnecessary anxiety as a result of overestimating the significance of a particular gene
    C) parents subjecting to unnecessary anxiety as a result of overestimating the significance of a particular gene
    D) parents being subjected to unnecessary anxiety as a result of having overestimated the significance of a particular gene

TEST EXERCISE:

Directions: Answer the questions that accompany the following passage.

The All Quiet Event

The sun has gone **(1)** <u>quiet, some would say too quiet</u>. In the **(2)** <u>middle of a period of time we call the 'solar maximum'</u> — the period in the sun's 11-year cycle when it is most active — one would expect the sun to be teeming with sunspots. Yet now, there seems to be hardly a sunspot in sight. In an image taken July 18th, 2014 by NASA's Solar Dynamics Observatory, there is a tiny brown spot near the center where a small sunspot appears to be developing. But just one day before, there was nothing. July 17th was a totally spotless day.

(3) <u>This "All Quiet Event," as solar physicist Tony Phillips has dubbed it,</u> has stirred mixed opinions about the state of Sol, the central star of our solar system. **(4)** <u>Is this development ordinary, or is it a new and worrisome development</u>?

1. A) NO CHANGE
   B) quiet — some would say too quiet.
   C) quiet; and some would say too quiet.
   D) quiet (some would say too quiet)

2. A) NO CHANGE
   B) middle of the time called "solar maximum"
   C) middle of the "solar maximum"
   D) middle of the period known as the "solar maximum"

3. A) NO CHANGE
   B) This "All Quiet Event" — as solar physicist Tony Philips has dubbed it,
   C) This "All Quiet Event": as solar physicist Tony Philips has dubbed it,
   D) This "All Quiet Event", as the solar physicist Tony Philips has dubbed it;

4. A) NO CHANGE
   B) Either this is a new and worrisome development or it is ordinary.
   C) Is this an ordinary development, or is it something new and worrisome?
   D) Is this a more ordinary development, or a new and more worrisome development?

"It is strange, but it isn't incredibly strange," said Phillips,. "A spotless day during solar maximum is odd, but this solar maximum we are in has been very weak." According to Phillips, this **(5)** not only is the weakest solar maximum to have been observed in the space age, but the weakest of the past hundred years. **(6)**The spotless day is thus an aberration from the norm.

Sunspots are **(7)** caused on the surface of the sun by highly concentrated magnetic fields. These magnetic fields **(8)** are cooler than the surrounding surface of the sun, and range from the relatively small 10-mile spots to spots that exceed 100,000 miles in diameter. **(9)** On the other hand, they appear to be darker than the rest of the sun.

5. A) NO CHANGE
   B) is not only the weakest solar maximum to have been observed in the space age, but also the weakest of the past hundred years.
   C) not only the weakest solar maximum to have been observed in the space age, but also the weakest one in the past hundred years.
   D) is not only the weakest solar maximum to have been observed in the space age but also is the weakest in the past hundred years

6. Which of the following can be inferred given the information in the paragraph?

   A) NO CHANGE
   B) Thus, the spotless day was not a complete surprise.
   C) Scientists were taken completely aback.
   D) There are many theories that say the solar maximum will soon surge again.

7. A) NO CHANGE
   B) on the surface of the sun, caused by magnetic fields which are highly concentrated.
   C) caused by magnetic fields on the highly concentrated surface of the sun.
   D) caused by highly concentrated magnetic fields on the surface of the sun

8. A) NO CHANGE.
   B) are cooler than the surrounding surface of the sun, and ranged
   C) were cooler than the surrounding surface of the sun, and range
   D) , cooler than the surrounding surface of the sun, and range

9. A) NO CHANGE
   B) Despite this evidence,
   C) Because of this,
   D) In addition,

[1]These spots are of interest to solar scientists because they are the regions where solar activity originates. [2] You may wonder what solar activity is. [3] This activity is caused by the magnetic fields' energy becoming too tightly wound. [4] When the sun releases that energy, it does so in an impressively explosive manner: **(10)** <u>with a solar flare, a giant flash of light; or a coronal mass ejection, a firing of</u> material from the sun into space. {**11**}

Alex Young, a heliophysicist at Goddard Space Flight Center, said it is hard to say what is unusual — and isn't — when it comes to the sun. "We've only been observing the sun in lots of detail in the last 50 years," he said. "That's not that long considering it's been around for 4.5 billion years."

10. A) NO CHANGE
    B) with solar flares, giant flashes of light, or with a coronal mass ejection, when the sun fires
    C) with a solar flare — a giant flash of light — or a coronal mass ejection, a firing of
    D) either with a solar flare, a giant flash of light, or a coronal mass ejection; a firing of

11. Which of the following sentences should be eliminated in order to improve the focus of the paragraph?

    A) Sentence 1
    B) Sentence 2
    C) Sentence 3
    D) Sentence 4

BLUE WRITING LESSON 14: PARALLELISM
Race to the Finish

HOMEWORK EXERCISE 1:

Directions: Find and correct any errors in each of the following sentences. Some sentences may not have any errors.

1. There are many differences between a story told in a book and how a movie tells it.

2. Watching a movie doesn't give you the same depth of understanding as having read a book.

3. A book allows the reader insight into characters' thoughts, feelings, and how they develop throughout the story.

4. On the other hand, the movie provides visual effects and ones you can hear.

5. When you go to the movies, you embark on a night out, while reading a book is done at home.

6. On the other hand, reading allows you both to stay home and you can get other things done.

7. Reading not only gives you a richer experience, it also helps to generate greater mental acuity in other activities.

8. The key ingredient of reading is that the reader is a more active participant rather than just watching and listening

9. Many students find that not only are their language arts skills improved with more reading, but their math skills are too.

10. The skills that have been shown to be bettered by reading are pattern recognition, conversational comprehension, and how many words people understand.

11. Unfortunately, most students would prefer to either watch a movie or staying at home to watch TV.

12. One advantage of movies is they can be attended individually, in pairs, or can be watched in large groups.

13. The social aspects of movie-going give it a unique advantage over when you read a book.

14. Oddly, even though many books are less expensive than a movie ticket, many people would rather pay for a movie than books.

15. Around the world, the nationalities that watch the most movies are the Americans, the Japanese, French and Russians.

16. The people in these countries attend the most movies because they have both opportunity and the citizens have ample free time.

17. Watching a movie, reading a book, or when you watch TV are all times you are seeking entertainment.

18. It's up to you whether that entertainment helps you become smarter or if it is just wasted time.

HOMEWORK EXERCISE 2:

Directions: Answer the questions that accompany the following passage.

Chagas: The Kissing Bug Disease

When Jenny Sanchez was pregnant, she asked her doctor in Virginia to test her for Chagas, also known as the "kissing bug disease." She was worried about **(1)** <u>passing it on to her unborn son and about placing him at risk</u> of future heart disease. In her home country of Bolivia, expectant mothers were routinely screened for Chagas, but her American doctor **(2)** <u>had never even heard of it.</u>

After cursory research, the doctor told her to not worry, telling her that Chagas is transmitted by triatomine insects **(3)** <u>endemic to Latin America, to Virginia not at all</u>. However, Sanchez **(4)** <u>knew well the disease and how it</u> could live in the body for decades without producing any symptoms and could be passed from mother to child.

When Sanchez was finally tested, the results were negative. Yet her experience got her thinking: How many other immigrants were living in Virginia without knowing if they had the deadly disease? Research by the World Health Organization indicates that Bolivia has the highest rates of Chagas disease in the world, and estimates from the U.S. Census Bureau show that **(5)** <u>more Bolivians call Virginia home than call any other state in the country</u>, including California and New York combined.

1. A) NO CHANGE
   B) passing on to her unborn son and, thus, placing him at risk
   C) passing it on to her unborn son and place him at risk
   D) passing it on to her unborn son and placing him at risk

2. A) NO CHANGE
   B) never even having heard of it
   C) never even heard of it
   D) had never been hearing of it

3. A) NO CHANGE
   B) endemic to Latin America, not endemic to Virginia
   C) endemic to Latin America, not Virginia
   D) endemic to Latin America not Virginia

4. A) NO CHANGE
   B) knew the disease well — and how it
   C) knew the disease well — and she knew how it
   D) knew the disease well, and also she knew it

5. A) NO CHANGE
   B) more Bolivians call Virginia home than Bolivians in any other state in the country
   C) more Bolivians call Virginia home than they do any other state in the country
   D) more Bolivians call Virginia home than they call home any other state in the country

[1] American doctors, unfamiliar with the disease, do not routinely screen for it, and many **(6)** <u>potential carriers of the undocumented disease are immigrants</u> without health insurance. [2] It wasn't until 8 years after Jenny Sanchez was tested that the first documented case in the United States of a mother transmitting Chagas to her baby occurred in Northern Virginia. [3] The number of people with Chagas disease in this area is small — according to local doctors, about two dozen cases — but experts wouldn't be surprised if the numbers were higher. **{7}**

According to the World Health Organization, almost 8 million people have **(8)** <u>Chagas disease worldwide, most of them live</u> in Latin America. The triatomines, or the so-called kissing bugs, live in the cracks of walls in rural houses made of mud **(9)** <u>and thatched roofs biting people at night</u>. The bite itself is painless, and many people never show any signs of the disease. A third of those with Chagas, however, develop heart disease and, if untreated, die from what appear to be sudden heart attacks. **{10}**

Because of migration, patients with Chagas are showing up everywhere **(11)** <u>from Spain and Italy to Japan and Australia</u>. The Centers for Disease Control and Prevention estimates that 300,000 people are infected with Chagas in the U.S. Cardiologist Dr. Rachel Marcus asserts that Northern Virginia could be "ground zero" for Chagas disease, because of the volume of immigrants from Bolivia. In 2012, she gave up her private practice to focus on patients with Chagas disease. If colleagues thought she would never find a patient with a tropical disease near Washington D.C., she says, they were wrong.

6. A) NO CHANGE
   B) potential carriers of the disease are undocumented immigrants
   C) potential diseased immigrants are undocumented
   D) undocumented carriers of the disease are potential immigrants

7. In which order should the sentences of this paragraph be arranged to aid the flow of the essay?

   A) NO CHANGE
   B) 2, 1, 3
   C) 3, 2, 1
   D) 2, 3, 1

8. A) NO CHANGE.
   B) Chagas disease worldwide, while most of them live
   C) Chagas disease worldwide, most of them
   D) Chagas disease worldwide, yet most of them live

9. A) NO CHANGE
   B) with thatched roofs, and they bite people at night
   C) with thatched roofs that bite people at night
   D) with thatched roofs, sometimes they bite people at night

10. Which of the following sentences below provides the best support for the previous sentence?

   A) The WHO estimates that 11,000 people die each year from Chagas.
   B) Other causes of heart disease are poor diet and lack of exercise.
   C) Chagas doesn't seem to be spreading very far.
   D) This is similar to how mosquitoes spread malaria.

11. A) NO CHANGE
    B) from Spain, then Italy, to Japan, finally Australia
    C) from Spain to Italy and Japan to Australia
    D) from Spain, Italy, and Japan, to Australia

BLUE WRITING LESSON 15: CHECKPOINT

LET'S CHECK IN

Congratulations! We are now three-fourths of the way through this book!

Today's lesson isn't really a lesson — it's a checkpoint to see how far we've come since the first lesson.

On the following pages, you'll find a series of writing passages and questions. Each set is designed to reflect the types of passages and questions that are common to the SAT writing section. Many of the questions will look familiar because they cover information we've already studied, but some of the questions may be new question types that we'll cover in later lessons.

As you work through each practice set, be sure to mark any questions that you find particularly challenging so that you and your teacher can review them in greater depth when you've finished this checkpoint lesson.

BLUE WRITING LESSON 15: CHECKPOINT

PRACTICE EXERCISE 1:

Directions: Answer the questions that accompany the following passage.

What is Lost as Handwriting Fades

According to many educators, handwriting has little significance in the modern world. The Common Core State Standards **(1)** , which have been adopted in most states, call for teaching legible handwriting, but only in kindergarten and first grade. After that, the emphasis quickly shifts to keyboard proficiency. Supporters of this new emphasis on keyboarding rightly note that **(2)** todays' higher education institutions and workplaces require strong typing skills, but psychologists and neuroscientists say it is far too soon to **(3)** speculate that handwriting is a relic of the past.

{4} New evidence suggests that the links between handwriting and broader educational development run deep. Using advanced tools such as magnetic resonance imaging, **(5)** researchers have been able to find that writing by hand is more than simply a means of communication. The practice helps with learning letters and shapes, can improve idea composition and expression, and may aid fine motor-skill development.

Writing activates a unique neural circuit in the brain, and it seems that this circuit contributes to learning in ways scientists did not previously realize. A 2012 study led by Karin James, a psychologist at Indiana University, supported this view. Children who **(6)** had yet to learn to read and write were presented with a letter or a shape and asked to reproduce **(7)** them in one of three ways: trace the image on a page with a dotted outline, draw it on a blank white sheet, or type it on a computer. They were then placed on a brain scanner and shown the image again.

1. A) NO CHANGE
    B) which have been adopted in most states
    C) , that have been adopted in most states,
    D) , that have been adopted in most states

2. A) NO CHANGE
    B) today's
    C) todays
    D) two days'

3. A) NO CHANGE
    B) suggest
    C) declare
    D) relegate

4. Which choice most effectively establishes the main topic of the paragraph?

    A) Handwriting must still be taught because it is important to broader learning.
    B) Handwriting is an important educational tool.
    C) Handwriting has been proven to be better for humans than other methods of writing.
    D) New computer imaging has proven that handwriting activates the brain in unique ways.

5. A) NO CHANGE
    B) researchers are working to find
    C) researchers hope to find
    D) researchers are finding

6. A) NO CHANGE
    B) hadn't learned ever before
    C) had had no chance to ever learn
    D) had never been able to learn

7. A) NO CHANGE
    B) these
    C) it
    D) those

Researchers found that the initial duplication processes strongly affected brain activity. **(8)** <u>Children who had drawn the letter freehand exhibited increased activity in three areas of the brain that are activated in adults when they read and write.</u> **(9)** <u>Researchers hoped to carry out this same study with adults to compare and contrast the results.</u>

A separate study that followed children in grades two through five found that printing, cursive writing, and typing on a keyboard are all associated with distinct brain patterns. **(10)** <u>When children composed text by hand, they not only consistently produced more words more quickly than they did on a keyboard, but expressed more ideas.</u> Brain imaging suggested that the connection between writing and idea generation went even further. Children with better handwriting exhibited greater neural activation in areas associated with working memory, reading, and writing.

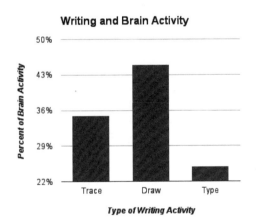

Writing and Brain Activity

8. Based on the sentence and the graph below, which of the following inferences is the most logical?

   A) If children traced and typed, they would see a combined increase in brain activity greater than that from drawing.
   B) It is always better to draw than to type.
   C) For children who are learning to read and write, drawing letters seems to activate the brain the best for learning.
   D) Tracing becomes a better method for learning as children grow older.

9. Which choice most effectively concludes the paragraph?

   A) NO CHANGE
   B) Remove this sentence and conclude the paragraph with the previous sentence.
   C) Their brain activated in three key areas of the brain that adults use when reading and writing.
   D) By contrast, children who typed or traced the letter showed no such effect.

10. Which element from the graph best supports the sentence?

   A) The fact that tracing and typing together produce more brain activity than does drawing on its own.
   B) The fact that drawing produces the most brain activity.
   C) The fact that all three activities are effective at triggering brain activity.
   D) The fact that typing shows the least brain activity.

PRACTICE EXERCISE 2:

Directions: Answer the questions that accompany the following passage.

Google Glass in the Operating Room

Before scrubbing in, Dr. Selene Parekh, an orthopedic surgeon at Duke Medical Center, slipped on a pair of sleek, black glasses — Google Glass **(1)** <u>, which is the wearable computer with a built-in camera and monitor.</u> He gave the glasses a voice command to start recording and turned to the motorcycle crash victim on the operating table. Dr. Parekh has been using Glass since Google began selling test versions of the device. **(2)** <u>He now uses it to record and archive all of his surgeries,</u> and soon he will use it to stream live feeds of his operations to hospitals in India as a way to **(3)** <u>train then educate</u> orthopedic surgeons there.

{4} At Duke and other hospitals, a growing number of surgeons are using Glass to stream their operations online, float medical images in their field of view, and hold video consultations with colleagues as they operate.

1. A) NO CHANGE
   B) ; this is a wearable computer with a built-in camera and monitor.
   C) , the wearable computer with a built-in camera and monitor.
   D) , this is a wearable computer with a built-in camera and monitor.

2. A) NO CHANGE
   B) It is now used to record and archive all of his surgeries
   C) Now being used to record and archive all of his surgeries
   D) Surgeries are now all being recorded and archived with Google Glass

3. A) NO CHANGE
   B) train and educate
   C) train, educate, and instruct
   D) take uneducated orthopedic surgeons there and educate them

4. Which choice most effectively establishes the main topic of the paragraph?

   A) Google Glass has already proven its worth for doctors to the extent that all doctors have recognized its benefits.
   B) Google Glass is cool in concept, but many doctors see its benefits more as gimmicks than as boons to the profession.
   C) The best aspect of Google Glass is its range of software.
   D) The range of possibilities for how doctors can use Google Glass is huge, leading more and more doctors to make use of it.

Software developers have been working to create programs that transform Glass into a medical wonder, allowing Glass to display **(5)** <u>patient vital signs, lab results that are urgent, and surgical checklists</u>; stream live feeds from paramedics to trauma surgeons to avoid potentially fatal delays in treatment; or store patient data using HIPAA-compliant programs to ensure patient privacy.

[1] Many hospitals see Glass as a relatively low-cost and versatile innovation, much like smartphones and tablets. [2] Because Glass is voice-activated and hands-free, it may be particularly well suited for the surgical suite, where camera-guided instruments, robotics, and 3D navigation systems have been commonplace for years. [3] More than half of all health care providers already use these to get access to patient data and other medical information. [4] Glass can float X-rays or CT scans in the surgeon's field of view, allowing the surgeon to reference imaging results without shifting attention from the operation. {6}

Not all members of the medical community **(7)** <u>have embraced</u> Glass. Some are concerned about potential distractions, pointing out that Glass's web-surfing capabilities may tempt doctors to take multitasking to dangerous new levels. Others point out that similar technology, such as navigational displays used to locate tumors, can induce a form of tunnel vision, making doctors less likely to notice problems unrelated to the task at hand. **(8)** <u>All in all, these concerns confirm that the risks are too great for doctors to commence using Google Glass in operations.</u>

5. A) NO CHANGE
   B) patient vital signs, urgent lab results, and surgical checklists
   C) vital signs of patients, urgent lab results, and surgical checklists
   D) vital signs of patients, lab results that are urgent, and checklists that are surgical

6. Which choice most effectively organizes the sentences in the paragraph?

   A) NO CHANGE
   B) 1, 3, 2, 4
   C) 4, 3, 2, 1
   D) 1, 4, 3, 2

7. A) NO CHANGE
   B) had embraced
   C) will embrace
   D) will have embraced

8. Which choice most effectively concludes the paragraph?

   A) NO CHANGE
   B) No concluding sentence is necessary.
   C) Still others point to Google's privacy issues, noting that patient privacy cannot yet be completely guaranteed with Glass.
   D) These complaints are really the same as those already leveled at employing smartphones and tablets in the operating room.

Dr. Oliver J. Muensterer, a pediatric surgeon **(9)** <u>that</u> recently published the first peer-reviewed study on the use of Glass in clinical medicine notes a few issues that must be overcome before Glass **(10)** <u>should be</u> useful in medical practice. "I'm sure we're going to use this in medicine **(11)** <u>." he says.</u> "Not the current version, but a version in the future that is specially made for health care with all the privacy, hardware and software issues worked out."

9. A) NO CHANGE
    B) who
    C) which
    D) whose

10. A) NO CHANGE
    B) couldn't be
    C) shall be
    D) could be

11. A) NO CHANGE
    B) " he says.
    C) he says.
    D) , he says.

PRACTICE EXERCISE 3:

Directions: Answer the questions that accompany the following passage.

Biofuel Tools added to Household Products

With the development of new biological technologies, the meaning of the term "natural" is up **(1)** to debate. Consumer products containing ingredients made using an advanced form of engineering known as synthetic biology are beginning to show up more frequently in grocery and department stores.

(2) Originally created in order to find a way to produce biofuels, this technology has been available for about 20 years, but applications have only recently begun to emerge across several industries, including **(3)** cosmetics, flavoring, and those that produce scents.

(4) While products derived from synthetic biology have become more common in household products, they are rarely labelled as synthetic products, creating confusion over the very meaning of "natural."

For example, a liquid laundry detergent made by Ecover, a company that makes green household products, contains an oil produced by algae **(5)** who'se genetic code was altered in order to force the organisms to produce an oil that they would not otherwise produce in nature. Ecover calls the algae-produced oil a "natural" replacement for palm kernel oil, which is an unsustainable resource. While many environmental groups and consumer activists applaud Ecover's attempts to find an alternative to unsustainable palm kernel oil, they question the ethics of labelling the synthetically-derived alternative as "natural."

1. A) NO CHANGE
   B) for some
   C) for
   D) upon

2. A) NO CHANGE
   B) A method to produce biofuels,
   C) First thought of as a method by which to produce biofuels
   D) Originally aimed at producing biofuels

3. A) NO CHANGE
   B) cosmetics, flavorings, and perfumes
   C) those responsible for the production of flavorings, perfumes, and scents.
   D) perfumes, flavoring-producers, and the ones who make scents.

4. A) NO CHANGE
   B) Since
   C) If
   D) When

5. A) NO CHANGE
   B) who is
   C) who's
   D) whose

[1] Because this technology is so new, there is almost no government oversight or regulation over synthetic biology. [2] In the absence of such regulation, manufacturers are free to label ingredients engineered from synthetic organisms in whatever way they choose. [3] Ecover, for example, justifies calling its algal oil "natural" because the ingredient itself is not synthetic, merely the organism producing the ingredient. [4] Other companies sidestep the issue entirely.

[5] Peter Thomas Roth, which produces a product made from a synthetic biology ingredient called squalane, says the ingredient is derived from a fermentation process involving sugar cane. [6] It does not say the sugar cane is first consumed by a microorganism whose genetic code was altered in a lab. {6}

In fact, (7) even the makers of such ingredients shies away from clearly identifying the technologies by which they create these products. Solazyme, the company that makes the algal oil used in Ecover's laundry detergent (8) ; used to describe itself as a synthetic biology company but has taken the term off its website. Rather than identifying the organism that produces the oil as an engineered organism, the company calls it an optimized strain of single-cell algae that (9) has been in existence for millennia, language that seems specifically (10) described to hide the fact that this algae contains DNA created on a computer.

Without clear regulations to draw a line between "natural" and "synthetic," consumers have no way of knowing (11) the origins of their product. The real question seems to be whether such regulations will be set in place before these ingredients overwhelm the marketplace.

6. Which sentence would serve as the best topic sentence for the paragraph?

A) Sentence 1
B) Sentence 2
C) Sentence 4
D) Sentence 6

7. A) NO CHANGE
   B) even the makers of such ingredients shied
   C) even the maker of such ingredients shy
   D) even the makers of such ingredients shy

8. A) NO CHANGE
   B) ,
   C) Delete it. It is unnecessary.
   D) :

9. A) NO CHANGE
   B) is being
   C) have been
   D) has always been

10. A) NO CHANGE
    B) denoted
    C) designed
    D) defined

11. A) NO CHANGE
    B) the origins of its product
    C) the origin of its product
    D) the origins of their products

PRACTICE EXERCISE 4:

Directions: Answer the questions that accompany the following passage.

Crickets Go Silent

In 2003, a number of male field crickets on the Hawaiian island of Kauai were born without the ability to chirp. Two years later, the same thing happened on Oahu. **(1)** <u>Speculating,</u> researchers believed the events were related, theorizing that a genetic mutation may have spread from one island to the other through commercial transport or via a flying cricket that found its way to the second island. Recent studies have contradicted these theories. **(2)** <u>The studies have suggested that humans were responsible for genetically engineering the mutant crickets.</u>

Nathan Bailey, a biologist at the University of St. Andrews in Scotland and an author of the new study, calls **(3)** <u>this an example</u> of convergent evolution. "It's exciting because we are catching this mutation as it's happening in the wild," he says. The earliest stages of convergent evolution are generally difficult to observe in the wild, limiting scientists' understanding of the genetic architecture underlying such evolutionary changes. **(4)** <u>In some ways,</u> this particular example of convergent evolution may provide unique insight into the means by which such changes occur in nature.

Male crickets have specialized structures at the ends of their wings. When they rub them together, **(5)** <u>the structures engages</u> one another to make the chirping sound. The physiology is comparable to running a fingernail along the teeth of a comb. The mutant male crickets have modified wing structures that render them unable to chirp, but Bailey and his colleagues found that different gene markers **(6)** <u>were responsible for</u> this mutation.

1. A) NO CHANGE
   B) Secondly,
   C) Delete it. It is unnecessary. Capitalize Researchers.
   D) Initially,

2. Based on the information in the passage, which of the following sentences provides the best transition between the first and second paragraphs?

   A) NO CHANGE
   B) The studies have shown that some of our previous assumptions about cricket evolution may have been wrong.
   C) Instead, it appears that the mutant males on each island stopped singing independently, through two similar but distinct adaptations.
   D) Actually, the scientists believe that they need more research before they can make any conclusions.

3. A) NO CHANGE
   B) these an example
   C) these examples
   D) this examples

4. A) NO CHANGE
   B) Therefore,
   C) However,
   D) Moreover,

5. A) NO CHANGE
   B) the structure engages
   C) the structure engage
   D) the structures engage

6. A) NO CHANGE
   B) founded
   C) caused
   D) ended up making

{7} More interestingly, although the species, *Teleogryllus oceanicus*, is found throughout Polynesia and Australia, the silencing effect has only been seen in Hawaii. Bailey believes that this geographic isolation is because the crickets **(8)** had adapted to become less vulnerable to a parasitic Hawaiian fly that is attracted to the males' chirp. The fly larvae burrow into the cricket, causing it to die within a week.

Males that cannot chirp are far less likely to be attacked by this parasite **(9)** , but this mutation has a downside. Male crickets chirp in order to attract mates, and those crickets that cannot chirp have difficulty attracting females. Natural selection would dictate that males that cannot attract mates would be unable to pass their DNA on to future generations. Why, then, does this adaptation persist?

Bailey says that the mutated male crickets have adjusted their mating behavior. **(10)** Rather than to attract mates by chirping, they gather near males that chirp. When females are attracted to the chirping, the silent males intercept the females. Whether this will result in a decrease in the population of singing male crickets, and how that might affect the mating habits of female crickets **(11)** , will certainly be interesting to observe.

7. Which choice most effectively establishes the main topic of the paragraph?

A) Scientists have not studied this cricket species in Polynesia and Australia enough to know if crickets there are adapting in the same way as the Hawaiian ones.
B) The adaptation of Hawaiian crickets will likely spread to the same crickets elsewhere because it is an important protection method.
C) Scientists are witnessing an adaptation unique to Hawaiian crickets which is occurring because the change is a response to a parasitic Hawaiian fly.
D) While the adaptation does protect against a parasitic Hawaiian fly, it also makes it more difficult for the cricket to mate.

8. A) NO CHANGE
   B) have adapted
   C) has adapted
   D) adapted

9. A) NO CHANGE
   B) , this mutation
   C) ; although this mutation
   D) , but these mutations

10. A) NO CHANGE
    B) Rather then attracting
    C) To attract
    D) Rather than attracting

11. A) NO CHANGE
    B) ; this will
    C) , this will
    D) will

PRACTICE EXERCISE 5:

Directions: Answer the questions that accompany the following passage.

My Experience with Online Networking

[1] Regardless, I am always looking forward in my career and thinking about what the next step entails. [2] I am in an enviable position because I love my job. [3] When this happens, I always apply; after all, it can't hurt! [4] I am not actively pursuing new **(1)** <u>positions, every</u> now and then a job posting comes to my attention and piques my interest. **{2}**

The truth is that when I submit my resume through the normal channels, it usually does not get forwarded on to the hiring manager for **(3)** <u>him or her</u> to review. I may feel certain that I can do the **(4)** <u>job do it well, and even enjoy it but</u> if my experience and education do not match the listed qualifications, my application will be automatically rejected. Recently, however, I learned how to use the career-networking website LinkedIn **(5)** <u>to overcome some of these barriers and grab the attention of hiring managers without even submitting an application.</u>

My first step was to find the director of the office in which this position was located. I looked him up on LinkedIn and searched the Internet for **(6)** <u>the scoop</u> about him. I found a couple articles he had written and read them.

1. A) NO CHANGE
   B) positions every
   C) positions, but
   D) positions but

2. The paragraph would be most cohesive if the sentences are placed in which order?

   A) 1, 2, 3, 4
   B) 2, 1, 4, 3
   C) 2, 4, 3, 1
   D) 4, 3, 1, 2

3. A) NO CHANGE
   B) them
   C) they
   D) he or she

4. A) NO CHANGE
   B) job do it well, and even enjoy it, but
   C) job, do it well, and even enjoy it, but
   D) job, do it well, and even enjoy it but

5. Which version results in the sentence with the clearest and most appropriate statement of the passage's main idea?

   A) NO CHANGE
   B) to cheat my way into being offered a job I did not want
   C) to make a connection that had nothing to do with a job that I was interested in
   D) to learn the differences between applying for a job online and applying in person

6. In the context of the passage, which word has the most appropriate tone and meaning?

   A) NO CHANGE
   B) information
   C) propaganda
   D) testimony

Next, I changed and updated my LinkedIn profile to match the position's requirements and the manager's interests. This is one of the benefits of websites like LinkedIn. A **(7)** <u>resume, being as it is limited to one sheet of paper,</u> is difficult to change and **(8)** <u>has</u> limited space, but in the experience section of an online profile, you can provide more targeted details. For instance, you can highlight the activities you are involved in even if they aren't a part of **(9)** <u>their</u> official job.

Once my profile was updated and organized to make me look like a great candidate, I sent the director a request to connect. When sending such a request to someone you do not know, it is important to offer him or her another reason to accept the request other than to discuss the position. {**10**} Even if we were not able to discuss the position, we could both benefit from the connection.

Within three days, we were talking on the phone about the position and the field in general. I had not even submitted my application, and I was basically having an interview! Impressed with my passion for the job, **(11)** <u>I was flown out</u> for an official in-person interview a week later.

The end result was that I was offered the position. Without the excellent user interface provided by LinkedIn, I doubt that the hiring manager would have ever seen my resume, much less considered me for the position. Ultimately, I turned down the position, but the experience was still extremely beneficial.

7. Which version is the clearest and most concise version of the underlined phrase?

   A) NO CHANGE
   B) resume, on a single sheet of paper,
   C) resume with a limit of one sheet
   D) one-page resume

8. A) NO CHANGE
   B) may contain
   C) having
   D) have

9. A) NO CHANGE
   B) your
   C) you're
   D) they're

10. Which information, if added here, would best support the ideas contained in the paragraph?

    A) I also made sure to proofread my message, as grammar and spelling errors give a negative impression.
    B) In this case, I expressed interest in discussing his articles and in sharing resources about our field.
    C) I wanted to appear to be confident and friendly but not cocky or sycophantic.
    D) To do so, I asked the manager if he shared my hobbies of gardening and coin collecting.

11. A) NO CHANGE
    B) a plane flew me out
    C) we flew out
    D) the company flew me out

BLUE WRITING LESSON 16: LOGICAL COMPARISONS
Getting Your Feet Wet

Directions: The following questions are intended to serve as a brief diagnostic exam.

1. Politicians' opinions should be considered no more important <u>than private citizens'</u>.

   A) NO CHANGE
   B) than private citizens
   C) than their opinions of private citizens
   D) than private citizens' opinions of politicians

2. Michael works faster <u>than anyone I know</u>.

   A) NO CHANGE
   B) than everyone I know
   C) than anyone I know works
   D) than anyone else I know

3. The view from this apartment is not nearly as spectacular <u>as from my office</u>.

   A) NO CHANGE
   B) as the view from my office
   C) as from my office windows
   D) as my office

4. Jackie always gave her sister more affection <u>than her brother</u>.

   A) NO CHANGE
   B) than she gave her brother
   C) then her brother
   D) than her brother's

5. The houses and shops I saw in Japan were just <u>like any town</u> in America.

   A) NO CHANGE
   B) like any other town
   C) like those of any town
   D) like towns

Blue Writing Lesson 16: Logical Comparison
Wading In

TOPIC OVERVIEW: LOGICAL COMPARISONS

Logical comparison questions on the SAT will test your ability to recognize and correct incomplete, inconsistent, or unclear comparisons.

TOPIC OVERVIEW: INCOMPLETE COMPARISONS

At least two items are needed for a comparison to be complete. Incomplete comparisons will make the reader guess at which two things are being compared. For example:

<u>Example 1</u>: The University has received more applications this year.

At first glance, this sentence might seem logical, but it doesn't complete the comparison. The University received more applications than what? More applications than it received in another year, or more applications compared to other schools?

Completed comparison:

The University has received more applications this year *than in the previous two years combined.*

Let's look at a trickier example:

<u>Example 2</u>: Lisa won the solo in this year's performance because she sings louder than anyone in the choir.

In this example, the two things being compared are "Lisa" and "anyone in the choir"—but since Lisa won the solo, she's probably in the choir, right? In this case, we're comparing Lisa to herself!

Completed comparison:

Lisa won the solo in this year's performance because she sings louder than *anyone else in the choir.*

TOPIC OVERVIEW: INCONSISTENT COMPARISONS

Comparisons must also be consistent in that they need to compare apples to apples rather than apples to oranges. Let's look at an example:

Example 3: The farmers' market peaches are cheaper than Whole Foods.

If someone said this to you, you would know what the sentence meant, but it terms of proper English conventions, this sentence is incorrect. This sentence compares peaches to Whole Foods—that doesn't make sense!

Consistent comparison:

The farmers' market peaches are cheaper than Whole Foods' peaches.

Inconsistent comparisons can often be addressed by simply making something possessive. For example, in the sentence above, it would also be correct to say:

The farmers' market's peaches are cheaper than Whole Foods'.

TOPIC OVERVIEW: UNCLEAR COMPARISONS

Finally, comparisons must be clear. A reader needs to be able to tell exactly which two things are being compared. Let's look at an example:

Example 4: My mother gives me more homework help than my brother.

In this example, the meaning is unclear. The sentence could mean that my mother gives me more homework help than she gives my brother, or it could mean that my mother gives me more homework help than my brother gives me.

RECOGNIZING LOGICAL COMPARISON QUESTIONS

Logical comparison questions can be identified by the use of key comparison words and phrases, such as:

- like
- less than
- that of
- as
- more than
- those of
- compared to
- other

You should also look for adjectives and adverbs in the comparative form (such as "bigger" or "longer").

ANSWERING LOGICAL COMPARISON QUESTIONS

The SAT presents logical comparison questions in two ways. Either the underlined portion will contain both items that are being compared, or the underlined portion needs to be altered to be logically compared to some other part of the sentence or paragraph.

Regardless of the presentation of the question, the process for finding the correct answer remains the same:

1. Identify the items that are being compared. Determine whether the error is the result of an incomplete, inconsistent, or unclear comparison.
2. If the comparison is incomplete, eliminate any answer choices that fail to logically complete the comparison.
3. Eliminate any answer choices that compare two items that are not similar. Look out for possessives because a seemingly inconsistent comparison can often be corrected by using possessives.
4. Eliminate any answer choices that create an unclear comparison.
5. Choose the best answer from the remaining choices.

<u>Example 5</u>:

Shakespeare's plays are different <u>from any other playwright</u> of his era because they exhibit an exceptional mastery of verse.

A) NO CHANGE
B) than any other playwright
C) from those of any other playwright
D) from any other plays by other playwrights

1. Shakespeare's plays are being compared to other playwrights. The comparison is inconsistent.
2. None of the answer choices are incomplete comparisons.
3. Answer Choices A and B can be eliminated because they do not create a consistent comparison.
4. The difference between Choices C and D is the way in which the information is presented. Though both provide consistent, clear, and complete comparisons, Choice D is redundant and choice C is concise. Choice C is the best answer.

Example 6:

I think that the winner for "Best Documentary" had <u>greater emotional impact</u>.

A) NO CHANGE
B) greater emotional impact than the other nominees.
C) more emotional impact.
D) greater emotional impact than film critics.

1. The winner for "Best Documentary" is being compared, but the comparison is incomplete, so we don't know what it is being compared to.
2. Both answer Choices A and C contain incomplete comparisons, so we can eliminate them.
3. Answer Choice D can be eliminated because it compares a film (the winner for "Best Documentary") to film critics, so the comparison is inconsistent.
4. Answer Choice B is the only remaining answer.

WRAP-UP: LOGICAL COMPARISON

Logical comparison questions can be answered using the following steps:

1. Identify the items that are being compared. Determine whether the error is the result of an incomplete, inconsistent, or unclear comparison.
2. If the comparison is incomplete, eliminate any answer choices that fail to logically complete the comparison.
3. Eliminate any answer choices that compare two items that are not similar. Look out for possessives because a seemingly inconsistent comparison can often be corrected by using possessives.
4. Eliminate any answer choices that create an unclear comparison.
5. Choose the best answer from the remaining choices.

BLUE WRITING LESSON 16: LOGICAL COMPARISON
Learning to Swim

CONCEPT EXERCISE:

Directions: Correct the errors in the following sentences. Some sentences may not have errors.

1. In the years before the Civil War, Northerners were far more likely to have careers in business, medicine, or education.

2. Most Southerners worked in agriculture, largely because the South enjoyed more fertile soil and a warmer climate than Northern farmers.

3. As a result, the South had many more large-scale farms than the smaller, subsistence farms of the North.

4. These large-scale farms were made possible by the widespread use of slave labor, though slave ownership in the South was not as common as many believe it to be.

5. In fact, slavery was in practice as far north as New Jersey until the Civil War, though Northerners owned far fewer slaves.

6. In the North, slaves were replaced by immigrants who were willing to work for far less pay than any workers.

7. The South had more talented military men than the Northern army did.

8. In fact, Confederate General Robert E. Lee was widely considered to be more gifted than any military strategist.

9. The North, having manufactured 97% of the country's firearms in 1860, had far greater firepower.

10. The South's agrarian economy allowed Southerners easier access to food than Northern farmers.

11. Because most battles were fought in the South, Confederate soldiers knew the land far better than the Union army.

12. At the same time, Southern civilians were at greater risk because the battles were so near to home.

13. During the Civil War, the North won more battles, which eventually led to the South's surrender.

14. Confederate General Robert E. Lee's military experience was far greater than the Union generals.

15. The Union was better equipped than Confederate soldiers.

16. The military and political objectives of the Union were much more difficult to accomplish.

17. If Virginia had chosen not to secede, the North may have won the war sooner because Robert E. Lee would have become a Union general.

18. When Abraham Lincoln issued the Emancipation Proclamation, the Union cause became much stronger than it had been early in the war.

19. The South's recovery from the Civil War took many decades longer than the North.

20. In fact, the early years of the Reconstruction Era, the period following the Civil War, were just as difficult for Southern civilians.

BLUE WRITING LESSON 16: LOGICAL COMPARISON
Diving into the Deep End

PRACTICE EXERCISE:

Directions: Answer the questions that accompany the following passage.

The Dangers of Lead

Lead is a naturally occurring toxic metal. Low blood levels of lead have been linked to low IQ, decreased academic achievement, and increased emotional and behavioral problems as well as delayed physical development in adolescents. Children are often exposed to lead because of human activities, including burning fossil fuels, mining, and manufacturing. In the United States, lead exposure comes more from lead-containing products, such as paint and caulking in older homes, **(1)** than pollution. Chinese children, **(2)** unlike America, suffer from lead exposure more often related to air pollution.

Many studies have examined the health effects of lead on IQ and physical development. Until recently, the U.S. Centers for Disease Control and Prevention (CDC) identified 10 micrograms per deciliter (μg/dL) of blood in children as a "level of concern." **(3)** However, after more comprehensive studies, CDC now advises that children with only 5 μg/dL of lead in their blood be considered at risk and that actions such as reducing sources of lead in the environment should be taken.

The effects of low blood lead levels, particularly on childhood behavior and emotional problems, aren't **(4)** as well understood as other toxins. A research team at the University of Pennsylvania and collaborators in China explored these associations.

1. A) NO CHANGE
   B) than in the environment
   C) than from pollution
   D) and from pollution

2. A) NO CHANGE
   B) unlike American children
   C) like America
   D) unlike American air

3. A) NO CHANGE
   B) Although, after more
   C) However, after the most
   D) Contrary to its more

4. A) NO CHANGE
   B) well understood like other toxins
   C) as well understood as others
   D) as well understood as those of other toxins

The scientists used data collected from more than 1,300 preschool age children in the Jiangsu province in China. A blood sample was taken from each child for lead testing between the ages of 3 and 5 years. Behavioral problems were assessed at age 6, during the last month of preschool, by both parents and teachers. The results of the assessments were compared to **(5)** the samples.

The average blood lead level in the children was 6.4 µg/dL. The researchers found **(6)** higher average blood lead levels in boys than blood levels in girls. The higher the blood lead levels, the **(7)** more emotional, anxiety, and behavioral problems the children exhibited. Even a small increase in blood lead concentrations of 1 µg/dL was associated with significant increases in teacher-reported emotional and anxiety problems. Girls exhibited more internalizing problems such as anxiety and depression. **(8)** Compared to these problems, boys were **(9)** the most likely to have externalizing problems, such as attention and conduct issues.

"This research focused on lower blood lead levels **(10)** than most other studies and adds more evidence that there is no safe lead level," says Dr. Kimberly Gray of the National Institute of Environmental Health Sciences.

The researchers suggest that continued monitoring of blood lead concentrations during regular pediatric visits may be more important **(11)** than previous years.

5. A) NO CHANGE
   B) the children's blood.
   C) the samples from the children.
   D) the results of lead tests on the blood.

6. A) NO CHANGE
   B) higher average blood lead levels in boys than in girls.
   C) the highest average blood lead levels in girls.
   D) the higher average blood lead levels in boys than girls.

7. A) NO CHANGE
   B) higher the children's problems in emotion, anxiety, and behavior.
   C) most emotional, anxiety, and behavioral problems the children showed.
   D) more emotional issues and anxiety were exhibited by the levels.

8. A) NO CHANGE
   B) Compared to those,
   C) In contrast to these problems,
   D) Compared to the girls,

9. A) NO CHANGE
   B) more likely
   C) likeliest
   D) more likelier

10. A) NO CHANGE
    B) than more studies
    C) than studies of other blood levels
    D) than the levels of most studies

11. A) NO CHANGE
    B) than monitoring previous visits.
    C) than monitoring has been in previous years.
    D) than tests run in previous years.

TEST EXERCISE:

Directions: Answer the questions that accompany the following passage.

The Advantage of Specialized Schools

It's a given: parents will fight to get their children into the best schools because they want their kids to have good careers. Starting children out at highly-ranked schools gives them plenty of opportunities to capitalize on: the best teachers, excellent student-teacher ratios, and classmates **(1)** that are as achievement driven as their own. What may surprise you, however, is how early this process starts. **(2)** In addition, in New York, many parents are doing their best to make sure that their children get into highly prestigious preschools—which means helping **(3)** your three-year-old toddlers practice for admissions tests.

Parents' desire for their kids to go to the best schools is **(4)** nothing new; as most people believe, getting into a good primary and secondary school paves the way to admission into a prestigious college and fine careers thereafter. What is new is that parents are starting almost fourteen years early to secure their children's success. New York has its share of excellent secondary schools, such as Stuyvesant High School, Brooklyn Latin School, and the Bronx School of Science, that have admissions rates to **(5)** college that are much higher than other schools. However, getting into these schools is not as easy as being in the right school district; each of these schools requires standardized test scores from the SHSAT, the Specialized High Schools Admissions Test.

1. A) NO CHANGE
   B) that are as achievement-driven as other classmates
   C) who are as achievement-driven as they are
   D) who are as achievement-driven as their parents'

2. A) NO CHANGE
   B) Indeed,
   C) However,
   D) Meanwhile,

3. A) NO CHANGE
   B) one's
   C) their
   D) yours

4. A) NO CHANGE
   B) nothing new, most people believe
   C) nothing new, as most people believe,
   D) nothing new; so as most people believe

5. A) NO CHANGE
   B) college that are much higher than that of other schools
   C) college that are much higher than those of other schools
   D) college that are much higher than other colleges

For those who are willing to spend the money, New York also boasts a selection of **(6)** <u>some of the finest private schools</u> in the country. The price tag can be high—Horace Mann, an elite prep school in the Bronx, has a tuition of just over $40,000 per semester, even at the kindergarten and pre-K levels. Students at these schools have a higher admission rate to tech schools such as CalTech and MIT **(7)** <u>than other states in the country.</u>

But **(8)** <u>admission to any of these schools requires</u> readiness—and starting early is the new trend in vogue. Three-year-olds take achievement tests and participate in observed play groups in order to test their potential as students. There is, one might say, one side benefit—your children may be enrolled **(9)** <u>with those of the New York financial elite</u>—and several parents have admitted this factor also plays a role in their attempts to win their students a place at the table. Mostly, though, New York parents desire the best for their children's abilities to get high-paying careers, even when said children have yet to learn to read, write, or add.

[1] Statistics compiled by the New York State Education Department **(10)** <u>imply students aren't working hard enough:</u> only 38.4% of students who have graduated in 2013 from New York public schools were considered "ready for a college or career." [2] Meanwhile, attendees at New York's elite schools entered top colleges at a rate of 21%. [3] The choice for many parents is clear. [4] Faced with these statistics, anxious parents will take the path that leads to the best possible education and career for their children. **{11}**

6. A) NO CHANGE
   B) some of the best of the finest private schools
   C) a smorgasbord of the finest private schools
   D) the finest private schools

7. A) NO CHANGE
   B) than schools in other states in the country
   C) than do students in other schools around the country
   D) than other states' students around the country

8. A) NO CHANGE.
   B) admission to any of these schools require
   C) admissions to any of these schools requires
   D) admission to any of these schools required

9. A) NO CHANGE
   B) with the New York financial elite
   C) with the children of those of the New York financial elite
   D) with the schools of the New York financial elite

10. Which of the following choices is most appropriate in the context of the passage?

    A) NO CHANGE
    B) show encouraging signs
    C) show a grim prognosis
    D) are cause for celebration

11. Which of the following sentences should be eliminated in order to improve the focus of the paragraph?

    A) Sentence 1
    B) Sentence 2
    C) Sentence 3
    D) Sentence 4

BLUE WRITING LESSON 16: LOGICAL COMPARISON
Race to the Finish

HOMEWORK EXERCISE 1:

Directions: Find and correct errors in the following sentences. Some sentences will not have any errors.

1. Derek Jeter is more talented than any player in the league.

2. Laura was awarded the solo for our recital because she sings louder than anyone in the choir.

3. My iPhone has more issues than any of my electronic devices.

4. Sara's grades were just as good as her brother.

5. In informal writing, the use of contractions is more acceptable than formal writing.

6. The novels of Mary Brunton are not nearly as well-known as Jane Austen, though the two authors were contemporaries.

7. Bicycling in Portland, unlike many other cities, is made safe by the prevalence of dedicating cycling lanes.

8. I like homemade meals better than any restaurant.

9. The platypus is stranger than any animal I've ever seen.

10. The interest and fees offered by the loan company are higher than the bank.

11. Simba, the zoo's oldest lion, is friendlier than any other animal at the zoo.

12. I think that apple trees have prettier blossoms than oranges.

13. Thanks to a recent referendum, firemen's salaries are now almost twice as high as policemen.

14. Mariah thinks more of you than Hannah.

15. The winters in the north tend to be far more severe than the south.

16. The prices at that new boutique are much higher than the outlet mall.

17. People in the U.S. do not follow soccer as obsessively as other countries.

18. The English grammar rules are far more confusing than many other languages.

19. During the holidays, our house is lit brighter than any house on the block.

20. Most students like Miss Hanover's class better than Mr. Gregory's, even though she assigns more homework.

HOMEWORK EXERCISE 2:

Directions: Answer the questions that accompany the passage.

Amazons: Myth or History?

(1) <u>Are the Amazons fact or fiction?</u> One school of thought insisted that the real Amazons were probably beardless Mongoloids, mistaken for women by the Greeks. Another insisted that they were a propaganda tool used by (2) <u>them</u> during times of political stress. The Freudians believed that the Amazonian myths held the key to the innermost neuroses of the Athenian male. None of the theories adequately explained the origins of the Amazons. If these warrior women were merely a figment of Greek imagination, there still remained the question of what (3) <u>inspires</u> such an elaborate fiction.

1. Which of the following choices best introduces the passage?

   A) NO CHANGE
   B) Historians have long debated whether the Amazons, a nation of all-female warriors referenced in Greek mythology, are fact or fiction.
   C) Sometimes history can be rooted in myths, as in the case of the Amazons, a group of all-female warriors featured in Greek mythology.
   D) Historians have always wondered whether some Greek myths, like the Amazons, might be real.

2. A) NO CHANGE
   B) politicians
   C) warriors
   D) the Greeks

3. A) NO CHANGE
   B) was inspiring
   C) had inspired
   D) inspired

{4} In Homer's poems, Amazonian women were considered worthy opponents of Homer's male heroes. Future generations of poets gave the Amazons a role in the fall of Troy, the foundation of Athens, and the story of Hercules. By the mid-sixth century B.C., the foundation of Athens and the defeat of the Amazons had become **(5)** <u>inextricably</u> linked.

[1] The more important the Amazons became to the Athenian national identity, the more the Greeks searched for evidence of their vanquished foe. [2] The fifth century B.C. historian Herodotus located the Amazonian capital in what is now northern Turkey. [3] Herodotus is commonly considered to be the father of history. [4] According to Herodotus, the Amazons divided their time between pillaging as far as Persia and founding towns closer to **(6)** <u>home. An</u> encounter with the Greeks at the Battle of Thermodon ended this existence. [5] Three shiploads of captured Amazons ran aground near Scythia, and the two groups eventually intermarried. [6] Their descendants became nomads who eventually founded a new race called the Sauromatians.

[7] Herodotus writes that the Sauromatian women continued to observe Amazonian customs, hunting on horseback and taking part in battles. {7}

4. Which of the following most effectively establishes the main idea of the paragraph?

   A) The first recorded references to the Amazons were in Greek poems.
   B) References to the Amazons in Greek poetry established the Amazons as part of Greek history.
   C) Because the first records of the Amazons are found in Greek poetry, many believe that the Amazons are merely a myth.
   D) The Amazons were the only women considered worthy of inclusion in Ancient Greek poetry.

5. A) NO CHANGE
   B) inexorably
   C) inexplicably
   D) indistinguishably

6. Which of the following would most effectively combine these sentences?

   A) home, until an
   B) home, and an
   C) home, finally an
   D) home; an

7. Which sentence should be eliminated in order to improve the focus of the paragraph?

   A) Sentence 2
   B) Sentence 3
   C) Sentence 5
   D) Sentence 7

Until the early 1990s, the writings of Herodotus were the only evidence of the Amazons' existence. Then, while excavating 2,000-year-old burial mounds near Kazakhstan, a team of archaeologists discovered over 150 graves belonging to the Sauromatians and their descendants, the Sarmatians. Among the burials of "ordinary women," the researchers uncovered evidence of warrior women who had been buried with their weapons. The presence of wounds and daggers was amazing in and of **(8)** <u>itself; but</u> the most unique find was that the warrior females measured 5 feet 6 inches, making them preternaturally tall for their time.

(9) <u>In conclusion,</u> after years of mystery, here was hard evidence of the women warriors that could have inspired the Amazon myths. **(10)** <u>Things that were found later</u> have confirmed that this was no anomaly. **(11)** <u>Though clearly not a matriarchal society, the ancient nomadic peoples of the region that valued strong women lived within a flexible social order.</u> Here were true Amazons.

8. A) NO CHANGE
   B) itself—but
   C) itself, but
   D) itself. But

9. A) NO CHANGE
   B) Certainly
   C) Ultimately
   D) Finally

10. A) NO CHANGE
    B) Subsequent finds
    C) Future discoveries
    D) Discoveries made after the find near Kazakhstan

11. A) NO CHANGE
    B) Though clearly not a matriarchal society that valued strong women, the ancient nomadic peoples of the region lived within a flexible social order.
    C) Though clearly not a matriarchal society, the ancient nomadic peoples that valued strong women of the region lived within a flexible social order.
    D) Though clearly not a matriarchal society, the ancient nomadic peoples of the region lived within a flexible social order that valued strong women.

BLUE WRITING LESSON 17: INTRODUCTIONS, CONCLUSIONS, AND TRANSITIONS
Getting Your Feet Wet

Directions: The following is intended as a diagnostic exam. Answer the questions that accompany this passage.

{**1**} Not only do the world's bees produce products like honey and beeswax, but they also pollinate well over one-third of the agricultural products humans consume. In addition, bees ensure the biodiversity of ecosystems across the globe by helping to pollinate more than 80% of the world's plant species.

{**2**} The USDA estimates that the United States is home to just 2.5 million honeybee colonies today, down from 6 million in 1947. Other countries have seen similar declines, with European bee keepers reporting that up to 40% of their hives are collapsing each winter. If these declines continue unabated, many of the world's species — including humans — will feel the effects.

With so much at stake, efforts to investigate reasons for this global pandemic have been robust. A new government study blames a combination of factors for the mysterious and dramatic loss of bees, including climate change, increased pesticide use, shrinking habitats, multiple viruses, and even cell phone towers. **(3)** <u>As a result</u>, according to a recent EPA-USDA study, the biggest cause is a parasite called the Varroa destructor, a type of mite found to be highly resistant to insecticides.

Humans have inadvertently helped this parasite in its war against bees. In 1987, when the Varroa mite was first discovered in the U.S., large chemical companies such as Monstanto and Dow began selling genetically modified insecticides to remedy the parasitic invasion. These chemicals also weakened the bees' natural genetic defenses to fight off the parasite. Thus the cure has been worse than the disease.

Such insecticides are hardly the only chemicals that are harming bees. A separate USDA study found 35 pesticides and fungicides, some at lethal doses, in the pollen collected from bees that were used to pollinate food crops in five U.S. states. Further research has confirmed that bees that contact pollen contaminated with such chemicals are up to three times more likely to be infected by parasites associated with Colony Collapse Disorder, a term used to describe the death of entire colonies of bees. {**4**}

1. Which of the following, if inserted at the beginning of the first paragraph, would provide the best introduction to the passage?

   A) Since bee populations are declining drastically, it is important that we find a way to replace them before they become extinct.
   B) Use of chemicals is contributing to a severe decline in bee populations.
   C) Anyone who has ever been stung by a bee might rejoice to hear that the world's bee population is experiencing a severe decline, but a world without bees would be an incredibly difficult place to inhabit.
   D) Humans are killing bees at unprecedented rates, and this must stop.

2. If inserted at the beginning of this paragraph, which of the following sentences would provide the best transition from the first to the second paragraph?

   A) Despite the importance of bees, their populations have been in severe decline for decades.
   B) Because of the amount of work bees must do, their populations are in decline.
   C) Since the world's biodiversity has long been in decline, bees are less necessary, and their populations are shrinking.
   D) Although bees are important, man-made chemicals are killing them off.

3. A) NO CHANGE
   B) In comparison
   C) Accordingly
   D) However

4. Which of the following, if added to the end of the passage, would provide the best conclusion?

   A) If people don't stop killing bees, there won't be any bees left to pollinate crops, which could lead to widespread starvation as a result of food shortages.
   B) Though chemicals are certainly not the sole cause of the dramatic decline in global bee populations, they are clearly a primary contributor to the problem and should be better regulated in order to ensure the continued survival of the world's bees.
   C) This is yet another example of how the widespread use of agricultural chemicals is harming our environment; other examples include the contamination of groundwater and the evolution of spray-resistant weeds, bugs, and diseases.
   D) If we cannot find and address all of the causes of Colony Collapse Disorder, including chemical use, then it may not be possible to save the bees, which could have drastic consequences for all creatures on Earth.

BLUE WRITING LESSON 17: INTRODUCTIONS, CONCLUSIONS, AND TRANSITIONS
Wading In

TOPIC OVERVIEW: INTRODUCTIONS, CONCLUSIONS, AND TRANSITIONS

These questions represent another type of organization question. As we discussed in Lesson 8, the SAT will test your ability to improve the logic of a passage. In Lesson 8, we discussed questions that ask you to move or delete sentences or paragraphs to improve a passage's logic; the questions we'll discuss in this lesson are somewhat similar, but they typically ask you to change or add sentences or transitions to improve the logic of the passage.

TOPIC OVERVIEW: INTRODUCTIONS

A good introductory sentence will introduce the information contained in the first paragraph (and possibly in the passage as a whole) without giving away everything in the passage.

RECOGNIZING INTRODUCTION QUESTIONS

Introduction questions will ask you to either add a sentence to the beginning of the passage or to change an existing sentence in the beginning of the passage. Look for the words "introduction" or "introduce" to help you identify these questions.

ANSWERING INTRODUCTION QUESTIONS

Once you've identified the question as an introduction question, follow these steps to find the correct answer:

1. Consider the tone and style of the passage as a whole. Eliminate any answer choices that do not fit with the tone or style of the passage.
2. Eliminate any answer choices that refer to information that is not at all related to the main ideas of the passage as a whole.
3. Carefully read the first paragraph. Eliminate any answer choices that are not at all related to the information in the first paragraph.
4. Examine the remaining answer choices. Choose the choice that is most closely related to the information in the first paragraph and that provides the most natural introduction to the passage.

TOPIC OVERVIEW: CONCLUSIONS

A good conclusion will summarize the main ideas of the passage as a whole. Depending on the content of the passage, a good conclusion might also clearly state the author's main claim.

RECOGNIZING CONCLUSION QUESTIONS

Conclusion questions will ask you to either add or change a sentence at the end of the passage in order to create a strong conclusion for the passage. Look for the words "conclusion" or "conclude" in the question.

ANSWERING CONCLUSION QUESTIONS

Once you've identified the question as a conclusion question, follow these steps to arrive at the correct answer:

1. As with introduction questions, eliminate any choices that do not suit the overall tone and style of the passage.
2. Consider the main claim, purpose, or idea of the passage. Eliminate any answer choices that do not relate to or agree with the main claim of the passage.
3. Eliminate any answer choices that make claims that cannot be supported by information in the passage.
4. Examine the remaining answer choices. Choose the one that best summarizes the main ideas of the passage or that makes a claim that is most clearly supported by the information and tone of the passage.

TOPIC OVERVIEW: TRANSITIONS

Transition questions will test your ability to utilize transitional strategies in order to improve the smooth progression of ideas within a passage. Though many transition questions will focus on the transitional words and phrases that you are most familiar with, others will ask you to select the best transition sentence to connect two paragraphs.

RECOGNIZING TRANSITION QUESTIONS

Transition questions appear in two forms:

The first form is similar to that of many grammar or convention questions on the SAT; these questions will have a transitional word or phrase underlined within the passage and will ask you to select the best transition for that part of the sentence. Such questions will typically require that you provide the best transition between two sentences rather than between two paragraphs.

The second form asks you to select the best sentence to provide a smooth transition from one paragraph to another. Sometimes, the question will refer to a place in the passage where a transitional sentence does not yet exist; other times, the question may refer to an underlined transitional sentence and will ask you to either change that sentence or replace it with a different sentence. These questions will often include the word "transition," but you should also look for related words and phrases, such as "flow" or "progression of ideas."

ANSWERING TRANSITION QUESTIONS

Below is a table containing some of the common transitions and their functions:

FUNCTION	EXAMPLES
Similarity	also, in the same way, just as…so too, likewise, similarly
Contrast	but, however, in spite of, on the one hand…on the other hand, nevertheless, nonetheless, notwithstanding, in contrast, on the contrary, still, yet
Sequence	first, second, third, next, then, finally, after, afterward, at last, before, currently, during, earlier, immediately, later, meanwhile, now, recently, simultaneously, subsequently
Example	for example, for instance, namely, specifically, to illustrate
Emphasis	even, indeed, in fact, of course, truly
Position	above, adjacent, below, beyond, here, in front, in back
Cause/Effect	accordingly, consequently, hence, so, therefore, thus
Support or Evidence	additionally, again, also, and, as well, besides, equally important, further, furthermore, in addition, moreover
Conclusion	finally, in a word, in brief, in conclusion, in the end, in the final analysis, on the whole, thus, to summarize, in summary

For questions that ask you to choose the best transitional word or phrase for an underlined portion of a sentence, follow these steps to find the correct answer

1. Carefully read the sentence containing the transition and the sentences immediately before and after that sentence. Determine which two sentences are being connected by the transition.
2. Once you've identified the two sentences being connected, consider the relationship between the two sentences. Eliminate any answer choices that don't reflect that relationship. For example, if the two sentences are in agreement with each other, you would eliminate transitions that suggest contradiction, such as "on the other hand" or "however."
3. Examine the remaining answer choices. Select the transition or transitional phrase that best reflects the relationship between the two sentences.

For questions that ask you to select the best sentence to transition between two paragraphs, follow these steps to find the correct answer:

1. Consider the style and tone of the passage as a whole. Eliminate any answer choices that do not suit the style or tone of the passage.
2. Identify the main ideas of each of the paragraphs being connected. Eliminate any answer choices that either disagree with those ideas or are completely unrelated to those ideas.
3. Look at the remaining answer choices. Eliminate any choices that reference information found in paragraphs other than the two paragraphs being connected.
4. Examine the remaining answer choices. Select the option that most logically and clearly connects the information in the two paragraphs.

BLUE WRITING LESSON 17: INTRODUCTIONS, CONCLUSIONS, AND TRANSITIONS
Learning to Swim

CONCEPT EXERCISE:

Directions: Answer the questions that accompany the following passage.

Crazy Ants

{1} Outside the office, Rasberry saw a few hundred ants traveling in erratic swirls. Not thinking anything of the ant colony, he sprayed them and moved on. The following summer, he was called back to the same spot. Now there were millions of them. The ants quickly sprouted in surrounding areas, transported in landscaping and soil, building materials, or on cars. Rasberry called state and federal agencies in an attempt to raise the alarm, but the government did little.

1. Which of the following provides the best introduction to the passage?

    A) The aptly named crazy ant was discovered in Pasadena, Texas, in 2002 by a man named Tom Rasberry.
    B) Tom Rasberry first spotted the crazy ants while on an exterminating job at a chemical plant in Pasadena, Texas, in 2002.
    C) Crazy ants, which are aptly named because of their erratic movements, were first spotted in 2002 by Tom Rasberry, a Texas exterminator.
    D) In Texas in 2002, Tom Rasberry saw an ant colony exhibiting erratic behavior, so he started calling them "crazy ants."

{2} In 2003, he collected samples of the ant at the Pasadena chemical plant and sent them off to a lab at Texas A&M to be identified. **(3)** <u>Finally</u>, scientists at Texas A&M and elsewhere debated the classification and origin of the ants, but it was not until 2012 that the ants were finally identified as Nylanderia fulva, a species native to Brazil. **(4)** <u>Meanwhile</u>, as the academics and bureaucrats hemmed and hawed over the problem, the crazy ants spread through Texas, Louisiana, Mississippi, Florida, and Georgia. **(5)** <u>These ants are called crazy ants because of their erratic, seemingly psychotic behavior.</u>

Entomologists report that crazy ants, like other ants, seem drawn to electronic devices, but unlike other ants, so many will stream inside a device that they form a single, squirming mass that completes a circuit and shorts the device. Crazy ants decimate native insects, overtaking beehives and destroying whole colonies. **(6)** <u>In particular</u>, they may also smother baby birds and have even been known to obstruct the nasal cavities of chickens and asphyxiate the birds.

2. Which of the following, if added here, would provide the best transition from the first paragraph to the second paragraph?

A) Rasberry was discouraged by the government inaction, but knew there was nothing he could do about it.
B) Rasberry was very concerned about the rate at which these ants had spread, so he wanted to learn more.
C) Rasberry was frustrated by the governmental lack of concern about these potentially dangerous insects.
D) In the absence of official action, Rasberry decided to learn more about this mysterious new insect.

3. A) NO CHANGE
   B) For months
   C) In the meantime
   D) For years

4. A) NO CHANGE
   B) Furthermore
   C) Regardless
   D) In fact

5. Which of the following changes to the underlined sentence would create the best transition between the second and third paragraphs?

A) Delete the sentence because it is not necessary to create a smooth transition.
B) Move the sentence to the beginning of the third paragraph.
C) Replace the sentence with a sentence that explains how the ants spread to other states.
D) Move the sentence to the end of the third paragraph.

6. A) NO CHANGE
   B) In contrast
   C) In addition
   D) For example

{7} <u>Some experts worry that it may already be too late to stop the crazy ants.</u> They have spread so far, so fast that the opportunity to stop the infestation while it was still localized has passed. Rasberry is convinced that the next wave of crazy ant damage will be ecological: they will decimate ground-dwelling bird species just as fire ants devastated Texas' quail.

{8} Entomologists speculate that crazy ants may eventually run into predators along the Gulf Coast. If that happens, their populations may be reduced to a more manageable size, allowing extermination measures to have greater effect, but the damage done before that happens could be enormous. **(9)** <u>Comparatively,</u> it may be that this is as dystopian as the ant situation gets, and Nature will solve the problem on her own. {10}

7. Which sentence provides the best transition between the third and fourth paragraphs?

A) NO CHANGE
B) This sort of behavior is potentially devastating for ecosystems.
C) Many experts believe that the spread of crazy ants can still be halted.
D) Crazy ants may never be stopped.

8. Which of the following, if added here, would provide the best transition between the fourth and fifth paragraphs?

A) Others believe Rasberry lacks the expertise to make accurate predictions on this matter.
B) Most people believe Rasberry's predictions are wrong.
C) Others are more optimistic.
D) Crazy ants will likely continue to spread.

9. A) NO CHANGE
B) On the other hand,
C) Otherwise
D) For this reason,

10. Which of the following provides the best conclusion to the passage?

A) We understand so little about these crazy ants that no one truly knows what's possible or where they'll go next.
B) Who knows what will happen?
C) The only thing we know for certain is that if the government had acted when Tom Rasberry first raised the alarm, none of this would have happened.
D) Crazy ants may well destroy entire ecosystems before Tom Rasberry gets the government to take action.

BLUE WRITING LESSON 17: INTRODUCTIONS, CONCLUSIONS, AND TRANSITIONS
Diving into the Deep End

PRACTICE EXERCISE:

Directions: Answer the questions that accompany the following passage.

The Golden Age for Hiring?

{1} It may be harder after 50, but there is hope and opportunity. The key to getting and succeeding at interviews was proving that, regardless of age, I had mastered the four R's — Relevance, Resiliency, Responsibility and business 'Rithmetic.

(2) The first of these is "Responsibility," and it is approached in a new and different manner by people who do the interviewing today. Behavioral interviewing is more the norm than years ago with hiring managers asking situational questions and looking for the potential employee's response in handling supervisors, difficult co-workers, and (3) direct orders. In one interview, I was asked how I'd handle a difficult client—a question that I didn't nail and I was not invited back for the second round of interviewing.

1. Which of the following, if inserted here, would best introduce the passage?

A) I cringe whenever I hear pundits tell audiences that unemployment after age 50 is a career death sentence.
B) Getting a job when you're older can be a real challenge.
C) I never found anything to be as difficult as getting a job.
D) After 50, the prospects for getting a job fall right off the cliff.

2. Which of the following sentences would provide the most effective transition between the first and second paragraphs?

A) NO CHANGE
B) Of the four of these, "Responsibility" is approached by new interviewers in a different manner.
C) "Responsibility" is approached in a new manner by today's interviewers.
D) The interviewers of today approach the first of these in a different manner.

3. Which of the following provides the best transition between the sentences?

A) NO CHANGE
B) direct orders, therefore in one interview.
C) direct orders, leading to an interview where
D) direct orders.

(4) <u>Secondly, "Resilience" also comes up</u> a lot in the behavioral interviewing process with recruiters frequently asking how you handled a failure. In one screening I was asked to describe a nightmare marketing situation. I answered by saying, "I can tell you how I dealt with projects that did not meet expectations at key milestones."

(5) <u>My answer, although lengthy, demonstrated good project management</u>, planning, and communication skills as well as the need to manage expectations both with employees and senior management. **(6)** <u>In that situation, I passed</u> the screening and became the top candidate for the open post, until I was asked the next question in the final round with the CEO. **(7)** <u>As I walked down the hallway, I felt the pressure building.</u>

[1] The CEO wanted to know why he should hire me over every other candidate. [2] The question was repeated in almost every subsequent interview. [3] Sometimes the question was phrased, "Why are you right for this position over others?" {8} [4] Then, I realized the question was simply: "What makes you special?"

4. A) NO CHANGE
    B) Another one of the 4 R's is "Resilience." It also comes up
    C) "Resilience," which also comes up
    D) "Resilience" also comes up

5. Which of the following provides the best transition between the two paragraphs?

    A) NO CHANGE
    B) My answer demonstrated good project management
    C) It seemed to me that my answer demonstrated good project management
    D) I clearly demonstrated good project management

6. A) NO CHANGE
    B) Therefore, I aced
    C) By showing the interviewers those skills, I flew through
    D) Luckily, I passed

7. Which choice below provides the best transition from this paragraph to the next?

    A) NO CHANGE
    B) Rewrite the sentence to read "I felt the pressure building as I walked down the hallway."
    C) Move this sentence to the beginning of the next paragraph.
    D) Remove the sentence.

8. Which sentence, if inserted here, would best connect sentences 3 and 4?

    A) The question was confusing, and I didn't know what it had to do with me.
    B) I was never fully sure how I should go about answering this question.
    C) I could not understand why the CEO couldn't know the answer by this point.
    D) When first asked this question, I was uncomfortable answering.

"Relevant" is the hardest arena for older workers. {9} I countered this with a strong digital profile on LinkedIn, a broad digital presence on Twitter and other social networks, and a deep digital footprint with a dynamic web site, digital portfolio, and involvement with new digital endeavors.

{10} In addition, I volunteered for the digital committee of a well-known marketing organization, got recertified in digital marketing, took online classes, and led various digital marketing groups.

{11} The difference in getting the offer became 'Rithmetic, or my ability to apply metrics to prove progress in project management. Because I had these skills and the other candidate didn't, I found myself with a new job. It turned out that my age was a factor in only one of the jobs I applied for. For someone past fifty, this really is the Golden Age for hiring.

9. Which of the following sentence would provide the best transition between the two sentences?

A) It becomes more difficult to show relevance as you get older.
B) People don't understand how old skills translate to new jobs.
C) Many hiring managers assume that older employees get stuck in old ways of thinking and working.
D) Older workers struggle when placed next to younger professionals.

10. Which sentence, if inserted here, would best begin the paragraph?

A) I took it upon myself to prove those hiring managers wrong.
B) There were ways for me to prove my digital competence.
C) Hiring managers began to recognize the effort I put into my digital portfolio.
D) I invested time, energy, and dollars into proving that I was still technologically relevant.

11. Which of the following, if inserted, best serves to introduce the final paragraph?

A) This made my resume and experience stand out over others'.
B) All of that got me to the final round between me and the other candidate.
C) This left it all up to the final R.
D) My digital skills made me a shoo-in for the executive-level position.

TEST EXERCISE:

Directions: Answer the questions that accompany the following passage.

How Amateur Thieves Stole New York's Most Precious Gems

On the night of October 29, 1964, two men crept onto the grounds of New York City's American Museum of Natural History while a lookout drove around the block. Clinging to a rope above a 4th floor window, one of them swung to a partially open window and **(1)** had used his feet to lower the sash. They had breached the J.P. Morgan Hall of Gems and Minerals, **(2)** which has since been partitioned into staff offices.

Allan Dale Kuhn and Jack Roland Murphy **(3)** (better known as Murf the Surf) used a glasscutter and duct tape to gain access to three display cases. **(4)** Their haul included the milky-blue Star of India, the DeLong Star Ruby, and the Midnight Star. Fearing they'd tripped a silent alarm, the pair retraced their steps and caught separate getaway cabs.

1. A) NO CHANGE
   B) was using
   C) used
   D) using

2. A) NO CHANGE
   B) home to some of the world's most precious stones.
   C) which is now known as the Morgan Hall of Gems.
   D) a popular museum attraction.

3. A) NO CHANGE
   B) , better known as Murf the Surf,
   C) — better known as Murf the Surf —
   D) better known as Murf the Surf

4. A) NO CHANGE
   B) Their haul included several priceless and irreplaceable gems.
   C) Their haul, which included the Star of India, the DeLong Star Ruby, and the Midnight Star, would be very difficult to trace.
   D) Their haul included the milky-blue Star of India, the world's largest sapphire; the DeLong Star Ruby, the world's most flawless ruby; and the Midnight Star, the world's largest black sapphire.

{5} In a press conference the day the heist was discovered, the director of the museum **(6)** <u>confided</u> that security was "not good." Batteries in the display-case burglar alarm had been dead for months. The tops of all of the gem hall's 19 windows were left open two inches overnight for ventilation, and none had burglar alarms. After years without a single burglary, even the precaution of locking a security guard into the gem room at night had lapsed.

5. Which choice, if added to the beginning of the paragraph, provides the most effective transition?

A) Such precautions proved unnecessary since the museum's security was sadly neglected.
B) Museum workers discovered the theft the following day.
C) Clearly the museum lacked security.
D) The great jewelry theft made headlines the next day.

6. A) NO CHANGE
   B) conceded
   C) acquiesced
   D) commented

{7} A police detective heard from an informant who had attended a party thrown by Kuhn, Murphy, and their lookout, Roger Clark. The trio had thrown the party in a pricey hotel suite and **(8)** were spending money with **(9)** abandon. They were displaying their newfound wealth rather than keeping a low profile. After obtaining a warrant, detectives searched the hotel suite. They were interrupted by the arrival of Roger Clark, who promptly caved and revealed that Murphy and Kuhn had flown to Florida.

The authorities apprehended Murphy and Kuhn, but were not able to hold them for long because the judge felt that the case against them was weak. Finally, in January of 1965, the pair was arrested for a Miami burglary. Authorities faced a **(10)** dilemma: The suspects were under lock and key, but their help was necessary in order to recover the missing jewels. With Kuhn's help, 10 of the 24 most valuable gems were recovered. The rest were never found. Kuhn, Murphy, and Clark were each sentenced to three years at Rikers Island.

Today, the Star of India, the DeLong Star Ruby, and the Midnight Star are on display at the Natural History Museum. The gems that once graced tabloid covers are displayed in a subdued room, and the plaques describing the gems offer no hint of their past **(11)** renown.

7. Which choice most effectively establishes the main topic of the paragraph?

   A) Through thorough and careful police work, the authorities soon caught up to the would-be thieves.
   B) Two of the three thieves quickly left town in order to find a safe way of selling the stolen jewels.
   C) Everything seemed to be going according to plan for the would-be thieves, but they were amateurs and lacked discretion.
   D) The would-be gem thieves might have gotten away with their crime.

8. A) NO CHANGE
   B) was spending
   C) spending
   D) have been spending

9. Which choice most effectively combines the sentences at the underlined point?

   A) abandon; they were displaying
   B) abandon, and they were displaying
   C) abandon, which meant that they were displaying
   D) abandon, displaying

10. A) NO CHANGE
    B) dilemma, which was that the
    C) dilemma — the
    D) dilemma. The

11. A) NO CHANGE
    B) fame
    C) notoriety
    D) reputation

BLUE WRITING LESSON 17: INTRODUCTIONS, CONCLUSIONS, AND TRANSITIONS
Race to the Finish

HOMEWORK EXERCISE 1:

Directions: Answer the questions that accompany the passage.

Comics and Censorship

{1} Educators saw comics as a bad influence on their students' reading abilities and literary tastes.   Church and civic groups protested these books as well, citing "immoral" content that would pervert the minds of innocent children everywhere.   Parents couldn't help but agree — the covers of these comic books often displayed scantily clad women, acts of gruesome violence, or ghastly illustrations of shambling zombies and rotting corpses.

{2} In 1954, the mental health expert Fredric Wertham published a book called *Seduction of the Innocent*, declaring comic books as one of the main sources of juvenile delinquency.   He advocated banning the sale of comic books to minors, saying that the content of these books desensitized young minds to violence.

1. Which of the following provides the best introduction to the passage?

    A) In the 1940s, many people became concerned about America's youth, in part because of the popularity of scandalous comic books.
    B) Although comic books had existed in one form or another since the 1830s, it was not until the 1940s that people began to recognize their negative impacts on young readers.
    C) By the 1940s, many developmental psychologists had expressed concern over the negative impacts that comic books were having on America's youth, and educators, church leaders, and parents agreed.
    D) In the 1940s, American parents, educators, and pastors aimed their sights on an industry they believed was warping the minds of the nation's youth: the burgeoning comic book industry.

2. If added here, which of the following would provide the best transition from the first to the second paragraph?

    A) These concerns gained additional support when experts expressed their agreement with the potential harms of comic books.
    B) Many people chose not to judge comic books until the experts offered their professional opinions.
    C) Unfortunately, these concerns lacked evidence for many years.
    D) Comic books publishers ignored these concerns until experts began to contribute support.

(3) <u>Wertham become famous for his ideas about comic books.</u> Following the book's release, public hearings were held in the Senate, where Wertham took the comics industry to task for its 'pernicious influence.' **(4)** <u>Henceforth,</u> public opinion turned against the comics industry, with many parents and concerned groups actually arranging for public burnings of comic books.

(5) <u>Seeing a huge dip in their sales, major comics publishers such as Marvel, DC, and EC comics decided to take matters into their own hands.</u> They established the Comic Magazine Association of America, which had a strict regulatory code. Many of the prohibitions were reasonable. **(6)** <u>In fact,</u> the rules forbade horrific violence or overt depictions of sexual acts. **(7)** <u>In reality,</u> other regulations were not quite as sensible: comics could no longer use "horror" or "terror" in their titles, nor could they show vampires, werewolves, ghouls, or zombies. One rumored story said that comics with robots were banned, because of the religious beliefs of the head of the CMAA that "only man was granted the ability to think." **(8)** <u>Of course</u> other publishers could publish comics that did not adhere to the code, many stores and retailers refused to sell comics that did not have the official CMAA seal of approval.

3. Which of the following changes to the underlined sentence would create the smoothest transition between the second and third paragraphs?

   A) NO CHANGE
   B) Delete the sentence because the transition is smoother without it.
   C) Replace the sentence with one that reads, "Wertham's book became a bestseller and remained popular for many years."
   D) Replace the sentence with one that reads, "Whether or not Wertham's case had credence, it caught the attention of the nation."

4. A) NO CHANGE
   B) In effect
   C) Before long
   D) With this in mind

5. Which of the following changes to the underlined sentence would create the smoothest transition between the third and fourth paragraphs?

   A) NO CHANGE
   B) Move it to the end of the third paragraph.
   C) Replace it with a sentence that reads, "As a result, major comics publishers such as Marvel, DC, and EC experienced a huge dip in their sales."
   D) Delete the sentence because it does not improve the transition between the paragraphs.

6. A) NO CHANGE
   B) Surprisingly
   C) For example
   D) Such as

7. A) NO CHANGE
   B) However
   C) Otherwise
   D) While

8. A) NO CHANGE
   B) In spite of
   C) Given that
   D) Although

(9) <u>Though</u> initially an industry-led organization, the CMAA soon became a despised entity within the comic publishing world. **(10)** <u>Similarly</u>, Bill Gaines, head publisher of EC Comics and a founder of the CMAA, soon became so disenchanted with the comics industry that he left it altogether. Throughout the national debate over the morality of comic books, Gaines had been depicted by the media as America's most amoral publisher. When EC was effectively driven out of business, Gaines focused his attention on his new project: *Mad* Magazine, which, as a magazine, was exempt from the rulings of the CMAA. Though Gaines enjoyed a long career with *Mad*, it is a shame that the comic industry lost such a talented leader.

{11}

9. A) NO CHANGE
    B) Unlike
    C) Despite
    D) While

10. A) NO CHANGE
    B) In fact
    C) Especially
    D) Markedly

11. Which of the following would provide the best conclusion for the passage?

    A) *Mad* Magazine is still popular today, proving once and for all that comic books were never necessary in the first place.
    B) By the 1980s, the CMAA had largely stopped policing comic book content, which is why modern comic books are filled with violence.
    C) Though the comic industry has long since recovered from its troubled past, it is a shame that critics like Wertham were able to effectively censor comic book publishers, forever altering an entire industry.
    D) It was only a matter of time before other long-standing members of the comic book world left to start magazines as well, which is why the comic book industry was never again as popular as it was in the 1940s.

HOMEWORK EXERCISE 2:

Directions: Answer the questions that accompany the passage.

The Quiet German

On a summer afternoon at the Reichstag, soft Berlin light filters down through the great glass dome, **(1)** <u>passed tourists</u> ascending the spiral ramp, and into the main hall of parliament. At least half of the seats are empty. At the podium, a slightly hunched figure in a magenta jacket and black pants is unabashedly reading a speech straight from a binder. Angela Merkel, the Chancellor of the Federal Republic of **(2)** <u>Germany is the world's most</u> powerful woman. {**3**}

"As the federal government, we have been carrying out a threefold policy since the beginning of the Ukraine **(4)** <u>crisis" Merkel says staring</u> at her speech. Her delivery is purposefully toneless, **(5)** <u>inducing</u> her audience into losing its focus. "Besides the first part of this triad, targeted support for Ukraine, is, second, the unceasing effort to find a diplomatic solution for the crisis in the dialogue with Russia." For the first few years of public office, speaking in front of crowds was visibly painful to Merkel. In particular, her hands were an enormous source of trouble. Eventually, Merkel learned to bring her fingertips together in a diamond shape over her stomach. {**6**}

1. A) NO CHANGE
   B) past tourists
   C) passed tourist's
   D) past tourist's

2. A) NO CHANGE
   B) Germany, is the world's most,
   C) Germany is the world's most
   D) Germany is the world's most,

3. If inserted here, which choice most effectively establishes the main topic of the paragraph?

   A) Despite the seriousness of the topic at hand, Merkel seems to be making every conceivable effort to be uninteresting.
   B) Germany has long been considered one of the most progressive countries in Europe.
   C) Merkel's climb to her government position is a huge win for feminists around the world.
   D) Despite her bland means of dressing, Merkel is a fiery leader.

4. A) NO CHANGE
   B) crisis" Merkel says, staring
   C) crisis", Merkel says, staring
   D) crisis," Merkel says, staring

5. A) NO CHANGE
   B) reducing
   C) deducing
   D) inferring

6. Which sentence most effectively concludes the sentence and the paragraph?

   A) NO CHANGE
   B) Delete it. It is unnecessary.
   C) distracting her from the speech she was giving
   D) focusing on the crowd in front of her as she spoke.

{7} She recounts a meeting, in Brussels, of the Group of Seven, an informal bloc of industrialized democracies including the United States, Canada, France, Germany, Italy, Japan, and the United Kingdom. The Group of Seven had just expelled its eighth member, Russia, over the war in Ukraine. "We will be very persistent when it comes to enforcing freedom, justice, and self-determination on the European continent," she says. "Our task is to protect Ukraine on its self-determined way, and to meet old-fashioned thinking about spheres of influence from the nineteenth and twentieth century with answers from the global twenty-first century." Merkel has reached the **(8)** climax of her speech — indicated by a slowing of her intonation and an extending of her fingers. To the non-German, she could be reading out regulatory guidelines for the mining industry or the rules of a complicated board game.

The Chancellor finishes to lengthy **(9)** applause, and takes a seat with the members of her cabinet. Merkel has recently lost weight — bedridden last winter after fracturing her pelvis in a cross-country-skiing accident, she gave up sausage sandwiches for chopped carrots and lost twenty pounds. Her slimmer face, with its sunken eyes and longer jowls, **(10)** betray her fatigue. She's been Chancellor since 2005, having won a third term last September, with no challenger in sight.

[1] After Merkel, it's the opposition's turn to speak, to substantially lesser applause. [2] One by one, members of Parliament come forward to defend Merkel. [3] Despite her subdued manner, Merkel has Parliament firmly under her control. [4] Merkel crushes her opposition into submission with every speech she gives. {11}

7. Which of the following provides the best transition from the previous paragraph?

   A) NO CHANGE
   B) Merkel wholeheartedly supports the Ukraine.
   C) Merkel's fingers divert her from thoughts of the previous weekend.
   D) At the lectern, Merkel continues addressing parliament.

8. Which of the following words could NOT replace the underlined word in the context of the paragraph?

   A) pinnacle
   B) nadir
   C) highpoint
   D) apex

9. A) NO CHANGE
   B) betrays her fatigue
   C) are betraying her fatigue
   D) have betrayed her fatigue

10. A) NO CHANGE
    B) applause, she takes
    C) applause and takes
    D) applause; and takes

11. In the context of the last paragraph, Sentence 4 should be

    A) left where it is now.
    B) placed before Sentence 1.
    C) placed between Sentences 2 and 3.
    D) deleted, it is unnecessary.

Blue Writing Lesson 18: Coordination and Subordination
Getting Your Feet Wet

Directions: The following questions are intended as a short diagnostic exam.

1. Although humans have been observing the night sky for <u>thousands of years, we have only</u> recently found planets outside our solar system.

   A) NO CHANGE
   B) thousands of years, yet we have only
   C) thousands of years; we have only
   D) thousands of years we have only

2. Polaris is located on the north <u>celestial pole, it appears</u> as a fixed point around which other stars rotate.

   A) NO CHANGE
   B) celestial pole; it appears
   C) celestial pole, therefore it appears
   D) celestial pole, but it appears

3. Many objects we see in the night sky are not <u>stars at all, but satellites,</u> planets, and nebulas.

   A) NO CHANGE
   B) stars at all but satellites
   C) stars at all; but satellites
   D) stars at all, whether satellites

BLUE WRITING LESSON 18: COORDINATION AND SUBORDINATION
Wading In

TOPIC OVERVIEW: COORDINATION AND SUBORDINATION

For this lesson, you should review the concepts you learned back in Lesson 3 on repairing run-on sentences and fragments.

When connecting two independent clauses, we have to arrange and punctuate those clauses to ensure that we do not end up with a run-on sentence. There are two choices: coordinate the independent clauses or make one of them subordinate.

TOPIC OVERVIEW: COORDINATION

Sometimes in writing we want to show that two ideas are closely linked or improve the flow of an essay by varying the sentence structure. For example, look at the two sentences below.

Example 1: I don't have to go to school in the summer. I sleep late every day.

Taken like this, we have two random statements that may or may not be related to one another. The structure is simple. The sentences are boring. Let's try combining them instead:

Example 2: I don't have to go to school in the summer, **so** I sleep late every day.

Now that both clauses are part of the same sentence, we can see that the ideas are more closely linked — in fact, one caused the other.

There are two main ways to coordinate independent clauses in one sentence.

- Use a comma and a coordinating conjunction.
  - Pigs are surprisingly clean animals, **and** they make wonderful pets.
- Use a semi-colon.
  - Computer programming is not as hard as you may think; many schools offer courses for beginners.

When coordinating independent clauses be careful to choose only ONE method of coordination — mixing methods will result in a grammatical error. If we use a comma, we'll use one coordinating conjunction (FANBOYS). If we use a semi-colon, we won't use any conjunctions at all.

coordinating conjunctions		
for	and	nor
but	or	yet
	so	

Example 3: Noor wants to major in art history**; yet** she took AP Calculus in tenth grade.

Example 4: Annu doesn't have any pets **so** she offers to walk her neighbors' dogs.

In both of these examples, the author has failed to coordinate properly; in Example 3 she used a semi-colon AND a coordinating conjunction, and in Example 4 she forgot to use a comma before the coordinating conjunction.

We also want to be sure that when we are coordinating, we use the conjunction that is most appropriate in the sentence itself.

Example 5: Raghav wanted to see *Guardians of the Galaxy* at 7:10**, so** there were no more tickets when he arrived.

These sentences do not have a cause/effect relationship, which means that *so* does not really work in context. It would be more appropriate to use *but* because there is a contrast between what was expected and what actually happened.

TOPIC OVERVIEW: SUBORDINATION

Another way to combine two independent clauses in one sentence is to make one of the clauses dependent — a sentence can have any number of dependent clauses and still be correct.

Dependent clauses can be formed by omitting the subject or verb or by adding a subordinating conjunction. Here are some common subordinating conjunctions, as given to you in Lesson 3:

Subordinating Conjunctions		
After	Although	As
Because	Before	Even
How	If	In order that
Now that	Once	Provided
Rather than	Since	So that
Than	That	Though
Unless	Until	When
Whenever	Where	Whereas
Wherever	Whether	While

Joining independent clauses with subordinating conjunctions is not much different than joining them with coordinating conjunctions.

Example 6: He completed his homework **because** he wanted to pass the test.

In Example 6 we have two clauses, *He finished his homework* and *because he wanted to pass the test.* The first clause is independent and is our main clause in this sentence. The second is dependent because of the subordinating conjunction. When a dependent clause follows an independent clause in a sentence, there is no need for commas.

Example 7: **When** the holiday season begins**,** she will hire ten new managers.

In Example 7 the dependent clause comes first, so we have to put a comma between it and the independent clause.

As with coordination, make sure that the subordinating clause in the sentences makes sense in context.

Example 8: There will be a celebration after the game **unless** our team wins.

The conjunction here implies that the team will only celebrate if it loses—it's much more likely that there will be a celebration *if* the team wins.

WRAP-UP: COORDINATION AND SUBORDINATION

To answer questions about coordination and subordination, it's important to identify the different types of clauses in the sentence and to understand the rules that tell you how to connect them. Here is a short summary of the information in this lesson:

1. Two independent clauses can be joined by **either** a semi-colon **or** a comma and a coordinating conjunction (FANBOYS).
2. One of the clauses can be made dependent by adding a subordinating conjunction.
3. A dependent clause can be attached to the front end of an independent clause with a comma, or to the back end without a comma.
4. Make sure that the conjunction you choose makes sense with regard to the relationship of the clauses.

BLUE WRITING LESSON 18: COORDINATION AND SUBORDINATION
Learning to Swim

CONCEPT EXERCISE:

Directions: Find and correct errors in the following sentences. Some sentences may have more than one error, while others will not have any errors.

1. After King George III of England signed the Proclamation of 1763 colonists were prohibited from establishing settlements west of the Appalachian Mountains.

2. In 1764, the English Parliament passed the Sugar Act, which increased taxes on sugar and other goods, in order to increase revenue to help pay for the French and Indian War.

3. While the colonists had been paying British merchants with practically worthless paper money, the Currency Act of 1764 prohibited the colonists from issuing any paper money.

4. By the time the colonists had been angered by several of the English Parliamentary Acts passed in the 1760s, it was the Stamp Act of 1765 that first united large segments of the colonial population against the British.

5. The Stamp Act was quickly followed by the Quartering Act, which required that colonists house and feed British troops; but the Quartering Act was successfully circumvented in all colonies except for Pennsylvania.

6. Most daily business and legal transactions in the colonies ceased, when the Stamp Act went into effect, because nearly all colonists refused to use the stamps.

7. In March of 1766, King George III signed a bill repealing the Stamp Act, after much debate in the English Parliament.

8. The English did not want to seem as if they had given into the colonists' demands; yet they also passed the Declaratory Act, which stated that the British government had total power to legislate the American colonies.

9. News of the repeal of the Stamp Act resulted in boisterous celebrations but the colonists relaxed their boycott of imported English goods.

10. In 1767, the English Parliament passed the Townshend Acts, which included new taxes on items such as paper and tea, because it wanted to punish New York for refusing to comply with the 1765 Quartering Act.

11. Many colonists believed that they should not have to pay taxes to the English government, as long as the colonists were not represented in Parliament.

12. While protesting the various acts of Parliament the colonists engaged in some questionable behavior.

13. In June of 1768, patriots locked a customs official in the cabin of a ship called *Liberty*; so the patriots could illegally unload a shipment of wine without paying the necessary taxes.

14. In 1772, when a British ship ran aground off Rhode Island, colonists rowed out to the ship and attacked it, before they burned the ship.

15. In 1770, a group of British soldiers fired their muskets into a crowd, because a mob had been harassing the soldiers; this became known as the Boston Massacre.

16. The British repealed the Townshend Acts after the Boston Massacre.

17. Several years later, the British once again tried to tax the colonists through the Tea Act; yet the Tea Act imposed duties on imports of tea.

18. Because of the Tea Act the patriots organized the Boston Tea Party, during which the patriots disguised themselves as Mohawks and dumped tea into Boston Harbor.

19. In response to the Boston Tea Party, an angry English Parliament passed the Coercive Acts and the colonists called these the Intolerable Acts.

20. The First Continental Congress met in Philadelphia, after the passage of the Intolerable Acts.

BLUE WRITING LESSON 18: COORDINATION AND SUBORDINATION
Diving into the Deep End

PRACTICE EXERCISE:

Directions: Answer the questions that accompany the following passages.

The Aerial Origins of Batman

On February 27, 1935, a 24-year-old daredevil named Clem Sohn stood in a plane 12,000 feet above Daytona Beach, Florida. He had attached a harness to his back, **(1)** <u>while connected</u> a metal bar across his chest to several feet of canvas that hung behind his waist. He wore two parachutes. **(2)** <u>Until jumping</u>, Sohn put on large scuba-style goggles. He raised his arms to his sides, straightening out the canvas into the unmistakable shape of wings. Sohn descended expertly with open wings for 10,000 feet. **(3)** <u>About 2,000 feet from</u> the ground, he tugged one of his parachute ripcords and calmly fell the earth.

(4) <u>Whereas seven months</u>, young male skydivers across the country were trying to outdo Sohn. The press called them "Bat Men."

Bob Kane, the co-creator of Batman, was a 14-year-old boy when Sohn and his fellow aerial performers filled American newspapers. **(5)** <u>But four years later</u>, in response to Superman's creation one year prior, DC Comics asked the young cartoonist to come up with another hero. Kane's initial sketches had "a pair of stiff wings" that his creative partner Bill Finger encouraged him to change to **(6)** <u>a cape, although "stiff wings"</u> is a phrase that reporters also used to describe the stretched canvas used by Sohn & Co.

1. A) NO CHANGE
   B) whereas he connected
   C) which connected
   D) when he connected

2. A) NO CHANGE
   B) After jumping
   C) While jumping
   D) Before jumping

3. A) NO CHANGE
   B) Until 2,000 feet from
   C) About 2,000 feet until
   D) Around 2,000 feet off of

4. A) NO CHANGE
   B) About seven months later
   C) Until seven months
   D) Within seven months

5. A) NO CHANGE
   B) And four years later
   C) Four years later
   D) Until four years later

6. A) NO CHANGE
   B) a cape; coincidentally, "stiff wings"
   C) a cape, and "stiff wings"
   D) a cape, and it is no accident that "stiff wings"

(7) <u>Throughout their lives</u>, the two artists attributed Kane's sources to the radio show *The Shadow*, to two movies, *The Mark of Zorro* (1920) and *The Bat Whispers* (a 1930 picture about a cape-wearing criminal who flashed a bat **(8)** <u>insignia), but to a</u> Leonardo da Vinci drawing of a flying machine that Kane said "looked like a bat man." **(9)** <u>And prior to</u> the character's first May 1939 appearance, the average American, and surely Kane and Finger to some degree themselves, would have visualized a specific image when hearing the term "Bat Man": the daredevils who headlined popular air shows across the country.

(10) <u>Whether or not it directly</u> influenced Batman, this subculture of performers captured the American imagination in much the same manner as the comic-book crime fighter who would later share their name. Superman and Batman were instant hits with the American public. In July of 1939, two months after the caped crusader's debut, the publishing industry reported that there had been a "sharp increase" in "comic magazine" subscriptions. **(11)** <u>In addition to Superman who</u> came from outer space, Batman was born to a public enamored with the idea that any human could fly.

7. A) NO CHANGE
   B) Within the span their lives
   C) During their lives
   D) In the midst of

8. A) NO CHANGE
   B) insignia), to a
   C) insignia), and to a
   D) insignia), yet to a

9. A) NO CHANGE
   B) Although prior to
   C) Also prior to
   D) But prior to

10. A) NO CHANGE
    B) Even if they directly
    C) Assuming that it directly
    D) Although it directly

11. A) NO CHANGE
    B) As opposed to Superman, who
    C) In opposition to Superman, who
    D) Just like Superman, who

TEST EXERCISE:

Directions: Answer the questions that accompany the following passage.

The Knowledge of London

{1} Until technology made Matt McCabe's career choice no longer as relevant, he had spent the last three years of his life thinking about one **(2)** thing: London's roads, its landmarks, and how to navigate between them. In the process, he had logged more than 50,000 miles on motorbike and on foot, nearly all within central London's dozen boroughs and financial district. He was studying to be a London taxi driver, devoting himself full-time to the challenge that would put him behind the wheel of one of the London's famous black taxis.

(3) In fact, "challenge" is not quite the word for the trial undergone to become a London cabbie. **(4)** It has been called the hardest test, of any kind, in the world. It is without question a unique intellectual, psychological, and physical ordeal, demanding unnumbered thousands of hours of immersive study, as would-be cabbies undertake the task of committing to memory the entirety of London. To demonstrate that mastery, a progressively more difficult sequence of oral examinations—a process which, on average, takes four years to complete, and for some, much longer than **(5)** that, is undertaken.

1. Which of the following, if added to the beginning of the paragraph, would best explain technology's role in McCabe's possible career change?

   A) GPS, or global positioning systems, have sharply reduced the amount of information today's drivers need to memorize.
   B) The advent of computers and the Internet has greatly affected modern life, and taxi drivers are no exception.
   C) Now that nearly everybody owns a car, taxi driving has become a much less profitable source of income.
   D) Technology is thought of as a boon to everybody, but taxi drivers may be an exception to the rule.

2. A) NO CHANGE
   B) thing. London's roads
   C) thing; London's roads
   D) thing, so London's roads

3. A) NO CHANGE
   B) However,
   C) But,
   D) Delete the underlined portion, then capitalize "Challenge".

4. Within the context of the sentence, which of the following is the best replacement for the underlined word?

   A) challenge
   B) trial
   C) cabbie
   D) taxi

5. A) NO CHANGE
   B) that is
   C) that—is
   D) that—are

The six-mile radius from Charing Cross, the **(6)** <u>allowed</u> center-point of London marked by an equestrian statue of King Charles I, is the focus of the examination. The area includes some 25,000 streets. London cabbies need to **(7)** <u>know all of them and how to drive it</u>—the direction they run, which are one-way, which are dead ends, where to enter and exit traffic circles, and so on. **(8)** <u>But</u> cabbies need to know everything on those streets. Examiners may ask a would-be cabbie to identify the location of any restaurant in London. Any pub, any shop, any landmark, no matter how small or obscure—all are fair game. One taxi driver told me that he was asked the location of a statue, just a foot tall, depicting two mice sharing a piece of cheese. It's on the facade of a building in Philpot Lane, on the corner of Eastcheap, not far from London Bridge.

{9} Some trace the test's creation to the Great Exhibition of 1851, when London's Crystal Palace played host to hundreds of thousands of foreign visitors. These tourists, the story goes, inundated the city government with complaints about the ineptitude of its cabmen. As such, London authorities were prompted to institute a more demanding licensing process.

But the Knowledge is not simply a matter of way-finding that any technological device can do. The key is a process called "pointing," studying all those places "a taxi passenger might ask to be taken." Knowledge boys have developed a system of pointing that some call "satelliting," **(10)** <u>whereby</u> the candidate travels in a quarter-mile radius around a run's starting and finishing points, poking around, identifying landmarks, making notes. By this method, the theory goes, a Knowledge student can commit to memory not just the streets but the streetscape—the curve of the road, the pharmacy on the corner, the mice nibbling on cheese in the architrave. {11}

6. A) NO CHANGE
   B) presumed
   C) invented
   D) imagined

7. A) NO CHANGE
   B) know, and how to drive, all of them
   C) know it and how to drive them
   D) know how to drive each of them

8. A) NO CHANGE
   B) Additionally,
   C) However,
   D) Similarly,

9. Which choice most effectively establishes the main topic of the paragraph?

   A) The origins of the Knowledge are unclear—lost in the obscurity of Victorian municipal history.
   B) London's cabbies were not always as sharply detail-oriented as they are now.
   C) There is a lot of murkiness involved in a test so difficult, of course.
   D) The name of the test is steeped in both shame and mystery.

10. A) NO CHANGE
    B) likewise
    C) alternatively
    D) consequently

11. Which of the following sentences, if added, would best conclude the passage?

    A) Taxi drivers in London are unlike those anywhere else.
    B) This may be London's most important gift to society.
    C) I challenge you to find a more difficult test than The Knowledge.
    D) However, with the advent of GPS, this unique method may be lost forever.

BLUE WRITING LESSON 18: COORDINATION AND SUBORDINATION
Race to the Finish

HOMEWORK EXERCISE 1:

Directions: Find and correct errors in the following sentences. Some sentences may have more than one error, while others will not have any errors.

1. Before the Great Depression stock prices rose by about 40 percent; but these price increases were largely artificial.

2. On October 24, 1929, the stock market collapsed, but investors began dumping shares in large numbers.

3. Millions of stock shares ended up worthless; and many investors were wiped out completely.

4. As consumer confidence vanished the downturn in spending and investments led businesses to slow production and begin firing their workers.

5. Those who were lucky enough to remain employed saw their wages cut; for the combination of unemployed and underpaid workers meant that consumers had no purchasing power.

6. The number of foreclosures and repossessions rose dramatically, because people had to buy on credit and went into large amounts of debt.

7. President Herbert Hoover insisted that the economic crisis would resolve itself in time, or the federal government failed to take action to address the problem.

8. Large numbers of newly homeless Americans established settlements made up of tents and shacks, which they called Hoovervilles, because they blamed President Hoover for the economic crisis.

9. Some of the men who lived in Hoovervilles possessed construction skills and were able to build their homes out of stone nor most people built their residences out of scraps of wood, cardboard, and metal.

10. Since Hoovervilles existed in many cities, the largest Hooverville was located in St. Louis.

11. The St. Louis Hooverville had four distinct sectors and an unofficial mayor, but residents formed churches and other social institutions.

12. By 1931, the number of unemployed workers had reached 6 million; and homelessness was rampant.

13. In 1933, with more than 13 million workers unemployed, Democrat Franklin D. Roosevelt became President, before winning the election by an overwhelming margin.

14. Rather than taking a hands-off approach, as Hoover had, FDR initiated a program known as the New Deal.

15. In addition to various economic policies, FDR attempted to restore public confidence through a series of weekly radio addresses called "fireside chats," but actions like these made FDR one of America's most popular presidents.

16. Because historians still debate the effects of the New Deal many programs provided immediate relief to the unemployed.

17. The Tennessee Valley Authority employed many workers to build dams and hydroelectric projects to control flooding and provide electric power to the impoverished Tennessee Valley region; and the Works Project Administration employed 8.5 million people from 1935 to 1943.

18. Because most of the world's economies, including the American economy, relied on the gold standard, America's Great Depression spread to the rest of the world.

19. Since global economic hardship fueled the rise of extremist political movements throughout European countries; some argue that the Great Depression caused World War II.

20. Whether or not the Great Depression caused World War II, World War II certainly brought about the end of the Great Depression and led the U.S. into its most prosperous economic era.

HOMEWORK EXERCISE 2:

Directions: Answer the questions that accompany the passage.

Women in STEM Workplaces

Women may be underrepresented in science and technology not because they are less skilled in those areas or because they face specific gender barriers to entering these fields, but because they may find better opportunities elsewhere. According to researchers, women have **(1)** <u>wider</u> intellectual talents, which provide them with more occupational options.

{**2**} Among **(3)** <u>these</u> who had highest scores on both the verbal and the math sections of the SAT, for example, nearly two-thirds were female, while only 37% were male. Among those who excelled in one area but not the other, 70% of those with high math and lower verbal scores were male, while 30% were female. For high verbal skills but lower math scores, the numbers were exactly reversed: 70% of high verbal scorers who didn't do as well in math were female, compared with 30% for the males.

Of those who scored best across the board, 34% choose a career in science, technology, engineering or mathematics (STEM) — but 49% of those who did better in math than in language skills chose a STEM career. Given the gender difference among those scoring higher in math than in **(4)** <u>language; that</u> meant fewer capable women wound up in science and mathematical fields. {**5**}

1. A) NO CHANGE
    B) more diverse
    C) broader
    D) less focused

2. Which of the following would best introduce the main idea of the paragraph?

    A) Some studies examined this phenomenon.
    B) One study shows how men and women are different.
    C) Gender studies scientists are trying to answer these questions.
    D) One study found dramatic differences by gender in the areas in which men and women excelled.

3. A) NO CHANGE
    B) those
    C) this
    D) that

4. A) NO CHANGE
    B) language; that
    C) language. That
    D) language, that

5. Which of the following would best conclude this paragraph and provide a transition to the next?

    A) This piqued scientists' interests.
    B) This difference led researchers to question social factors.
    C) The scientists continued their research about social causes of this phenomenon.
    D) Researchers wondered how this difference could be explained and whether social factors played a role.

What interested the researchers most was that more women than men showed aptitude in both math and language skills, yet the rate of women choosing STEM careers remains low. **(6)** <u>Are women discouraged from these fields,</u> or are they simply not interested in them for other reasons? To find out, the scientists also questioned participants about their math and English "self concepts." People tend to play to their strengths: for those who think they are best at English, it may not matter that they may also be math geniuses when

(7) <u>compared by their peers.</u>

(8) Cultural stereotypes may be indirectly pushing women away from scientific fields. If **(9)** <u>one is</u> highly skilled in two areas, but one is more in line with social stereotypes and has **(10)** <u>richer</u> social support that affirms that skill, it's not surprising that would be the talent you chose to develop.

Women may find the support and options in non-science fields more appealing. If that's the case, then addressing the gender gap in STEM careers isn't so much about boosting women's aptitude in math and science—their results show that's not the issue—but **(11)** <u>to making careers</u> in these areas more welcoming, accessible and financially attractive.

6. A) NO CHANGE
   B) Women are discouraged from these fields,
   C) Are women being discouraged from these fields,
   D) Are men are keeping women out of these fields,

7. A) NO CHANGE
   B) compared with their peers
   C) compared next to their peers
   D) compared to their peers' talents

8. Which of the following would provide the best transition from the previous paragraph?

   A) This could explain the gender difference.
   B) That may be why fewer women enter STEM fields.
   C) The cause of this gender gap remains unknown.
   D) The study continues to search for answers.

9. A) NO CHANGE
   B) you are
   C) she is
   D) we are

10. A) NO CHANGE
    B) wealthier
    C) more successful
    D) advanced

11. A) NO CHANGE
    B) in making careers
    C) for making careers
    D) in order to make careers

C2 education
be smarter.

BLUE WRITING LESSON 19: IDIOMS
Getting Your Feet Wet

Directions: The following questions are intended as a short diagnostic exam.

1. When he won the cooking competition, he was <u>rewarded by</u> a scholarship to culinary school.

   A) NO CHANGE
   B) rewarded with
   C) rewarded for
   D) rewarded to

2. <u>Inside of the cave</u>, the explorers turned on their head lamps.

   A) NO CHANGE
   B) Inside at the cave
   C) Into the cave
   D) Inside the cave

3. Because my doctor told me to cut back on caffeine, I <u>stopped to drink a</u> Coke.

   A) NO CHANGE
   B) stopped for a
   C) stopped drinking
   D) stopped

4. You never <u>forget turning off</u> the stove once you've seen your house burn down due to a cooking accident.

   A) NO CHANGE
   B) forget
   C) forget turning
   D) forget to turn off

BLUE WRITING LESSON 19: IDIOMS
Wading In

TOPIC OVERVIEW: IDIOMS

The term **idiom** refers to any phrase whose meaning cannot be predicted based on the meanings of the words themselves. English has many colorful idioms like "get your feet wet" (meaning to gain experience in something new), but the SAT won't test those. Instead, it will test idiomatic prepositions, infinitives vs gerunds, and other English conventions that may not be addressed by standard grammar rules.

TOPIC OVERVIEW: IDIOMATIC PREPOSITIONS

There are certain verbs that require specific prepositions in order to convey their intended meanings—we refer to these as idiomatic prepositions because they cannot be predicted simply based on individual word meaning. The most common ones must be memorized.

Any time you see a preposition underlined in a sentence, you should ask yourself two questions:
1. Is this preposition necessary?
2. Is this the correct preposition for this phrase?

Example 1: Registration for the tournament will open <u>up</u> tomorrow morning.

Example 2: Adam cared <u>about</u> his grandmother after she broke her ankle.

In Example 1, the first step is to identify the preposition *up*. Is this preposition needed in the sentence? If you remove the preposition, does the meaning change? In this case, the preposition isn't actually required and can be eliminated.

In Example 2, a preposition is absolutely needed—if we remove it, the sentence loses some structure. However, it sounds odd to say Adam cares *about* someone after an injury. It would be more appropriate to say that he cared *for* her.

Here are some of the prepositions you should look out for when they are underlined in passages:

common prepositions				
at	before	for	over	until
above	behind	from	through	with
about	below	in	to	
against	between	of	toward(s)	
around	by	on	under	

TOPIC OVERVIEW: INFINITIVES VS. GERUNDS

The infinitive is the base, non-inflected form of the verb. In many Romance languages, infinitives are one word (Spanish *tener*, "to have") but in English, the infinitive is formed by the preposition *to* + verb.

Example 3: Raj wanted **to spend** his birthday at Six Flags.

The gerund is the form of the verb that ends in *–ing*. Gerunds function as nouns in subjects and prepositional phrases.

Example 4: Prem enjoys **reading** historical nonfiction.

The infinitive generally indicates a specific activity, a stronger connection between the subject and the action, and a specific purpose or intention. The gerund generally indicates a general class of activity, a less strong connection between the subject and action, and a general purpose or intention.

Because the use of infinitives and gerunds tends to be idiomatic, there is no 100% clear rule you can follow every single time to know which one to use. You will sometimes have to trust your ear for the language and use the form sounds the most natural or least awkward.

WRAP-UP: IDIOMS

To answer questions about idioms, it's important to identify the different types of idiomatic phrases you'll be tested on. Here is a short summary of the information in this lesson:

1. Identify common prepositions as they appear in underlined portions of text. Ask yourself if the preposition is necessary or if there's another preposition that would be more appropriate. Eliminate any answer choices that contain unnecessary or illogical prepositions.
2. If an infinitive or gerund is underlined in a sentence, ask yourself if the situation is more general or more specific—test the opposite construction and see if one verb form is more logical than the other or if the sentence flows more naturally with one over the other. Eliminate any answer choices that are illogical or very awkward.
3. Read the sentence with each remaining answer choice replacing the underlined portion. Eliminate any answer choices that sound clearly wrong or awkward.
4. Examine the remaining answer choices. Choose the one that is the most logical and sounds the most natural.

BLUE WRITING LESSON 19: IDIOMS
Learning to Swim

CONCEPT EXERCISE:

Directions: Find and correct errors in the following sentences. Some sentences may have more than one error, while others will not have any errors.

1. In 1776, Abigail and John Adams had a difference about opinion regarding women's suffrage.

2. Abigail Adams had implored her husband to "remember the ladies" when creating a code of laws for the new republic, but John Adams did not agree on this idea.

3. We can infer to John Adams's response, in which he referenced the "despotism of the petticoat," that he believed that women were inferior at men.

4. Prior with the adoption of the U.S. Constitution, women were allowed to vote in several states; after its adoption, women lost the right to vote in all states except New Jersey.

5. In 1807, even New Jersey stopped to allow women to vote.

6. Without the right to vote, women were entirely dependent to their husbands to voice their political opinions.

7. The Abolitionist Movement allowed women taking a greater role in politics by forming anti-slavery associations.

8. The Abolitionist Movement was intended on making people more aware of the horrors of slavery.

9. Unfortunately, women were barred from participating in the 1840 World Anti-Slavery Convention in London.

10. Due in part to the opposition with women's involvement in the anti-slavery movement, many women began to express their desire to gain the right to vote.

11. At the First Women's Rights Convention, held in 1848, attendees agreed with a Declaration of Sentiments that proposed equal suffrage for women.

12. Although leading suffragette Susan B. Anthony was opposed with the idea, women put aside suffrage activities to help the Civil War efforts.

13. In 1868, the newly ratified Fourteenth Amendment defined citizens as "male," to deal a blow to the women's rights movement.

14. The new Amendment effectively codified the idea that women were not citizens independent to their husbands.

15. Susan B. Anthony's suffrage activities met with great resistance, particularly when she was arrested for casting a ballot in 1872.

16. In 1896, Idaho granted women the right voting.

17. As a new century dawned, most women were still frustrated that they lacked of the right to vote.

18. Increasingly, women were growing impatient for their lack of voting rights, believing that their inability to vote was a sign that their country thought them incapable with making rational voting decisions.

19. In the early 20th century, several states, including New York and California, agreed to grant women the right to vote.

20. Finally, in 1920, Susan B. Anthony was posthumously rewarded by her efforts when Congress ratified the Susan B. Anthony Amendment, which granted women the right to vote.

BLUE WRITING LESSON 19: IDIOMS
Diving into the Deep End

PRACTICE EXERCISE:

Directions: Answer the questions that accompany the following passage.

Ask Not What You Can Do For Your Country

In November of 1960, Kennedy had won the election. All through the Christmas holidays that's all my family talked **(1)** <u>on</u>. Would the pope tell Kennedy how to run the country? Would Kennedy tell the pope what to do? Would Kennedy act **(2)** <u>according with</u> the pope's instructions?

My side of the family was Baptist. Lon, my best friend, finally put the question to rest when he asked my father, if he were president, would my father **(3)** <u>agree to everything</u> Billy Graham asked him to do. My father said that he wouldn't. "But that's beside the point," my dad said, beginning **(4)** <u>to get angry at</u> Lon. "I don't even know Billy Graham." Lon pointed out that Kennedy probably didn't know the pope, either. That was the end of that conversation.

Lon was a pretty smart kid, and very argumentative. Lon's adult conversation with my dad, about Kennedy and the pope, about my dad and Billy Graham, was pretty heady stuff for a twelve-year-old, and it was the first time I'd ever seen someone from my generation **(5)** <u>use adult rational</u> to take on an adult. And Lon had prevailed! I remember thinking that it would be OK to express my own opinions after that. And I often did.

1. A) NO CHANGE
   B) around
   C) for
   D) about

2. A) NO CHANGE
   B) according to
   C) in accords with
   D) according for

3. A) NO CHANGE
   B) agree on everything
   C) agree with everything
   D) agree as to everything

4. A) NO CHANGE
   B) to get angry on
   C) to get angry with
   D) to be angry with

5. A) NO CHANGE
   B) using adult rational
   C) use the rationale of an adult
   D) use adult rationale

On Inauguration Day, 1961, I was going **(6)** <u>thorough</u> the lunch line at Morningside Elementary School. Kennedy was making his inaugural speech. The principal, Mr. Jenkins, **(7)** <u>had rigged up</u> our public address microphone so that it picked up the sound from the TV set in his office. Just as I picked up a tray and was reaching for the silverware, I heard "Ask not what your country can do for you, ask what you can do for your country." **(8)** <u>I was the last student on line,</u> and my teacher was reaching for a tray right behind me. I told her that I thought what the president had just said would probably be printed in future history books. The student **(9)** <u>just ahead from me said,</u> "You're wrong. You have to be dead for anybody to remember what you said." The teacher said, "I don't think so, Bobby. People don't remember what modern day presidents say."

The Kennedy years were exciting; the front page was always **(10)** <u>occupied by</u> news about our problems with the Communists. There never seemed to be a dull moment. First, there was this invasion of Cuba called The Bay of Pigs. I didn't know much about what was going on at the time, but I remember hearing my father say that we never should have done whatever it was we did. Whatever it was we did must have really made the Cubans mad. It made the Russians mad, too. The next thing I knew, the Russians were sending nuclear missiles to Cuba. Kennedy went on national television and started talking about using nuclear missiles against the Cubans and the Russians. Ever since Kennedy became president we were involved in one **(11)** <u>international incident</u> after another.

6. A) NO CHANGE
   B) threw
   C) through
   D) throughout

7. A) NO CHANGE
   B) has rigged up
   C) had rigged on
   D) had rigged out

8. A) NO CHANGE
   B) I was the last student at line
   C) I was the last one on the line
   D) I was the last student in line

9. A) NO CHANGE
   B) just ahead of me said
   C) just to the head of me said
   D) just in front from me said

10. A) NO CHANGE
    B) occupied in
    C) occupied with
    D) occupied about

11. A) NO CHANGE
    B) international accident
    C) internationally incident
    D) internal incident

TEST EXERCISE:

Directions: Answer the questions that accompany the following passage.

Chief Joseph and the Nez Perce

The Nez Perce tribe of Indians, like other tribes too large to be united under one chief, **(1)** <u>was composed in</u> several bands, each distinct in sovereignty. It was a loose confederacy. **(2)** <u>Joseph was a</u> <u>quiet, kind, and humble young man, truly a dutiful son and loving</u> <u>father to his people</u>.

[1] The elder chief, in dying, had counseled his son Joseph, then not more than twenty-two or twenty-three years of age, never to part with their home, assuring him that he had signed no papers. [2] These peaceful, non-treaty Indians did not even know what land had been ceded until an agent read them the government order to leave. [3] Of course they refused.{3}

(4) <u>Despite the fact that the agent failed to move them</u>, he and the would-be settlers called upon the army to force them to be good, namely, to leave their pleasant inheritance in the hands of a crowd of greedy grafters. General O. O. Howard, the Christian soldier, was sent to do the work.

1. A) NO CHANGE
   B) was composed about
   C) was composed of
   D) was comprised of

2. Which of the following changes best maintains the focus of this paragraph in relation to the rest of the passage?

   A) NO CHANGE
   B) Many white speculators were interested in buying land for its mineral rights or other economic value.
   C) Joseph's father had on many occasions tried to reconcile with the other Nez Perce, but they were too independent.
   D) Joseph and his people occupied what was considered perhaps the finest land in that part of the country.

3. For the sake of the focus of the passage, how should the second paragraph ("The elder chief...they refused") be edited?

   A) NO CHANGE
   B) Move Sentence 1 after Sentence 3.
   C) Move Sentence 3 after Sentence 1.
   D) Move Sentence 2 before Sentence 1.

4. Which of the following is the most logical transition from the previous paragraph?

   A) NO CHANGE.
   B) When the agent failed to move them,
   C) The agent tried desperately to move them; yet despite his efforts
   D) Instead of the agent moving them,

He told Joseph and his leading men that they must obey the order or be driven out by force. We may be sure that he presented this hard alternative reluctantly. Joseph was a mere youth **(5)** <u>without experience of war</u> or public affairs. He had been brought up in obedience to parental wisdom and with his brother Ollicut had attended Missionary Spaulding's school where they had listened to the story of Christ and his religion of brotherhood. He now replied in his simple way that neither he nor his father had ever made any treaty disposing of their country, that no other band of the Nez Perces was authorized to speak for them, and it would seem a mighty injustice and unkindness to dispossess a friendly band.

(6) <u>General Howard told them in effect that they had no rights, no voice in the matter, they had only to obey</u>. Although some of the lesser chiefs counseled revolt then and there, Joseph maintained his self-control, seeking to calm his people and still **(7)** <u>grabbing for</u> a peaceful settlement of their difficulties. **(8)** <u>He finally asked for thirty days' time in which to find and dispose of their stock; which was granted</u>.

Joseph steadfastly held his immediate followers to their promise, but the land-grabbers were impatient and did everything in their power **(9)** <u>bringing</u> about an immediate crisis to hasten the eviction of the Indians. Depredations were committed, and finally some of the Indians retaliated, which was just what their enemies had been looking for. "Down with the bloodthirsty savages!" was the cry.

5. A) NO CHANGE
   B) without experience in war
   C) without experience from war
   D) without experiencing war

6. A) NO CHANGE
   B) General Howard was telling them, furthermore, they had no rights or voice, and that they should merely obey
   C) General Howard told them in effect that they had no rights, no voice in the matter: they had only to obey
   D) Speaking kindly, General Howard insisted that, in being as they had no rights or voice in the matter, they should probably obey

7. A) NO CHANGE
   B) holding out for
   C) grasping at
   D) manipulating toward

8. A) NO CHANGE
   B) He finally asked for thirty days' time in which he could find and then dispose of their stock, and this time he had asked for was granted.
   C) He finally asked for and was granted his stock, for thirty days' time.
   D) He finally asked for thirty days' time in which to find and dispose of their stock, and this was granted.

9. A) NO CHANGE
   B) to bring
   C) in the manner of bringing
   D) to have brought

Joseph told me himself that during all of those thirty days a tremendous pressure was brought upon him by his own people to resist the government order. "The worst of it was," said he, "that **(10)** <u>everything they said was true besides", he paused for a moment—"it</u> seemed very soon for me to forget my father's dying words, 'Do not give up our home!'" {11}

10. A) NO CHANGE
    B) everything they said was true; besides"—he paused for a moment—"it
    C) everything they said was true. Besides"—he paused for a moment—"they
    D) everything they said was true: besides"—he paused for a moment, "it

11. Given the passage as a whole, which of the following additions would provide the most appropriate conclusion?

    A) Knowing as I do just what it would mean to an Indian, I felt for him deeply.
    B) Regardless, Joseph eventually accepted his tribe's fate calmly.
    C) This fiery rhetoric aroused the neighboring Nez Perce to action.
    D) Realizing the threat to the Nez Perce was grave, General Howard relented.

BLUE WRITING LESSON 19: IDIOMS
Race to the Finish

HOMEWORK EXERCISE 1:

Directions: Find and correct errors in the following sentences. Some sentences may have more than one error, while others will not have any errors.

1. Even though it is used in almost everything they use on a daily basis, many people are oblivious of the ubiquity of mathematics.

2. Many students are taught, incorrectly, in school that they are not capable from learning math.

3. They are not even aware with the fact that anyone can learn math if he or she has the right teacher.

4. One particularly confounding aspect is that the higher levels of math are based with the foundational levels.

5. This means that if you are not familiar to the more basic concepts, the more difficult ones will be almost impossible to handle.

6. Students end up feeling disappointed with themselves after they get a poor grade on an exam.

7. In reality, they should be disappointed in the teacher who didn't teach them the basics more thoroughly.

8. Some teachers get impatient to their students' lack of understanding and move on without thoroughly teaching the subject.

9. When the students move on, they find that their skills are inferior against those of their peers.

10. According with a study done in high schools nationwide, the topic most students don't learn well is fractions.

11. A student whose skills at fractions are superior against her peers will find herself at a major advantage.

12. A topic similar with fractions, ratios can be helpful in many different situations as well.

13. Ratios are involved with unit conversions, percent questions, and scale calculations.

14. A student without a strong base in these topics finds himself occupied to the algebra instead of focusing on the more relevant points.

15. A survey of math teachers found that almost all concurred with the opinion that students need a better grasp of fundamentals.

16. In order to adapt from this situation, it is necessary for the teacher to provide the assistance the students need in order to overcome this deficiency.

17. After-school study sessions, extra worksheets, and mini-quizzes are just some of the ways that teachers can provide their students with this assistance.

18. If they put in the extra effort, both teachers and students will find they are rewarded to better grades and happier parents.

19. The advice here is intended with giving you an idea of why it's important to study math, even if it doesn't seem that way in class.

20. Just sitting around and waiting on something to happen will not get it done!

HOMEWORK EXERCISE 2:

Directions: Answer the questions that accompany the passage

Married at Work

[1]

Maybe it's not such a good idea to marry a doctor, especially if you're a doctor yourself. One of the hallmarks of modern marriage in America is that people tend to marry others who have similar educational **(1)** <u>attainments, for</u> this is particularly true of doctors. However, a new study suggests that doctor-doctor marriages may need more life-support than others.

[2]

In the biggest study of married doctors to date, the American College of Surgeons surveyed nearly 8,000 of its **(2)** <u>members, 90%</u> of whom were married. Of those, half had spouses or partners who did not work outside the home. About a third of the double-income couples were actually double-doctor duos, and in about a third of those marriages, both partners were surgeons. {**3**}

[3]

Who's better at understanding the stresses and strains of a physician's life than another physician? Luckily, there are more female surgeons than there have been before, so there are more around to marry. {**4**} No wonder that the study suggests surgeon-surgeon marriages are **(5)** <u>at the rise</u>.

1. A) NO CHANGE
    B) attainments, this
    C) attainments, that
    D) attainments. This

2. A) NO CHANGE
    B) members 90%
    C) members; 90%
    D) members. 90%

3. Which of the following, if added here, would best conclude Paragraph 2 and provide a transition to Paragraph 3?

    A) Many health professionals marry others.
    B) People tend to marry within their career field.
    C) In fact, the study notes that something like 50% of female surgeons are married to physicians.
    D) This tends to affect women more than men.

4. Which of the following, if added here, best supports the ideas of Paragraph 3?

    A) And since medical students are busy, they are more likely to socialize among their own kind.
    B) Students spend too much time working to date.
    C) Many medical students have similar backgrounds.
    D) Students marry other medical professionals for monetary reasons.

5. A) NO CHANGE
    B) on the rise
    C) in the rise
    D) all rising

[4]

You'd think that two-doctor families would be **(6)** <u>pragmatic</u>: not only are both parents competent at handling Baby's late night fever spike, but they can appreciate each other's latest bit of O.R. gossip and compete **(7)** <u>to beat Gregory House at</u> the correct diagnosis.

[5]

{8} "Surgeons in dual physician relationships had greater difficulty in balancing their parenting and career responsibilities," than those who had partners who stayed home or worked in other areas, the study says. Specifically, two-doctor couples were more likely to delay having children and to feel that their work did not leave enough time for a family life.

[6]

For surgeons married to other surgeons, the picture was even grimmer. They were more likely to report that child-rearing had slowed their career, and they were more "likely to stay home from work to care for a sick child and more often surrogated their career" in **(9)** <u>favor for</u> their partner's career, the study said.

[7]

Individuals from the **(10)** <u>two-surgeon</u> families felt about the same amount of burnout and depression as surgeons married to non-surgeons. This doesn't stop the study from concluding that "the higher prevalence of depressive symptoms and clinically significant lower mental quality of life among surgeons **(11)** <u>in marriages</u> or partnered to other surgeons suggests that the work-life hurdles could be taking a toll on their mental health."

6. Which of the following is the best replacement for the underlined word?

A) NO CHANGE
B) perfect
C) beneficial
D) ideal

7. A) NO CHANGE
B) to beat Gregory House to
C) to beat Gregory House after
D) to best Gregory House getting to

8. Which of the following is the most logical place for Paragraph 5?

A) Where it is
B) After Paragraph 2
C) Before Paragraph 4
D) After Paragraph 6

9. A) NO CHANGE
B) favor of
C) favor to
D) favoriting to

10. A) NO CHANGE
B) double-surgeon
C) twin-surgeon
D) two surgeons

11. A) NO CHANGE
B) who marry
C) married
D) who had wedded

BLUE WRITING LESSON 20: PRACTICE SECTION
LET'S CHECK IN

Congratulations! We've reached the end of this book!

Today's lesson isn't really a lesson — it's a checkpoint to see how far we've come since the first lesson.

On the following pages, you'll find a series of writing passages and questions. Each set is designed to reflect the types of passages and questions that are common to the SAT writing section. As you work through each passage, keep these tips in mind:

- No matter what kind of question you face, always eliminate any answer choices that do not suit the style or tone of the passage as a whole.
- If you find yourself struggling with a particular question, look at the surrounding sentences to see if there are context clues that might help you to eliminate additional answer choices.
- If you've eliminated every answer choice you can, and you still can't seem to decide which of the remaining options is correct, rely on your ear for the language. Read the appropriate part of the passage with each remaining answer choice inserted in the correct place and choose the answer that sounds best.

As you work through each practice set, be sure to mark any questions that you find particularly challenging so that you and your teacher can review them in greater depth when you've finished this lesson.

BLUE WRITING LESSON 20: PRACTICE SECTION

PRACTICE EXERCISE 1:

Directions: Answer the questions that accompany the following passage.

Population Growth and War

In 1870 Germany had a population of about 40,000,000. By 1892 this figure had risen to 50,000,000, and to 68,000,000 by June 30, 1914. In the years immediately preceding the war, the annual increase was about 850,000, of whom an insignificant proportion emigrated. This great increase was only rendered possible by a far-reaching transformation of the economic structure of the country.

(1) From being agricultural and mainly self-supporting, Germany transformed herself into a vast and complicated industrial machine, dependent for its working on the balance of many factors outside Germany as well as within. Only by operating **(2)** this machine, continuously and at full blast, could **(3)** she find occupation at home for her increasing population and the means of purchasing their subsistence from abroad. **(4)** By contrast, the population of America grew slightly less quickly during the intervening period, annually increasing by only 2%.

1. Does the underlined sentence support the previous claim?

   A) Yes, by showing the great increase in population.
   B) Yes, by demonstrating Germany's economic shift from an agricultural to an industrial economy.
   C) No, because it is wordy and unrelated to the previous sentence.
   D) No, it contradicts the previous claim.

2. Which of the following is the most precise replacement for the underlined phrase?

   A) this economy
   B) this war
   C) these many factors
   D) this great increase

3. In context, which of the following is the best replacement for the underlined word?

   A) Germany
   B) the United States
   C) Russia
   D) an industrial worker

4. Which of the following changes best maintains the focus of this paragraph in relation to the rest of the passage?

   A) NO CHANGE
   B) Industrialization had eventually reached Germany through Brussels, and ultimately from Great Britain.
   C) Despite this focus on industry, many in Germany, particularly in Bavaria, yearned for a more bucolic lifestyle.
   D) The German machine was like a top which to maintain its equilibrium must spin ever faster and faster.

(5) <u>To understand the present situation, we must apprehend with vividness what an extraordinary center of population the development of the Germanic system had enabled Central Europe to become.</u> Before the war the population of Germany and Austria-Hungary together not only (6) <u>almost</u> exceeded that of the United States, but was about equal to that of the whole of North America. In these numbers, situated within a compact territory, lay the military strength of the Central Powers. But these same numbers—for even the war has not appreciably diminished them—if deprived of the means of life, remain a hardly less danger to European order.

European Russia increased her population in a degree even greater than Germany. (7) <u>Russia grew from less than 100,000,000 in 1890 to about 150,000,000 at the outbreak of war in 1914; and in the preceding year, there was an excess of births over deaths in Russia as a whole.</u>

5. Which of the following sentences provides the most logical transition from the previous paragraph, considering the organization of the passage as a whole?

   A) NO CHANGE
   B) Let us now take a look at the cultural relationship between Germany and the rest of Europe.
   C) We can only applaud the Germans for their industry and fecundity.
   D) Compared with Germany, the rest of the world was hardly industrializing at all.

6. A) NO CHANGE
   B) substantially
   C) concretely
   D) previously

7. Does this sentence properly support the claim made in the previous sentence?

   A) Yes, by adequately appealing to the reader's emotion.
   B) Yes, by showing the population increase of Russia just prior to the Great War.
   C) No, because the time period is not specific enough.
   D) No, because the numbers stated do not support the claim.

The great events of history are often due to secular changes in the growth of population and other fundamental economic **(8)** <u>causes, which, escaping</u> by their gradual character the notice of contemporary observers, **(9)** <u>are attributed with</u> the follies of statesmen or the fanaticism of atheists. Thus the extraordinary occurrences of the past two years in Russia, that vast upheaval of Society, which has overturned what seemed **(10)** <u>most stable, religion, the basis of property, the ownership of land, as well as forms of government and the hierarchy of classes</u>—may owe more to the deep influences of expanding numbers than to Lenin or to Nicholas, and the disruptive powers of excessive national fecundity may have played a greater part in bursting the bonds of convention than either the power of ideas or the errors of autocracy. {11}

8. A) NO CHANGE
   B) causes. That
   C) changes are caused
   D) changes; caused in part

9. A) NO CHANGE
   B) is attributed for
   C) are attributed to
   D) are attributed by

10. A) NO CHANGE
    B) most stable, religion, the fact that people can own property, the ownership of land, as well as forms of government and the hierarchy of classes—
    C) most stable; religion, owning property, the ownership of land, in addition to various forms of government and the hierarchy of classes—
    D) most stable—religion, the basis of property, the ownership of land, as well as forms of government and the hierarchy of classes—

11. Which of the following best summarizes the main claim of the passage?

    A) The Great War was brought about as much by a population boom and industrialization as by any other cause.
    B) Germany had a population boom between 1870 and 1914.
    C) Although population was a significant factor in the outbreak of war in Europe, it was only minor compared to the diplomatic debacle caused by Archduke Ferdinand's assassination.
    D) Russia grew less quickly than did Germany in the pre-war period.

PRACTICE EXERCISE 2:

Directions: Answer the questions that accompany the following passage.

Rembrandt's Environment

Surprise is sometimes expressed that **(1)** <u>a more great artist</u> as Rembrandt passed all his time "in such a little country" as Holland, so far from the great artistic centers of northern Italy, and that he was not attracted to Italy or even to Flanders is regarded in some quarters as a sign of eccentricity. {2}

But Italy, though supreme, at any rate in repute, as an artistic center, **(3)** <u>was being</u> in all the elements that made the life of the seventeenth century absolutely devitalized, while since the beginning of the troubles between Spain and the Netherlands Flanders had retrograded. Antwerp about the time of Rembrandt's birth possessed only a shadow of its former greatness. **(4)** <u>Many still regarded Antwerp as the commerical engine of the Northern Renaissance.</u> It was a decayed country town, numerous still in population, but even in that point suffering a daily loss from emigration. The contrast in the early part of the seventeenth century between the southern or Catholic provinces and those of the north was **(5)** <u>quite striking</u> and was all in favor of Holland.

1. A) NO CHANGE
   B) a greater artist
   C) so great an artist
   D) such a person,

2. For the sake of the cohesion of the passage, which sentence best transitions between the first and second paragraphs?

   A) After all, most contemporary artists spent time learning from Italian masters.
   B) There are many other features of Rembrandt's life that are surprising.
   C) Fortunately, our evidence suggests that he was not considered odd for his time.
   D) Likewise, Jan van Eyck spent most of his life in Bruges.

3. A) NO CHANGE
   B) had almost been
   C) were
   D) was

4. Which of the following replacements best supports the claim made in the previous sentence?

   A) NO CHANGE
   B) It had become a deserted harbor through the closing of the Sheldt.
   C) Despite this fact, Antwerp and Brussels were closely aligned trading partners.
   D) The city first experienced an economic boom in the 12th century, when the rival port of Bruges started silting up.

5. A) NO CHANGE
   B) subtle
   C) somewhat remarkable
   D) like night and day

If the trading towns of the north so far surpassed the once opulent and splendid Flemish cities, it is clear that **(6)** <u>they</u> would be at least equal to any centers of secular life in Western Europe, and a contemporary authority reckoned Amsterdam at the beginning of the seventeenth century as the greatest commercial city of Christendom.**[7]**

We must remember that although Rembrandt never left his native Holland, he yet passed all his life in one or the other of the two chief towns of that country, at the epoch of its most vigorous political and intellectual activity. **(8)** <u>He was born and brought up at Leyden, which at the beginning of the seventeenth century was second only to Amsterdam in population, and rivaled it in industry; while it surpassed as an intellectual center all the cities of the Provinces.</u>

[1] As soon as he was established in his profession he settled in Amsterdam, where there was all about him the stir of an energetic burgher life that found its chief outlet in a world-wide commerce. [2] The Amsterdam of Rembrandt's days has been called 'Holland in miniature'. [3] With equal justice might the United Provinces as a whole be termed an epitome of the world of the seventeenth century. [4] Nonetheless, Rembrandt had little interest in the burgher life, and retreated to his easel to capture, instead, the lives of common people.

{**9**}

6. Which of the following words is the best replacement for the underlined word?

   A) the countries
   B) it
   C) the towns
   D) Rembrandt

7. Which of the following facts would best support the ideas presented in this paragraph?

   A) In 1843, Bruges handled ten times the trade volume that Antwerp did.
   B) By contrast, Istanbul dwarfed the former glory of Flanders.
   C) In terms of Renaissance art, however, Rome still held far more treasures than could be found in Amsterdam.
   D) Amsterdam's port experienced severe crowding in the 17th century from the volume of trade.

8. In relation to the previous sentence, what is the function of the underlined sentence?

   A) It acts as a transition to the following claim.
   B) It illustrates the previous claim.
   C) It is redundant and should be deleted.
   D) It provides background context for a claim made in another paragraph.

9. Which of the following changes would improve the focus of the paragraph?

   A) NO CHANGE
   B) Combine sentences 2 and 4
   C) Omit sentence 4
   D) Omit sentence 1

All that is distinctive of that century, activity in commerce and inventions, intellectual alertness, the prominence of the citizen and man of trade, religious antagonisms, would have been found there more in evidence than on **(10)** <u>any spot of earth</u>. One who then lived in Holland, and in Holland's chief seat of traffic, would have his finger on the pulse of the world and would feel the currents of the world's life stream back and forth. **{11}**

10. A) NO CHANGE
    B) any other spot on Earth
    C) any city in northern Europe
    D) all the Christian cities of the world

11. Considering the passage as a whole, which of the following additions to the final paragraph would provide the most suitable conclusion?

    A) At its height, the commercial power of Amsterdam eclipsed even that of 15th century Venice.
    B) Rembrandt's surroundings provided, therefore, ample stimulation for his art.
    C) However historians rank the cities of the northern Renaissance, Rembrandt's Antwerp remains a magnificent example of human achievement.
    D) Even modern tourists revel in the rich history of early center industry.

PRACTICE EXERCISE 3:

Directions: Answer the questions that accompany the following passage.

Caesar and Pompey

The history of the years 49 and 48 B.C., the period covered by this book, centers around two striking personalities: Gaius Julius Caesar and Gnaeus Pompeius. During this period Caesar subjugated Gaul by a series of brilliant campaigns, the details of which are familiar to all readers of the *Gallic War*. At the conclusion of this war keen observers began to recognize that the Roman world possessed a man of military capacity equal to that of Pompeius, and of personal qualities that outshone those of his rival. **(1)** His daring exploits, his profuse liberality, his attractive humanity, and the extraordinary versatility of his genius, in which he may be compared with the first Napoleon, made him subsequently the most striking figure in the world of his day. Pompeius, his son-in-law, was a great and successful soldier, having subdued the Far East, crushed the power of the pirates, and quelled a dangerous revolt in Spain. He had been three times Consul, yet he seems to have had no firm hold on the mass of his countrymen; his stiff formality stirred no enthusiasm, and his political vacillation made him generally mistrusted.

An open rupture between two such men, each at the head of a veteran army, one the popular democratic leader, the other, nominally at any rate, the champion of the senatorial order and of all who upheld the constitutional republic, **(2)** have been inevitable.

1. A) NO CHANGE
   B) He committed exploits of daring, being a profuse liberal, and his attractive humanity and genius
   C) His daring exploits, along with his profuse liberality, his humane attraction, and his ingenious versatility
   D) Having committed daring exploits, his profuse liberality and attractive humanity, and versatile ingenuity

2. A) NO CHANGE
   B) were
   C) was
   D) having been

[1]The Pompeian party eventually forced a vote to issue a decree that Caesar should disband his army by a fixed date. [2]Tribunes loyal to Caesar fled Rome to deliver the news to him at Ravenna, so he at once crossed the Rubicon. [3]Caesar was concerned about his legions in Gaul. [4]The great war had now begun. {3}

The three books of the *Bellum Civile* narrate the fortunes of the war from **(4)** its outbreak to the decisive battle of Pharsalus in June 48 B.C. The narrative may be regarded as in the main trustworthy, **(5)** though it is evidently intended by Caesar to justify his political action in the eyes of his countrymen, and **(6)** sometimes he appears to mis-state the political situation or understate a military reverse.

3. Which of the following changes would improve the focus of the paragraph?

   A) Merge Sentences 1 and 2 by a semicolon.
   B) Add information about the Gallic legions to Sentence 3.
   C) Move Sentence 2 so that it is between sSntences 3 and 4.
   D) Omit Sentence 3.

4. A) NO CHANGE
   B) it's
   C) they're
   D) their

5. Which choice most effectively combines the sentences at the underlined portion?

   A) NO CHANGE
   B) inasmuch as
   C) because
   D) despite the fact that

6. Given the context of the passage, which of the following facts would best support the claim made in the underlined portion of this sentence?

   A) Caesar admitted that his soldiers were no match for Pompeius' soldiers.
   B) Caesar intentionally downplayed his difficulty in maintaining his army's fighting morale during the march on Rome.
   C) In his public address to the Senate, Caesar humbly acknowledged that his troops were starving.
   D) Caesar understood that crossing the Rubicon meant war was inevitable.

Caesar's style is singularly clear, simple, and restrained, enlivened now and then by a touch of vivacity, emotion, or sarcasm. Perhaps its most **(7)** <u>prominent</u> characteristic is his constant use of the present tense, due to his vivid realization of the scenes that he describes. He sees **(8)** <u>as it were</u> the past event unfolding itself before his eyes. **(9)** <u>Just in the same manner as</u> all ancient historians, Caesar omits much that we should be glad to know. It probably never occurred to **(10)** <u>him</u> that in future ages his campaigns would be closely investigated by students {**11**}.

7. Which of the following is the best replacement for the underlined word?

   A) excellent
   B) featured
   C) notable
   D) insignificant

8. A) NO CHANGE
   B) albeit
   C) nevertheless
   D) in a manner of speaking

9. A) NO CHANGE
   B) Like
   C) As
   D) In similarity with

10. A) NO CHANGE
    B) Pompeius
    C) Modern historians
    D) Caesar's biographer

11. Considering the passage as a whole, which of the following additions to the final paragraph would provide the most suitable conclusion?

    A) In time, however, modern students will appreciate Caesar's writings.
    B) Caesar's own account of his struggle against Pompeius should, therefore, be viewed as entirely reliable.
    C) Pompeius, by contrast, provided a comprehensive account of his own downfall.
    D) His direct and engaging style will, nevertheless, ensure that Caesar's history remains a popular subject of study.

Unauthorized copying or reuse of any part of this page is illegal.

PRACTICE EXERCISE 4:

Directions: Answer the questions that accompany the following passage.

Honey Hunting

Andrew Newey has spent his career **(1)** apprehending the essence of disappearing traditions and cultures, but his most recent project, "Gurung Honey Hunters," was something of an enigma; photojournalists, such as Mr. Newey, play a factor in the dissapearance of traditions in not only central **(2)** Nepals remote villages', but other sheltered communities around the world.

Honey hunting dates back a millenia, but it was a relatively unknown tradition until the 1987 National Geographic documentary flooded the quiet area with tourists, film crews, and photographers. The exposure of this tradition allowed travel agencies to add Himilayan adventure package deals that included staged honey hunts for over $1,000 a person. These vacationers and adventurers, no matter how pure their intentions were, became a large factor in the declining of this tradition. {3}

Newey arrived in Nepal in October and spent the next three months in search of a honey hunt untainted by mass tourism. He found a small village in the Kaski district, surrounded by snow-covered mountains — he refused to reveal the name of the village. "If the name comes out, tourists will flock **(4)** there," said Newey, "That would be a disaster." {5}

1. Within the context of the passage, which of the following is the best replacement for the underlined word?

   A) NO CHANGE
   B) capturing
   C) grabbing
   D) seizing

2. A) NO CHANGE
   B) Nepal's remote villages
   C) Nepals' remote villages
   D) Nepal's remote villages'

3. Which choice most effectively establishes the main idea of the paragraph?

   A) Tourists cannot manage to keep their modern ways from influencing old traditions.
   B) National Geographic is at fault for the decline of cultures.
   C) Travel agencies profit the most from the exploitation of isolated pockets of culture and tradition.
   D) Unexpected exposure of secluded cultures generally results in harm regardless of the original intentions.

4. A) NO CHANGE
   B) there." said Newey.
   C) there" said Newey,
   D) there," said Newey.

5. Which of the following, if added here, would best support the ideas presented in the previous sentence?

   A) NO CHANGE
   B) Many journalists believed that exposure would benefit the remote villages, but it often led to the diminishing of a culture.
   C) It is common for reporters to not expose their sources.
   D) By not exposing his source, Newey inadvertently caused the decline of that culture.

He spent time gaining the trust of villagers who were guarded when around cameras and foreigners. When he finally swayed them with his good intentions, he joined them on the three-hour trek down the mountain to one of a few honey-hunting sites in the area.

{6} On the first day, a sheep is sacrificed to the cliff gods and prayers are lifted in hopes of a bountiful harvest. On the day of the hunt, the hunters then gather wood for small fires near the cliff's base to smoke the large Himalayan bees out of their hives. On the third day, the **(7)** <u>hunters</u> return home with their harvest.

[1] The cutter must climb up a 50-meter rope ladder that is fastened to the top and base of the cliff while carrying two seven-meter bamboo sticks called tangos. [2] He must then use one of the sharpened tangos to cut down visible honeycombs while the other tango steers a hanging wicker basket that catches falling pieces. [3] The process of gathering the opulent honey is an effort **(8)** <u>, that involves</u> dozens of people. [4] However, the "cutter" plays the hardest role. [5] The cutter cannot catch all of the falling combs in the basket, but the children below greet these misses with jubilant scrambling to feast on the fallen honey. {9}

The cutter on Newey's expedition was 58 years old — indicative of the **(10)** <u>elderliness</u> of traditional honey hunters. This, **(11)** <u>paired with</u> the migration of younger generations to cities, has also contributed to the decline of this tradition. The cutter on Newey's hunt served several neighboring villages whose veteran cutters were too old.

6. Within the context of the paragraph, which of the following provides the best transition from the previous paragraph?

A) NO CHANGE
B) Three days of hunting lies ahead of Newey.
C) The hunting starts and ends in three days.
D) Newey observed and recorded the three-day hunt.

7. A) NO CHANGE
B) hunter's
C) hunters
D) hunters's

8. A) NO CHANGE
B) that involves
C) , which involves
D) which, involves

9. The paragraph would be most cohesive if the sentences are placed in which order?

A) NO CHANGE
B) 1,2,5,3,4
C) 3,4,1,2,5
D) 3,4,5,2,1

10. A) NO CHANGE
B) crumbling
C) oldness
D) aging

11. A) NO CHANGE
B) being paired with
C) pairing
D) in pairs with

PRACTIC EXERCISE 5:

Directions: Answer the questions that accompany the following passage.

Online Literature in China

{1} [1] Anyone trying to learn how to dig up ancient artifacts by watching the *Tomb Raider* movies would find little practical help from Angelina Jolie traipsing around Cambodia's temples. [2] If you're an online-literature buff in China, you might have better luck. [3] Last spring, an unemployed 45-year-old man and his accomplices were arrested after having successfully dug up artifacts from a 15th century tomb just outside Beijing. [4] **(2)** That techniques were an exact imitation of those described in *Ghost Blows Out the Light*, a hugely popular Chinese online novel that was first published on the Web in December 2005 and **(3)** had been read by millions.

Behind the wild **(4)** success of *Ghost Blows Out the Light* is a booming internet-novel industry that is largely unique to China because of the greater freedom from censorship enjoyed online by writers and readers. Shanda Literature, a successful online publishing company in China, runs three popular online-novel websites and boasts a total readership of 25 million that is growing at 10 million per year, according the company. {5}

1. Sentence 3 should be placed

   A) NO CHANGE
   B) before Sentence 1.
   C) before Sentence 2.
   D) after Sentence 4.

2. A) NO CHANGE
   B) Those
   C) This
   D) Their

3. A) NO CHANGE
   B) having been read
   C) has been read
   D) will have been read

4. Which of the following is the best replacement for the underlined word?

   A) NO CHANGE
   B) achievement
   C) accolades
   D) profit

5. Which of the following should be added to conclude the paragraph and provide a transition to the next?

   A) This is a large growth rate for a relatively new industry.
   B) These novels receive more online traffic than Facebook in China.
   C) The industry could grow more if censorship laws loosen in China.
   D) There would be less Chinese literature if there were no online publishers.

The tradition of online literature in China goes back to the mid-'90s, when the bulletin-board system, or BBS, **(6)** <u>first appearing</u> on the Chinese Internet as a platform to share opinions and in many cases literary creations. The same rigid censorship that drove millions of users to BBS and other online forums likely also **(7)** <u>caused</u> many book readers into cyberspace. Although largely substituted now by social-networking sites like Facebook and Twitter in the West, the BBS still prevails in China today as a relatively free place to express dissidence, while no such leeway is allowed in the traditional media. "All books are required to go through three rounds of government-supervised editing, which could take months, before they can be published on the mainland," says Zhang Kangkang, a renowned novelist and vice chairwoman of the Chinese Writers Association. "Whereas online novels almost instantly reach the public at the click of a button."

{8} A growing trend in the business is to convert online postings into hard copies of books, plays, movies or even computer games. *Ghost Blows Out the Light*, whose book and online game versions both became best sellers, already has a movie and a play **(9)** <u>in the making</u>. A major part of our job now is to forage those online-novel websites for potential book ideas," says Xiang Zhuwei, the Beijing-based publisher of *Ghost Blows Out the Light*.

Shanda also expects to tap into China's **(10)** <u>increasingly trends</u> of cell-phone reading. Still, to expand readership in the long term, it may not be enough to rely solely on amateur writers and their largely similar tomb-raider or martial-arts novels. **{11}**

6. A) NO CHANGE
   B) first appeared
   C) had appeared first
   D) had been first seen

7. Which of the following is the best replacement for the underlined phrase?

   A) NO CHANGE
   B) made
   C) showed
   D) ushered

8. Which of the following would best introduce this paragraph and provide a transition between this paragraph and the preceding paragraph?

   A) This business is changing.
   B) Recently, online publishers have been expanding their business beyond novels.
   C) Online publishers are sticking to cyberspace to generate revenue.
   D) Despite this, online publishers are looking beyond the Web for customers.

9. A) NO CHANGE
   B) of the making
   C) to the making
   D) being made

10. A) NO CHANGE
    B) increasing trending
    C) increasing trend
    D) increasingly trendy

11. Which of the following would best support the main idea of the final paragraph?

    A) Studies show a more broad interest among young readers.
    B) Cell-phone sales are down in China.
    C) Students can't read on their phones in Chinese schools.
    D) Young readers read most of their literature on their cell-phones.

Contributors

A *Very Special Thank You* to the following contributors

Ashley Zahn (HQ)   Brian MacNeel (HQ)   Chris Thomas (HQ)

Kyle Hurford (Johns Creek, GA)   Micah Medders (HQ)   Monica Huynh (Johns Creek, GA)

Sarah Plunkett (Cumming, GA)

Abigail Burns (Johns Creek, GA)

Alicyn Henkhaus (Palos Verdes, CA)

Ankit Rawtani (Bridgewater, NJ)

Anne Hellerman (Coppell, TX)

Benjamin Yu (Bridgewater, NJ)

Brent Cash (Germantown, MD)

Brett Vigil (Johns Creek, GA)

Brian Cabana (Paramus, NJ)

Brian Hester (Roswell, GA)

Caitlin Pancarician (Middletown, NJ)

Casey Lynch (Livingston, NJ)

Christopher Muyo (New York)

Christopher Woodside (Edison, NJ)

Danielle McMullin (Clifton, NJ)

David Rutter (Snellville, GA)

Drew McKelvy (Olney, MD)

Edward Helmsteter (Westfield, NJ)

Eli Aghassi (Northridge, CA)

Elizabeth Peterson (Centreville, VA)

Erica Schimmel (West Portal, CA)

Erin Lynch (Coppell, TX)

Erin Short (Palo Alto, CA)

Greg Hernandez (Rancho Cucamonga, CA)

Heather Kelly (Issaquah, WA)

James Kyrsiak (Old Alabama, GA)

James Wagner (Los Angeles, CA)

Jeffrey Pereira (Scarsdale, NY)

Jessica Loud (Palos Verdes, CA)

Jin Park (Frisco, TX)

John F. Callahan (Parsippany, NY)

Kaleab Tessema (Coppell, TX)

Katharine Galic (Palo Alto, CA)

Kyla Bye-Nagel (Sterling, MD)

Kyle Mesce (Chatham, NJ)

Lane D'Alessandro (King of Prussia, PA)

May-Lieng Karageorge (Lorton, MD)

Michael Fienburg (Calabasas, CA)

Michael Lupi (Paramus, NJ)

Morgan McLoughlin (Brentwood, CA)

Nicole Lampl (Calabasas, CA)

Peter Lee (Hamilton Mill, GA)

Rachel Becker (Burke, VA)

Rachel Tucker (Naperville, IL)

Richard Faulk (Fremont, CA)

Robert Jedrzejewski (Timonium, MD)

Sam Anderson (Paramus, NJ)

Sean Llewellyn (Lynnwood, WA)

Thach Do (Monrovia, CA)

Tina-Anne Mulligan (Paramus, NJ)

Qi-lu Lin (Parsippany, NY)

Zack Arenstein (Livingston, NJ)

Zafar Tejani (Little Neck, NY)